CECIL BEATON

D37   Gordon Anthony, *Cecil Beaton in Fancy Dress Costume*,
1937 (Sotheby's, London)

A RETROSPECTIVE

Edited by Dr. David Mellor

A New York Graphic Society Book
Little, Brown and Company
Boston

First United States edition
Library of Congress Catalog no. 86–80445

New York Graphic Society books
are published by Little, Brown and Company (Inc.)

Printed in Great Britain

CONTENTS

This catalogue offers a revised account of Cecil Beaton and his visual imagination. It contains essays of critical and historical analysis as well as essays of celebration. Their emphasis is upon Beaton's extraordinary place in British cultural history, and this is one of the key elements in the introduction, *Beaton's Beauties*. In this I have tried to set out some of the broad lines of Beaton's strategies and their several contexts. This is followed by a detailed chronology, *Snapshots in Time*, compiled by Terence Pepper of the National Portrait Gallery, which provides an overview of Beaton's career until his death in 1980. His biographer, Hugo Vickers, has contributed a sketch of that most important aspect of Beaton as a man of letters, through a study of his diaries, in *A Fly in Amber*. The synonymity between Cecil Beaton and the institutions of fashion photography is a commonplace of the history of photography, and Philippe Garner of Sotheby's, London, offers a new study in *An Instinct for Style*. This is followed by a novel evaluation of Beaton as a gardener by Ian Jeffrey, Head of the Department of Art History, Goldsmiths' College, London, in *Landscape, Nation and Ideology*, which offers a different perspective on his life. Michael Parkin, who has advised in the selection of drawings and paintings, has done much by bringing Beaton's graphic works to the public eye through his gallery. Here he writes a celebration of Beaton's draughtsmanship, *Eggie's Pupil*. Amongst all of his activities that deserve re-appraisal perhaps it is Beaton's relationship to the theatre that will preoccupy future art historians; an initial examination of some of the issues has been outlined here by Ian Jeffrey and myself in *The Tyranny of the Eye*. Finally, the critic Stuart Morgan discusses the many personas of Cecil Beaton in *Open Secrets*. Taken together, it is hoped that these writings will open new ways of considering Beaton's achievements, in conjunction with the exhibition itself.

As curator of this retrospective exhibition, as well as editor of this book and catalogue, I have been greatly helped by those individuals already named who have aided me in the choice of exhibits. Terence Pepper has been my assistant during this period and I should particularly like to thank him for his tireless research. I have also valued the advice and support of this exhibition's American co-ordinating curator, William A. Ewing. The exhibition would not have been possible without the co-operation of Eileen Hose, whose advice and patient help have been invaluable. Sotheby's, London, kindly made available their Beaton Archive, together with numerous facilities, under the direction of Philippe Garner, who has overseen the selection of the fashion sections of the exhibition. I am grateful, too, to Condé Nast for their permission to use significant photographs from their archives in New York. Many private collectors have given freely of their time and have made generous loans to the exhibition, and while it is invidious to single any out, I feel I must particularly thank Paul Walter of New York, Leslie Esterman and Roy Astley, not least for their great enthusiasm for this project and for Cecil Beaton. Lastly, I am greatly obliged to Diana Vreeland for her observations.

One of the objectives of this book has been to provide catalogue entries for the exhibits which have been compiled by Terence Pepper and myself according to conventional procedure: dimensions are given in centimetres, height preceding width. Dimensions for colour transparencies are given in their standard imperial sizes. Inscriptions on a photograph or picture are transcribed literally and an attempt has been made to locate the original place of reproduction for as many of the photographs as possible. The citation 'Cuttings Books' refers to Cecil Beaton's extensive collection of cuttings books in the Victoria and Albert Museum. Finally, a bibliography of Beaton's published works is provided by Hugo Vickers.

Dr David Mellor,
School of English and American Studies,
University of Sussex

❧ FOREWORD ❧

At a time of deprivation and austerity, it might seem untimely to reflect upon an artistic character as flamboyant and grand as Cecil Beaton. Within six years of his death might also seem too proximate a time to attempt such a full retrospective as this exhibition. Yet it has become clear throughout the exhibition's development period that many have wanted to see Beaton seriously assessed against current historical criteria. While it is now easier to produce a more comprehensive and revised overview of his career than that possible at the time of the last retrospective at the National Portrait Gallery nearly twenty years ago, it is also apparent that his style was as attractive to his contemporaries in the twenties and thirties – the time of the Wall Street Crash and the Depression – as it is now to us in the eighties with over three million unemployed. Seen in the context of Post-Modern decorativeness and the present economic climate, Beaton's activities and the opulence of his style take on a new significance.

Cecil Beaton fed off the aura of our high society, reflected it, adorned it and gave it back a romantic, alluring sheen that fictionalized its existence. In *Brideshead Revisited*, Anthony Blanche refers to 'the great English blight . . . charm'. However, while Beaton did create a perfect image of a charmed existence, divorced from the rigours of the everyday, he also portrayed 'the skull beneath the skin', whether on the stage set, in front of the mirror or camera, even in the ballroom, palace garden or Western Desert. Unlike an artist who becomes associated with a particular era, and whose reputation in turn fades as the era fades, Beaton was so attuned to the changes of fashion as to be able to respond to, or even anticipate, its capricious movements and sufficiently connected to remain at ease with its architects throughout his life. He was equally a party to the capers of the Sitwells in the mid-twenties as those of the Rolling Stones in the mid-sixties; as able to photograph Picasso and Dali in the thirties or Monroe in the fifties when they were being lionized by the cultural élite as he was to build a more intimate and lasting relationship with celebrities like Garbo and the Windsors, as much in their heyday as in their later, less public years. The exhibition demonstrates this continuity through six decades.

The range of his work and his stature as Britain's first twentieth-century international media-artist, at home in Hollywood, London, New York and Paris, call for the reassessment that this exhibition attempts to achieve. Through a full retrospective which will, for the first time, contain examples from his entire oeuvre, it is hoped that he will no longer be seen merely as a photographer with an ability to dabble in other areas, but a highly skilled artist operating across several complementary fields; from royal portraiture and war reportage to design of opera and films.

Many of Beaton's friends and collectors have given valuable time and support to this exhibition and we are especially indebted to Eileen Hose for her encouragement. The initiative for the exhibition came from Dr David Mellor of the University of Sussex, who has mounted a far reaching analysis and reassessment of Beaton's activities. As curator and editor of this catalogue he has been assisted by Terence Pepper and he has received much help from Philippe Garner of Sotheby's, London, Ian Jeffrey, Michael Parkin, Hugo Vickers and William A. Ewing. David Bentheim has designed the exhibition's installation and Denny Hemming and Trevor Vincent for Weidenfeld and Nicolson have guided the catalogue through production.

John Hoole
Curator, Barbican Art Gallery

Remembering the Childhood Idyll
A3 *Cecil Beaton in Bed Reading, c.* 1910 (Sotheby's, London)

BEATON'S BEAUTIES

 SELF-REPRESENTATION, AUTHORITY AND BRITISH CULTURE

Dr David Mellor

——— I *A Precious Object* ———

Cecil Beaton's beginnings, as he narrated and published them, start with the founding act of his formation as photographer – and there stands a story which inaugurates all Beaton's histories. This is the memory of the first fixating moment when his childhood desire and an object – a photograph – came together. For Beaton's personal history, to use the title of his 1951 autobiography, is a *Photobiography*; a life pre-fixed and fixed upon the photograph.

'When I was three years old I used to be allowed to scramble in my mother's large bed and nestle close to her while she sipped an early morning cup of tea and opened her letters. One morning during this customary treat, my eyes fell on a postcard lying in front of me on the pink silk eiderdown and the beauty of it caused my heart to leap. The photograph was of Miss Lily Elsie . . . I started to make a collection of picture postcards of my heroine.'[1] The discovery of this photograph of a musical comedy actress initiates Beaton's history of himself, dedicated to a precious object of desire which must be glorified, protected and collected. The photograph, and photography itself, becomes in this way a point of origin, and a transcendental signifier for Beaton. But the first chapter of *Photobiography* is also a record of idyllic pleasure in the shared maternal bed, looking at the precious photograph, the effect of which was 'unbearably beautiful',[2] acting as a supplement to his mother.

Beaton's account of this experience bears a profound similarity to those autobiographies narrated in the form of pastiche psychoanalytic case studies of childhood by the Surrealists Salvador Dali[3] and Max Ernst.[4] In another autobiographic fragment, this time of 1944, Beaton dwelt upon the theme of the photograph as a double and as compensation for a woman's body: 'Though I saw few "actresses" . . . in the flesh, their photographs were for me an absorbing interest and an almost entirely satisfactory substitute.'[5] This initial displacement from a woman's body to the fascinating photograph, a displacement which began so close to mother, is then channelled, in Beaton's own account, into a 'passion' for theatre and musical comedy. And so a phantasy is installed which links Beaton to a pleasurable and scenic universe of 'Beauties' from theatre and society, and later, film and royalty. And this, arguably, defined Beaton's photographic project until the close of his life.

As Beaton narrates his story, the history of photography is rescued from relative decadence by an epic encounter between himself and the lowly genre of the theatre publicity postcard. Fixated by it from infancy, Beaton was imprinted with the institution of the publicity photograph from theatrical and society magazines. He had 'a passion for the code',[6] that is the British cultural codes of female dress, the stage and Empire – the codes of his Edwardian childhood – but a passion for them under their factitious guise as photographic representations, a passion for a world made up of photographs. His jubilation was understandable therefore, when at Harrow School he received from his parents the present of a folding Kodak 3A camera, which produced postcard-sied negatives now he could produce his own postcards of desire: 'It was a great moment.'[7] In Beaton's written beginnings we may picture him as a lover of photographs to the point of being a *photophiliac*, that is to say, one who is utterly fascinated by the image of the photograph itself and continually seeks his phantasies in that artefact. Once more in bed, this time in his New York hotel bedroom in the thirties, Beaton photographed himself smothered in newspapers and news photography – a veritable filmy bath of the media. On another occasion in the thirties, this time portrayed by Paul Tanqueray, he was represented with 10 × 8 inch photographic prints adhering to his suit – a photophiliac's body overlaid with photographs of himself.

Yet the argument should run beyond Beaton. We would fail entirely to grasp Beaton's context if we were to perceive him as being unique in his fascination for the photograph. This fascination was a cultural issue of the first magnitude, and one which was continually reflected upon at the time of Beaton's entrance into professional photography in the 1920s, from Noël Coward's plays to Walter Sickert's paintings.[8] In 1930 the glossy society weekly, *The Sphere*, coined a term to designate those figures of High Bohemia and the *beau monde* who were Beaton's sitters – 'The Photocracy'.[9] They formed a complex social mixture of heiresses, lionized artists, leading theatrical figures and the residues of the patrician class – the leisured inhabitants of a new world created by the mechanisms of publicity. The photocracy were themselves translated into photographic fictions, and in their

turn were fascinated by the photogenic.[10] Among those who composed the photocracy, some were indeed connoisseurs of the popular and mass-circulated photograph, such as Beaton's friend and companion, the Hon. Stephen Tennant. The latter possessed a revolving picture-postcard rack, which stood like a cult object or fetish on an ornate table amongst the mid-eighteenth-century furniture and statuary at his home, Wilsford Manor.

The chief focus of such connoisseurship was perhaps to be found in the use of the photo-album and scrap-album within the micro-culture of the photocracy. In this case Beaton was himself an exemplary figure, and his absorption in photo-albums was a recurrent topic in both his writing and his portrait studies. At his country house, Ash-combe, Beaton represented his weekend guests sprawling with photo-albums both indoors and out-doors; albums and scrapbooks are as indispensable for his construction of thirties' *fêtes champêtres* as the portable gramophone, and are always to hand. The introduction to *Photobiography*, entitled 'The Author, Self-Portrait', discloses Beaton as a noc-turnal peruser of such albums: 'his hobby is poring over scrap-books',[11] the magazine *Illustrated* poin-

479 N ROTARY PHOTO. E.C.   MISS GABRIELLE RAY.   W. & D. DOWNEY, LONDON, S.W. COPYRIGHT

The Musical Comedy Star and her Postcards of Desire
Miss Gabrielle Ray signing Postcard Portraits of Herself,
c. 1908 (Dr David Mellor)

ted out. In the rituals of country house culture, browsing through albums was continually reported by Beaton, especially in his published diaries for the twenties and thirties. Here he describes scenes where figures are enraptured by the power of the photograph,[12] scenes which call for a narrative, which in turn call for a text. In *The Wandering Years*, Beaton describes a visit to Stephen Tennant in the summer of 1937: 'we looked at scrap books of old photographs and he rhapsodised suitable texts. Some very ordinary pictures of Garbo were brought to life by "apt ecstasies"'.[13] Used like this, the album took on mnemonic form, and in the case of the Garbo pictures the reader of the diary is called upon to witness the witty appropriation of mute publicity stills from Hollywood's mass culture by the vivifying discourse of an ecstatic élite.

Country House Customs in High Bohemia
Looking at Photo-Albums, Ashcombe, late 1930s
(Sotheby's London)

Beaton's scrapbooks of the twenties show him extending his first project, begun at infancy, of collecting photographs of stage and film stars. This motif of collection, of the photophiliac's erotic desire for possession, was certainly present in press notices for his first exhibition at the Cooling Galleries in November 1927. As usual the society magazines listed celebrities present at the opening alongside those photographed and framed on the walls: 'He has collected most of our beauties', the *Tatler* eulogized.[14] His albums grew to be more heterogeneous than his early clippings of celebrities taken from *Vogue*'s 'Hall of Fame' series in the mid-twenties. By the thirties they had become running montages governed by comic rules of representation about history and fashion. Beaton took up photomontage as a means of ironizing those juxtaposed images which he culled from the photo media. He produced a dense intertextuality of reference, as on a 1940 album page where he joined photographs around the theme of *ancien régime* monarchy. He began this with a low-relief profile of Louis XIV, his face looking at a film re-creation of George III, while above, an image from *Life* magazine shows Marie Antoinette, impersonated by a film actress, who 'trips down the step of a moonlight Versailles-in-Hollywood'. These floating film simulations, souvenirs and impersonations, created a media-version of the *ancien régime*. The scrap-book form was operative in many of Beaton's publications, often assemblages of re-made magazine articles. For example, *Cecil Beaton's Scrapbook* (1937) was launched in New York with an exhibition of his photographs which were not framed, but pinned instead to the gallery walls as a large environmental version of a scrap-album.

In the thirties Beaton's scrapbooks and albums carried connotations of leisured image-scavenging, which disavowed the status of the photograph as a commodity and an industrial fragment. The album became a customized, crafted and ornamental piece, resuscitated from an earlier, nineteenth-century culture of leisure. Beaton maintained, in an essay on scrap-albums in the late thirties, that this was a product of the social élite of 'elusive' and 'exceptional' persons who were connoisseurs of scraps that 'they have thought fit to enshrine'.[15] Thus, in Beaton's imagination, the photograph returned to that especially adored and protected position as a precious object, where it was collected and revered almost as a Proustian keepsake, as a magical souvenir snatched from mass culture and transmuted by phantasies of origin, authority and love.

—— II *The Mirror Gazer* ——

To find Beaton's context, we must return to his own account, his self-representation of his early years. In 1926 Beaton definitely stood outside the circle of the privileged photocracy since he had been enrolled by his timber-merchant father into a City of London business life. But his diaries, constructed as a *Bildungsroman*, portray a youth's conflict with a bourgeois patriarch. They are built around a flight from the stigma of business, of 'trade', which had been imposed on him as his social identity. Beaton represents himself instead as struggling to adopt and be adopted by art, theatre, photography and design. This entailed entering the realm of High Bohemia, and his diaries and photographs embody this sole strategy. To quit middle-class patriarchy for that exotic, quasi-aristocratic and largely matriarchal milieu was his wish; to enter that ornamented scene of 'Beauty', a confined and much-photographed world like that glimpsed in his mother's bed, a world of pictures into which he could be inserted and in which he could see himself. His diary entry for 24 April 1926 recounted his wish to dine at the Eiffel Tower restaurant in Soho: 'the people who go there are smart, arty and the set I must get in with'.[1] These, then, were Beaton's elected social group, and we might speak of his narcissistic group identification with them, since he rapidly took the interests, anxieties, wishes and values of High Bohemia to heart. And beyond them he glimpsed representations of another group, the Arcadian British patrician class, who once again were 'the set I must get in with'. Allegorically just so, for Beaton was not only to depict them, but was also to get into the picture with them, as the Narcissus of High Bohemia, transmitting and magnifying this narcissism until it became the dominant element in the pictures for his first exhibition in November 1927.

In the catalogue for that show, Osbert Sitwell wrote of Beaton's sitters: 'even though they lack utterly what is known as the "narcissus complex", they can hardly help falling in love with their own reflection after the magic is complete.'[2] *The Sunday Herald* reported that at the opening, 'There was the enthralling spectacle of thrilling beauty trying to look exactly like its picture.'[3] And in his many press interviews around the time of the exhibition, Beaton undoubtedly replayed Osbert Sitwell's half-repressed invocation to Narcissus.[4] In his mother's drawing-room, he had found that the polished top of the grand piano 'makes a perfect reflection for a modern Narcissus',[5] a device used in his portrait of the Jungman twins (1927) and of Baba, Nancy and Mrs Beaton (1926), both of which appeared in the exhibition. To the mirroring lure and allure of the polished piano were added further reflections from tinsel, silver paper and oilcloth.

Reflected Enigma
The Secret of Beauty, Baba Beaton, 1926
(Cecil Beaton's *Cuttings Book*)

The Narcissus of '67: A mod at the Waterhole of Reddish
s23 *Gervase*, 1968 (Sotheby's, London)

This system of portraiture, with the reflection of the face doubled, opened up enigmas of representation. One example, a photograph of his sister Baba in 1926, arms akimbo and gazing at her reflection, pool-like, below her, was published with the caption 'The Secret of Beauty'.[6] This led Beaton directly to those specifically Surrealist images of Narcissus, as in his portrait of Dali's wife Gala, which adorned the front of Dali's catalogue for his 1937 exhibition at the Julian Levy Gallery in New York, entitled *The Metamorphosis of Narcissus*. Like those 'Beauties' of the photocracy who had been 'trying to look exactly like [their] picture' at his exhibition, Beaton himself had become fascinated by the theme of Narcissus. As Dali himself described the process with which Beaton had been concerned for ten years in his portraits, 'The body of Narcissus flows out and loses itself in the abyss of his reflection.'[7] Beaton obsessively drew sketches on the theme of mirror and double while working in the City office to which his father had farmed him out in 1926, making schemata for doubling his sisters in photographic compositions that would be 'all very modern'.[8] He was to repeat and develop this theme well into the sixties and seventies, when he revised his double portraits of sisters and twins from the twenties (for example, that of Zita and Theresa Jungman[9] or Baba and Nancy Beaton). But it is significant that in the sixties he extended this device to male sitters, like the Myers twins in 1967. They appear in a pastoral location – Arcadian even – under trees at Reddish, Beaton's country house from 1947, a propped-up mirror redoubling their duality as twins. At about the same time Beaton photographed a nude male model, Gervase, in the same landscape, but posed to parody the iconography of John the Baptist, with one finger pointing to the sky. Beaton also posed him indoors in the conservatory, gazing at his reflection in the fishpool, alluding once more – but forty years later – to Narcissus, and to a text laid down at the centre of Beaton's imaginary universe.[10]

With the use of mirrors,[11] Beaton insinuated himself literally into the picture and set, reflected alongside his ostensible sitter, whether this was Picasso in 1930 or Andy Warhol in the late sixties. Mirrors were symptomatically associated with him. Evelyn Waugh's fictional version of Beaton, David Lennox, in the novel *Decline and Fall* (1928), is represented as arriving at the house of the

High Bohemian Lady Beste-Chetwynde, where he 'made straight for the nearest looking glass'.[12] For according to the prevailing notions of 'conservative-modern' decoration, as theorized by his friend, the society hostess Elsie de Wolfe, mirrors were key elements which 'rejuvenated' house interiors.[13] In 1942 Beaton's mirror was set up like an altar on the table in his army tent, called 'The Ritz', in the Western Desert. He was the other hero of his reflection pictures; for he found himself and seduced himself in every mirror and in every place – whether in Emerald Cunard's apartment at the Dorchester, or at the Jain Temple at Jaipur, or in the plexiglass cockpit of an RAF bomber. He was, therefore, reflected in the scene as a willing victim and simultaneously as an omnipotent master of visual fictions, everywhere drawn into an 'entrapment in . . . the [reflecting] surfaces of appearance'.[14]

In the summer of 1944 Beaton made just such a seductive self-portrait in a mirrored bedroom at an Indian palace in Delhi, Faridkot House. It is a double portrait which includes, reflected in the walls and mirrors of the bedroom, the Supreme Allied Commander for South-East Asia, the charismatic Lord Louis Mountbatten. Like Beaton, Mountbatten was a master of artifice, a dashing Naval dandy impersonated by Nöel Coward in the contemporary film *In Which We Serve* (1942), for which Beaton had shot stills. In the photograph, Beaton and Lord Mounbatten lie on a bed in a bordello room – a room given over to visual phantasies (phantasies of auto-voyeurism) – from which vantage point Beaton takes the photograph, with his Rolleiflex reflected as a radiant point in the many mirrors. All this was with Mountbatten's obvious connivance, like a late episode in the games and parties of the Bright Young People which Beaton had photographed in the 1920s. As Beaton recorded in his diary, Mountbatten 'was in a light mood and only wished to make jokes. No intention of listening to China's troubles which Mrs C[asey] had asked me to expound upon but thoroughly frivolous about our photographing in the glass bed at Faridkot House'.[15] In the photograph a bolster lies between them, a diagonal spar in the reflected geometries; bedded but without contact, paired but barred off from one another. The double portrait was a supreme joke narrative and, moreover, a specular allegory on Beaton's aspirant desire to be embedded in 'the set I must get in with'.

Such a picture photographs the photographer. It is an auto-representation, and Beaton's Official War photographs contain many of these recurrent moments when, either through mirrors or delayed exposure, Beaton represents himself. There is in all of this an aspiration to masterful spectatorship, to a condition of becoming all-seeing within the picture itself through self-inclusion. In 1944 Beaton photographed himself before the mirrors at the Jain Temple in Jaipur, and the following year the picture was reproduced in the magazine *The Sketch*, with the punning caption 'Four Shows – Four Books',[16] commenting on his perennial exhibitionism. Beaton is credited with exhibiting himself not only in four published books and four theatrical productions ('Four Shows') but also in the punning sense that the autoportrait is 'for shows', literally 'for show'. *The Sketch*, a society magazine which had published Beaton's work since the mid-twenties, used his exhibitionist, self-referential and self-reflexive portraits, ones that would have been read, presumably, as lapses by Beaton's superiors at the Ministry of Information. 'In some of these five pictures', ran a wartime *Sketch* caption, 'he makes a game of his own game and of himself – quite a change from the splendid photographs of the three Services which he has taken . . . under the aegis of MoI.'[17] *The Sketch* presented such self-portraits as if they had issued from some playful counter-world, like that inhabited by the momentary frivolity of Mountbatten, which subverted briefly the high seriousness of war, and the rectitudes of authority.

Mirror, Bed and Camera
J13 *Self-portrait with Admiral Lord Louis Mountbatten, Faridkot House, Delhi,* 1944 (Sotheby's, London)

III *The Fictional Self*

In the twenties Beaton was caught up in the development of new modes of biography, and the dramatization of public or fictive personalities. Just as Lytton Strachey's project at this time was to ironize traditional biography, so Beaton seems to have undertaken to revise portraiture into a kind of comedy of egoism, narcissism and shifting identity. The historian Miles F. Shore has traced this moment when nineteenth-century biographic forms began to fissure in Anglo-American culture: 'In its Victorian version the official tone of deadly propriety was replaced by the irreverent "new biography", which by the late 1920s and early 1930s made biography a major literary form at least in terms of sales.'[1]

No sooner had irony been freed and the notion of an authoritative biography 'debunked', than the genre parodied itself. One monument to this, and a probable major influence on Beaton himself, was Virginia Woolf's novel *Orlando* (1928). It is, as Professor Quentin Bell has reminded us, 'a parody of that then fashionable literary form, the fictionalised biography; it leaps away from fact tracing

its hero's career from the late 16th century to the early 20th century.'[2] Although he was to write parodied historic biographies which celebrated an ironized aristocracy, such as *My Royal Past* (1939) and *Quail in Aspic* (1962), the significance of *Orlando* as a model for Beaton lay in other formal and thematic areas. Half-way through *Orlando* the hero becomes a woman; gender is displaced, like historical time in the novel. This theme of transvestism is well-grounded in the culture of the twenties, and loss of fixed gender (another blow against the epoch of the Victorian patriarch),[3] as well as the figure of the androgyne, are distributed throughout Beaton's works with great regularity. At Cambridge he played several transvestite roles on stage, and again in 1934, in travesty, photographed himself impersonating Elsie de Wolfe at Elsa Maxwell's ball in New York. In 1946 he portrayed Garbo as a sexless Pierrot, and even as late as 1968 rendered Mick Jagger as an androgyne[4] – another commonplace, this time of the late-sixties pop culture.

If gender is unstable in *Orlando* and in Beaton's productions, so too is identity, or rather identity is multiplied like Beaton's mirror reflections. Orlando has several historical identities, and in the twentieth century becomes the object of modern publicity and fame, a photocrat like a number of Beaton's debutante sitters from good patrician families of long lineage. 'I understand crops',

Idyllic Travesty: An Edwardian Past in a Feminine Disguise
A25 *Self-portrait, c.* 1926 (Sotheby's, London)

Orlando says. 'But (here another self came skipping over the top of her mind like a beam from a lighthouse) Fame! (she laughed) Fame! Seven editions. A prize. Photographs in the evening papers.'[5] In his diaries of 1924, Beaton had anguished over his appearances in Luigi Pirandello's play, *Henry IV*, which was performed for the first time by the Cambridge University Amateur Dramatic Company. What provoked his anxiety was not so much his stage appearance as its lack of media coverage: he was in danger of losing his other, duplicated, fictional self through the non-appearance of his photogenic self as an image in the newspapers. 'If I'd known there were to be no photographs in the press I wouldn't have acted', he wrote in his diary. 'It's all I care about – well, no but still it's one of those things I like best. Everyone sees them'.[6] But with his début in magazines and gossip columns in 1926 as one of the photocracy, 'Cecil Beaton' was born in the networks of publicity. Later, his absence from the newspapers was equally to become a cause for comment, as happened during the 1931 London society 'Season', when *The Bystander* noticed his non-appearance with astonishment: 'Cecil Beaton and his sister have done little or nothing to attract publicity.'[7]

At the centre of *Orlando*, and at the centre of a story which Beaton began to outline in the year of *Orlando*'s publication, 1928, was a 'fabulous woman', a representation framed and magnified like the actress Lily Elsie in that primal postcard, a fancy-dress woman wearing alternating costumes in historical settings and scenery. In the forties, fifties and sixties, that same woman would be multiplied as Anna Karenina and Eliza Doolittle. Beaton wished to write 'a story with times and periods jumbled together so that some fabulous woman would be sitting to have her portrait painted by Greco and Gainsborough simultaneously – enter celebrities of every period'.[8] That same year saw the publication of another narrative of a time-travelling female, *The Harlequinade: An Excursion*, by Dion Clayton Calthorp and Granville Barker, about a figure who progresses through a sequence of historical *tableaux* to the present. Works like this and *Orlando* were strictly analogous to Beaton's strategy of historical costume revival in those comic, over-abundant *tableaux vivants* that sustained his framed women. The recurrence of similar, related motifs in Beaton's work is manifest as late as 1969, when he worked on Vincente Minelli's film *On a Clear Day You Can See Forever*, which starred Barbra Streisand as Daisy, a twentieth-century woman haunted by a centuries-old English lady, Melinda; haunted, that is, through a set of picturesque and touristic historical environments and backdrops.

Narratives like this, and Beaton's revivalist costume photography, were mirrored in Virginia Woolf's *Orlando*, not only by the agency of the plot itself but by the novel's illustrations. These consisted of portrait paintings that were appropriated, photographed and re-captioned, together with a number of photographs of Vita Sackville-West posed in various portrait styles ranging from Italian Baroque,[9] to parodied versions of the portrait style of Julia Margaret Cameron, or Hill and Adamson.[10] Woolf's book had a final illustration, *Orlando at the Present Time*,[11] which had close similarities to some of Beaton's idyllic, mock-Gainsborough, conversation-piece-pastiche portrait photographs of the late twenties and early thirties. Photography, under Woolf's and Beaton's authorship, appears to devolve into a game of allusion and citation of historical signs and styles, and also records private 'fancy dress' jokes. Signs of the past and present are collapsed into 'costume', and meta-fictions proliferate.

Beaton's earlier, overwhelming lesson in this kind of Modernist meta-fictionality was learned during his participation as designer and actor in Luigi Pirandello's *Henry IV*. In this work 'the time of the play is today',[12] yet the dress is medieval, since the actors are engaged in a therapeutic charade to cure a traumatized player. The play became a kind of touchstone for Beaton, signifying scrambled levels of reality and in later life, in difficult social situations, he would refer to the anti-naturalistic drama of Pirandello as a paradigm for dislocation. *Henry IV* is a piece of theatre which plays with theatrical fictions. Its plot requires the impersonation of historical characters to be acted out, along with the mimicking of portrait paintings. To the contemporary twenties spectator, like Beaton for instance, it would have seemed most immediately comprehensible in terms of London society pageants, *tableaux* and charades, which were held for charity and attracted considerable news coverage. During these charity *tableaux*, such as 'The Pageant of Great Lovers' in 1927, titled ladies masqueraded as living personifications of Reynolds or Gainsborough or Watteau paintings; and Beaton himself designed and acted in pageants such as these at the close of the twenties.

Pirandello's play, concerned with 'a life of fiction',[13] contains a number of Beatonesque themes. For example, Henry refers continually to his portrait mirroring himself on the wall, confirming his double status. And as the doctor says of Henry, 'In his own eyes he must inevitably be an Image . . . a picture in his own imagination.'[14] Beaton acted the role of Donna Matilda, a matriarch impersonating a medieval aristocrat, and as Pirandello instructed, heavily made-up.[15] In this shifting meta-theatrical universe, Beaton's stage design for the drama added another important motif of authority, the iconography of The Throne. In *Henry IV* it was an imperial seat with baldachin, based on the twelfth-century court of Goslar. The throne motif generated an iconography which he was to elaborate throughout his career and it posed a crucial question in Beaton's system of substitutions and representations: what kind of authority can occupy the throne? The answer, boy kings, viceroys and sanctified queens, as in 1942 in Baghdad with the boy King Faisal, in 1944 in Bombay with the Governor General, and in Westminster Abbey and Buckingham Palace with Her Majesty Queen Elizabeth II in 1953. These are depictions of power theatricalized as an image of itself. In Beaton's imagination, *Henry IV* was possibly the crucial point of departure which led him towards a distinctly Modernist reading of the pageant genre – Beaton's genre – of the costumed and staged self. By being the arbiter of those detached signs of story-book history used in this genre, and thereby, in phantasy, Beaton acquired an exalted position, a throne; authority of a kind, perhaps.

A year after acting as one of the plural selves of *Henry IV*, Beaton impersonated another self to stand as signatory or author of his photographs. The name he took to sign his pictures was that of a Venetian Renaissance painter, Carlo Crivelli, a ratified artist. For Beaton was undoubtedly anxious over his name and over his family's social status; it was his father's name which provoked his anxiety. Did he come from a 'good' family or, as it seemed, a family 'in trade'? To compensate for this, Beaton claimed that his sisters were descendants of Mary Beaton, Lady-in-Waiting to Mary, Queen of Scots, and went as far as costuming them in this part for a charity ball. But Beaton's anxiety over his genealogy and lineage played upon his name and was focused upon his signature, his trade-mark. For Beaton felt that he lacked authority, hence the persona of Carlo Crivelli and the phantasy of courtly ancestry. He was fascinated by those contemporary, ennobled senior photographers who possessed well-established identities, particularly *Baron* de Meyer, who was ennobled by Edward VII, and *Baron* Hoyningen-Huene, together with *Colonel* Steichen of military caste. Not until 1972 would Beaton also be a titled photographer, *Sir* Cecil Beaton. In the early 1920s, his signature and his authorizing mark took on some significance. He copied the hieratic, quasi-oriental signature of de Meyer, associating himself with the latter's prestige. In the decayed universe of Pictorialist art photography in the twenties, autographs were still valued; but in the magazine world, in which Beaton was increasingly enmeshed at the end of the decade, the flourish of authorship was downgraded to a typeset name credit.

By 1926 he had dropped the fictive identity 'Carlo Crivelli', and in order to compensate, Beaton's signature swelled and enlarged. He contrived, as always, to place himself and his signature *inside* the frame. Thus Beaton acts as *scriptor* as well as *pictor*. There he *embeds* himself (as at Faridkot House), signified solely by his christian name, written large across the painted background and always adjacent to the portrait's sitter. On the other hand his father's name, florid and red, was written larger still, so inflated as if to disperse it, on the card frame of a portrait he entered for the London Salon of Photography in 1930. It was so large that a reviewer wrote that Beaton was 'thus reducing the photograph to background'.[16] Precisely. For the exhibiting multiple self must always occupy the foreground.

—— IV *An Exception* ——

Beaton represented himself as a prodigy, a figure who was seemingly untainted by the 'trade' connotations of the studio system, and aspired to the status of the courtly artist. This epic construction of Beaton's commenced with the publicity surrounding his first exhibition at the Cooling Galleries, London, in November 1927. Fifteen years later he contributed a short biographical essay to a book entitled *Photography as a Career*, along with other essays by professionals all of whom commended specialist training. But in this context, Beaton refused to recommend photography as a career, instead perceiving his experiences to be, in the words of the essay's title, 'The Story of an Exception'.[1] This phrase is symptomatic of that myth of Beaton's sheer exceptionality which was first written into the Beaton story by Osbert Sitwell, when he outlined Beaton's merit in his introduction to the Cooling Galleries' exhibition catalogue. Sitwell's tactic was to list contemporary photographers, but with a grudging allowance: Maurice Beck, E. O. Hoppé and Curtis Moffat are admitted by Sitwell to be 'famous' and 'excellent photographers in their own way'.[2] But Beaton is represented as wholly exceptional, a *Wunderkind*, and one who could not be judged alongside other photographers or be ranked with them since he 'does not belong to any school, but is absolutely individual'.[3] The biographic tropes in which Sitwell set Beaton were those of the over-reaching and the epic.

During the twenties, the work of London studio photographers was slowly becoming known, if only marginally so, through those major West End galleries and institutions which went beyond the club-like circles of Pictorialism. Of Beaton's listed rivals, E. O. Hoppé had held a one-man show at the Goupil Gallery in January 1922, and Maurice Beck and his partner Helen McGregor (the latter was a major influence on Beaton) had held a major exhibition at the Piccadilly Hotel in November 1923. These events formed a horizon of possibility for Beaton's West End display of photographs. Nevertheless, such shows were secondary to regular appearances of portrait work in the glossy society press, that is in *The Sphere*, *Tatler*, *The Sketch*, *The Bystander*, *The Graphic* and *Vogue*. 'Society' and theatrical portrait photography was consolidating its place in competitive journalism,[4] or so it seemed. For by the early thirties, with the onset of the Depression, the studio photographers entered a period of absolute economic decline, a decline from which Beaton was saved because of his idiosyncratic operating procedures: 'I have no studio of my own and send a great deal of my photographic work to a firm of excellent technicians. I have no qualms about studio staff languishing.'[5]

Like the dandy he was, Beaton passed on the laborious portion of photography – developing and printing – to others, to 'trade' in fact. In addition, he avoided the necessity of having a studio for portrait sessions by initially using his mother's drawing room and later his own residences or the private houses or apartments of his sitters. And, of course, there was always the *Vogue* studio itself.

With this particular division of labour, he reasserted the aesthetic claim of the photographer-as-artist, and excluded routine commercial work. He wrote, 'All artists speak the same language, so photographers should be considered in terms of artists . . . no great technician can make a photographer'.[6] Beaton stood at the terminus of the old studio portrait system which, as an industrial and commercial form, had run from the 1850s to the 1930s. His ability to pass from the phantasy of the romantic photographer-artist to being a corporate agent of *Vogue* and the Ministry of Information, without touching the uneasy base of the portrait studio at all, was perhaps one of his more important achievements, an eccentric case, certainly, within the economic and social history of British photography.

Yet Beaton stood in a nostalgic relationship to that very same studio system which he hoped to supersede and which, paradoxically, he celebrated in his own writing of the history of photography, *British Photographers* (1944). In his photographs he created comic and parodic homages to studio portrait practice, ironically incorporating it and affirming it as part of a wonderland of artifice in *My Royal Past* (1939), for which Beaton used props from the studio of Thomas Downey, the Edwardian portraitist. With immense reflexiveness he quoted and alluded to photographs by Hugh Cecil, Bertram Park and E. O. Hoppé, the kings of the big London portrait studios, while still remaining outside their pattern of organizing manufacture, and therefore outside 'trade'. The history of the form was conserved by Beaton even as he comically recounted it (and discounted it). He stood groomed as 'The Exception', and Beaton's career, in post-Second World War culture, was to act as a kind of conservator, a last custodian of the role of the artist-gentleman-photographer. This was a role that beckoned to him from the nineteenth century, and was exemplified by the Baron de Meyer, friend and courtier of Edward VII, and a figure who fascinated Beaton. It was in the guise of the *grand seigneur*-photographer that Beaton made a farewell gesture at the close of 1971, when he appeared dressed as Nadar, the French photographer of a whole century before, at the Proust Ball held by the Rothschilds. He was impersonating the lost functions of photography in a fancy dress role of exceptionality,[7] that of the artist-photographer.

A Fancy Dress Impersonation of a 'Classic' Portraitist
16 *Cecil Beaton as the Photographer Nadar, for the Rothschild 'Proust Ball'*
by Liliane de Rothschild, 1971 (Private Collection)

Others, senior to Beaton, had aspired to that paradoxical role of artist-photographer within the market-place of society and theatrical portraiture in the twenties. Curtis Moffat and Helen McGregor, both American High Bohemians, were regarded by Beaton as possible models to emulate. When he re-wrote his diaries in the early sixties, Beaton recounted his leap, in the spring of 1926, into a new kind of photography of narcissistic reflected doubles and disembodied heads under glass domes. He presented this development as being preceded by a critical visit to Helen McGregor. As Beaton plots it in his diary, the meeting with her resembled an encounter with 'one's Fairy Godmother'.[8] Just as his mother presided over his first discovery of the 'unbearably beautiful' photograph from her paradisical bed, so Helen McGregor introduced Beaton to another photogenic universe – the shimmering, dazzling and reflecting world of Orientalism. Beaton describes the visit as an inspiring, influential point of departure within his own photography; Helen McGregor sanctioned his efforts. 'She favours Chinese things I suppose . . . I looked around the studio at a large screen, which was prepared with silver foil, the lacquer chest and other oriental props I'd seen photographed by her in *Vogue*.'[9] This Aladdin's Cave afforded a second glimpse of that world of glittering props, reinforcing what Osbert Sitwell described as his fixation with 'theatrical glamour'.[10] It was the self-same glamour that began, in phantasy, with his mother's postcard: everything shines and reflects, like the pages of glossy magazines, the surfaces of photographic prints, or the sheen of postcards themselves – a filmy, mirrored world. But with McGregor there was a strong supplementary meaning which augmented the theatrical imagination, and that was the spectacle and mentality of Orientalism, which was to become Beaton's paramount discourse when he pictured the Empire at war in the Near and Far East in 1942, and again in 1944.[11]

The press reception for Beaton's November 1927 exhibition took up and further circulated Sitwell's characterization of Beaton's exceptionalism: 'Mr Cecil Beaton is uncommonly clever, so clever that he is afraid to let himself go',[12] commented the art critic of *The Morning Post*, who mistrusted the connotations of artifice and reflexiveness which multiplied themselves across Beaton's pictures. *The Sketch* carried four pages of reproductions at the end of the week in which the exhibition opened, while *Eve* and *Tatler* gave one page each. Often it was the many-sidedness and virtuosity of Beaton that provided the press with their headings: Beaton the draughtsman (he had included a room of drawings and paintings to enhance his credibility as an 'artist'); Beaton the stage-manager of *tableaux vivants* and impersonation. Like the media event that it was, the exhibition was composed of sensational novelty items, 'Weird and Novel Photographs of Celebrities',[13] to quote *The Star*'s headlines. There were items suited to all the diverse segments of the press. One of the surviving middle-class family journals of the late Victorian era, *Pearson's Magazine*, with its pre-existing categories of 'eccentric pictures' and trick photography (which had long been a component of the Edwardian period), chose to reproduce Beaton's *Miss Olga Lynn As Seen By The Angels*, a compressed and distorted high-angle view taken from a step ladder. Also selected was a portrait from the opposite, low-angle, foot-of-the-stairs view, entitled *Miss Nelson As Seen By a Dog*. If Beaton revived this kind of late-nineteenth-century grotesque photography (albeit in the age of Renger-Patzsch and Rodchenko), he also made allusions to Victorian spirit photography in his multiple-exposure portraits of 'heads floating about in a non-descript medium'.[14] He made a pastiche of the deathbed portrait, another Victorian genre, with his soon to become notorious photographs of Edith Sitwell and her brothers, looking dream-like and lying in state. These were Beatonesque citations of the visual fiction of spiritualism, and of the nineteenth-century cult of death, which bordered upon the concerns of Valentine Hugo's 1931 Surrealist photographs of the seemingly dead André Breton and Paul Eluard, 'passing over to the other side'.[15]

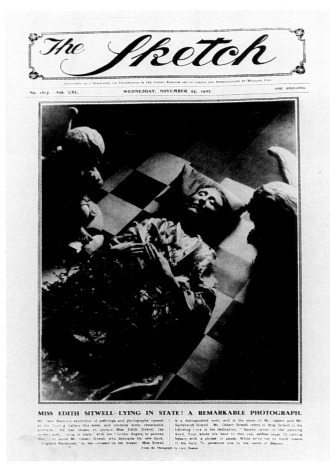

Effigy and Flesh – A Fancy Dress Memorial
for a High Bohemia Poetess
Edith Sitwell Lying in State, The Sketch, 23 November 1927

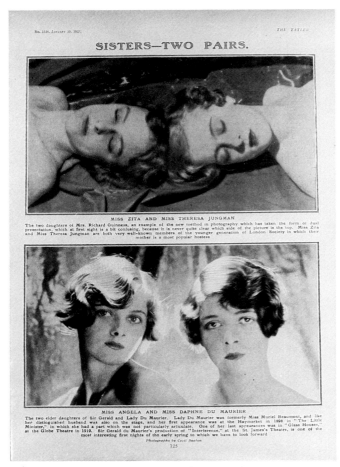

Debutantes Doubles and Redoubled
Zita and Theresa Jungman ; Angela and Daphne du Maurier,
from the *Tatler*, 19 January, 1927

However, the role in which Beaton was most often portrayed by the press, and in spectacular fashion, was as 'the latest addition to the ranks of Society Photographers'.[16] *The Standard* and *The Sunday Herald* presented the exhibition as simply one more mutation of codes in 'the latest phase of Society portraiture'.[17] Beaton's special commodity, his novelty product, was the doubling up of twins or sisters, or of debutantes reflected in lacquered piano tops (a pictorial donation from his 'Fairy Godmother', Helen McGregor). *The Standard* headlined this as 'A Double Face Business/ Young Artist Supplies Society with New Fad'.[18] In that cross-over sector between publicity and art, the habitat of High Bohemia which Beaton was at pains to join, portraiture was one of the key genres of the twenties. In sculpture, Frank Dobson was working on the heads of Osbert Sitwell, Tallulah Bankhead, Iris Tree and Sidney Bernstein, denizens of High Bohemian photocracy. Dobson's sculptures were invariably photographed during their production for the front covers of *The Graphic*, or for *The Standard*, alongside the sitters and Dobson himself, for he was a master of publicity ; ranged in echelon, heads and signs were tripled within the frame. In early November 1929 Beaton was pictured in the London newspapers together with his sculptured head and with Dobson, all profiled in a line, with the caption 'The Cecil Beaton Effect'.[19] This caption knowingly acknowledged the currency of Beaton's profiled double portraits, and opened up an abyss of reflexive references to media fame and the fictional self, as well as pointing back to that named exception – Beaton.

[22]

V *The Amateur as Photographer as Dandy*

After the spectacular and news-worthy aspects of the first exhibition had been circulated in the London press – the society ladies who attended the opening; the presence of the Sitwells; the cocktails served – there was one, single attempt to try to place Beaton within the context of current styles in photography. This was published in *Vogue* magazine, which headlined Beaton as a representative of the 'New Photography', in opposition to Pictorialism and to soft-focus gentility. With Beaton's photographs, they announced, 'The death knell of the foggy school of Impressionist photography is sounded'.[1] As a judgement, this followed in the steps of Obsert Sitwell's 'Appreciation' in which he polemically established Beaton's difference from all other practitioners in the field – his exceptionality. Following a Modernist line of argument, Sitwell commended Beaton's formalism and his specificity: 'The peculiar excellence of Mr Beaton's photographs is that they are so photographic . . . and there is no haze, no scotch mist through which the familiar features can lose themselves.'[2] Yet there was a Pictorialist residue in Beaton. The 'haze', we might say, reappeared, transferred to the interplay of translucencies in Beaton's props of tinsel and cellophane, and in the sitter's costumes: the shimmer and glitter which produced that dazzlement of illumination in his portraits of the late twenties. Paradoxically, Beaton entered photographs for the Pictorialist Salon exhibitions throughout this period. These were usually double-reflection portraits, and they finally drew a moralizing rebuke from the Pictorialist critic, 'Mentor', in *The Photographic Journal*. Beaton's allusive free play with styles, signs and representations angered 'Mentor', who argued that 'in all artistic work . . . it is essential that the motive be sincere and truthfully expressed . . . the aim of this print [a double portrait of Edith Sitwell] on the contrary seems to be the acquirement of notoriety'. There was 'nothing in the work except a manifestation of the author's willful eccentricity'.[3] 'Mentor' correctly suspected that Beaton's playing with signs, and his Modernist sensibility, were wholly at odds with such naturalistic, nineteenth-century criteria as 'sincerity' and 'truthfulness'.

Beaton's involvement with Modernist photography was contradictory. For example, probably taking his cue from Curtis Moffat, he made a series of photograms in 1926 which he called 'Dada-like designs by placing various objects on sensitised paper'.[4] Yet instead of the lexicon of objects which Man Ray and Moffat had used in their Parisian experiments in the early twenties – Bohemian signs like revolvers, wine glasses, masks and musical instruments – Beaton, like Fox Talbot in the 1840s, had gathered far more domestic elements: net curtains, lace doileys, flowers, glass animals and vases, all from his mother's drawing room. Similarly, his use of multiple-exposure techniques, as in *Tallulah Bankhead As The Divine Sarah*, were not grounded in continental vanguardist experimentation, but were rather an appropriation of the style of multiple-exposure photography combined with memories of Edwardian theatrical illusions and comic impersonations.

This naturalized joke-domestication of Modernist elements (the fragmented identity found comically in the drawing room, reflected decoratively in the piano lid) pointed to Beaton's distant and spasmodic contact with some of the issues concerning European photography. Modernity seemed a fashionable style, and not only a figurative style but a social one too, as a correspondent from *The British Journal of Photography* reported when he recounted a remark overheard at the Cooling Galleries exhibition: 'Everybody is modern now.'[5] From Germany, the centre of 'New Photography' in Europe, Beaton had contact with a young journalist, Paul Cohen-Portheim, who managed to sell Beaton's pictures to the leading photo-magazines in Munich, Frankfurt and Berlin.[6] At the important *Film und Foto* exhibition in Stuttgart in 1929, which surveyed a panorama of Modernist photo-

Signs of Germanness for a Bright Young Person
B7 *Nancy Beaton*, 1929 (Sotheby's, London)

graphy, Beaton was the only British photographer whose work was included.[7] His exhibits were all portraits, and in one of them, a portrait of his sister Nancy, Beaton responded to his new German context. While resorting to his customary image of the mirror-gazing sitter, he also jammed as many stereotyped signifiers of 'Germanness' into the frame as possible. Nancy was modelled on German film actresses seen in pin-up postcards, with drooping cigarette and blonde bobbed hair. She was posed by Beaton looking at a heavily-carved, late-Gothic, wooden-framed mirror, with medieval murals in the background — a film-world-cum-Gothic version of Germany. In 1929 and 1930, Beaton's photographs were on the covers of several German magazines, such as the *Münchner Illustrierte Presse*, as 'Ein Neuer Weg Der Porträt Photographie'[8] — 'a new way for portrait photography'. Here, and in the *Frankfurter Zeitung*'s supplement, *Für die Frau*,[9] Cohen-Portheim laboured to present Beaton as belonging to a mythical English aristocracy that was every bit as stereotyped as Beaton's view of Germany. According to Cohen-Portheim, Beaton was truly the fashionable gentleman-society-photographer that he phantasized himself to be, pictured in the German press attending a Royal Academy opening in top hat and tails, '*als Amateur*' — 'as an amateur'.

Beaton *als Amateur* indeed. But perhaps there is greater relevance in the Latin derivation of amateur as *amator*, lover of that good object photography and its accoutrements — its postcards, props, paraphernalia, cameras and its past. He also posed as an amateur in another sense: 'I don't understand speeds or apertures . . . I take an assistant who looks after details.'[10] And for the thirties circle of Bohemian Mayfair photographers, which included Beaton, Peter Rose Pulham and Francis Goodman, it was 'considered *mauvais goût* to be professional', as Goodman recently recalled. But the issue of professionalism was not to do with any lack of technical competence, so much as a wish to restore an earlier golden age of photography, as was seen in the nineteenth century before the arrival of rationalized industrial processes. In Beaton's remembrance and re-enactment of the supposed nineteenth-century 'amateurs' of photography, he hoped to bypass, or at least to re-negotiate, the prevailing commercial structure. This anachronistic stance was noticed immediately, and *The British Journal of Photography* criticized his pictures for resembling closely the products of 'amateurs of two generations ago'.[11] Throughout his first crop of interviews in December 1927 and January 1928, Beaton recurrently stated an aversion towards the routinizing that had resulted from the development of professional commercial practices in the twentieth century, in contrast to 'the best Victorian photographer [who] has us hopelessly beaten'.[12] Writing in 1927, and again in 1957 in his essay 'The

Devil's Instrument',[13] Beaton represented modern photography as hopelessly rushed and without the redeeming factor of inspiration, having become merely 'a brutal and relentless medium'.[14] Throughout his career Beaton revealed a persistent horror of an imagined threat: the threat of de-personalized photography. His phobia was directed towards 'zombie' sitters and models, and the practitioners themselves in their satanic studios where 'they have one sitter following another with the result that they become so deadened with routine work that there is no energy left for inspira-tion'.[15] Beaton's horror was, in essence, a dread of industrial mass society, of a world simply made up of 'trade'; a world contained in that paradigm of the twenties' imagination, the film *Metropolis* (1927). Nevertheless, resistance was possible: 'The tendency to uniformity that is so marked a charac-teristic of these years', Osbert Sitwell had written in support of Beaton, 'has not been able to swamp individual loveliness.'[16] Thus Beaton romantically perceived 'inspiration', 'individuality' and 'freedom' as being paramount over 'routine', and placed them in the foreground of his phantasies of amateur status – 'I am an amateur in the sense that I work by inspiration.'[17]

When he wrote his first extended history of photography, *British Photographers* (1944), those he most approved of were presented as quasi-amateurs. In Beaton's history, de Meyer 'begins' as an amateur and is then recognized by royalty; Beck and McGregor 'set about their work with a deep and unspoilt relish more generally found in the amateur'; Curtis Moffat and Olivia Wyndham have 'only a half-hearted professionalism'.[18] For Beaton, the 'Professional' was a caricature creature who belonged to the standardized, routine, mechanized universe associated with his father's world of business and efficiency, the dull 'trade' universe. Beaton dreaded a combination of the professional and the patriarchal as a form of dominant rationality, a dread which ran through his narratives like a Nemesis that he wished to escape from. But a more general fear, shaped by the culture of the twenties, was of technocracy, an anxiety over a fallen, mechanized, diabolic world – the Metropolis world. 'Perhaps', he wrote in 'The Devil's Instrument', 'it is all part of modern life. The camera is after all only a machine; and with the machine efficiency is too often valued above performance.'[19] Beaton's wish was to cleave to a rudimentary innocence, propped up and aided by the devices of his Edwardian and Georgian childhood, primarily his beloved Kodak 3A camera with which he continued to take professional photographs for *Vogue* and private sitters until 1929. We might see him as an *amator* of his Kodak, that beloved tool of a childhood before the Modern age. 'I love my old Kodak; I've had it for years . . . I refuse to hamper myself with expensive and complicated cameras',[20] he wrote. His 'toy camera', moreover, became a publicity gimmick which marked him as a news-worthy *faux-naïf* in the gossip columns of London and New York. Until, that is, Condé Nast, the patriarch of *Vogue*, decided to deprive him of his Kodak in December 1929, when he demanded a higher level of technical proficiency from Beaton, and the adoption of a pro-fessional 10 × 8 inch plate camera, a change of equipment which Beaton registered as a personal loss, as a symbolic castration.[21]

The year before, during his second visit to America, Beaton had made much in interviews of his disdain for routine portrait commissions, insisting that he was, in fact, a portrait painter and that he photographed for $500 a time only if, 'I can think of something amusing with a client'.[22] Otherwise, he claimed, he refused the commission. This motif of detachment, and of apparent abstinence from business unless 'amused', is perhaps the key which might unlock Beaton's dandyism. An attendant at the first Cooling Galleries exhibition of his portraits regularly warned visitors as they left the gallery that, 'we must not regard it as a commercial enterprise [since] under no conditions whatsoever did Mr Beaton accept commissions to take portraits'.[23] Like a dandy attempting to ward off boredom, Beaton told an *Evening News* reporter in November 1927 that he photographed 'just to pass the time'.[24] Instead of the production of goods, Beaton, like Oscar Wilde and an earlier generation of dandies, put forward performance and the exhibition of his charismatic self. But this was judged by the journalistic criteria of 'personality profiles' and the new gossip columns that had arisen in the early twenties. 'Gossip as we now have it', remarks a character in Wyndham Lewis's novel *The Apes of God* (1930) 'was invented about 1924',[25] and it was in the mental space of this new institution that Beaton emerged.

Luxury goods, and the mass circulation of images, were compressed and confounded in Beaton's *The Book of Beauty* (1930). Besides attempting to return systematically to Victorian formats with vignetted portraits, the preparation of the book's illustrations was made by the process of collotypy, which added the appearance of scarcity value and supplemented mass production processes. Dandyism in the production and consumption of luxury goods was always a part of Beaton's existence, and one salient aspect of this trait was the design of his own, his sisters' and his mother's clothing. Beaton's desired exclusion from mass society, demonstrated by posing as the dandified exception, was noticed as part of his construction as a celebrity by the press in the late twenties. The columnist William Gerhardie wrote in *The Graphic* in June 1928 that Beaton's shirt collars were a sign of his 'originality', 'a deliberate act of stamping one's personality on the herd mind, a conscious addition of inches . . . imaginatively and with grace'.[26] At this point, Proust, whose new volume in the series *À la recherche du temps perdu* had just been published, was cited by Gerhardie. Beaton's dandified collar, Gerhardie indicated, was exactly what Proust called a 'sentimental acquisition'.[27]

The association of nostalgic, aristocratic dandyism with a French sub-culture was significant. Once Beaton's friendship with Peter Watson was formed, he had a direct link to the great dandy taste-maker of Paris, Comte Etienne de Beaumont, one of Cocteau's great patrons, and in addition a role model for an élite of cultured cosmopolitan homosexuals.[28] De Beaumont was the leading European organizer of *tableaux* and costume balls, which were reported in *Vogue* and which Beaton attended. His immersion in Swinging London in the mid and late sixties was certainly derived from his perceived role as a kind of senior custodian of dandyism, and as a seasoned media celebrity of self-exhibiting 'style'. 'We all owe a great debt to Cecil', said David Bailey, 'for keeping the idea of "style" alive'.[29] Beaton's self-incorporation as a dandy was taken a step further in America in 1946, when, as well as designing Wilde's comedy, *Lady Windermere's Fan*, Beaton also acted in the play, taking the part of Cecil Graham. In the stage version, as he appears in publicity photographs, Cecil's Cecil Graham became a vengeful dandy persecuting bulky patriarchs. In Hollywood Beaton was photographed opposite the stout and stalwart Rex Evans, who played the role of a noble buffoon. Beaton, thin, painted, immaculate and with an insinuating leer, faced Evans, who appeared stunned and shocked by the Wildeian revenge of the dandy wit on the patriarch, amongst the matriarchal culture of Lady Windermere's milieu. At various moments in his career, Beaton had represented himself as the dandy he was now impersonating. It was Beaton who had instructed Cyril Connolly in that prerequisite 'sensibility' while at school, and in 1937 Connolly devoted an entire chapter of his book, *Enemies of Promise*, to 'An Anatomy of Dandyism' in recent British culture. There he directed his reader to the critical edge of dandyism that was manifest in a novelist like Ronald Firbank (one of Beaton's chief influences, especially through his novel, *The Artificial Princess*). Connolly argued that Firbank, 'like most dandies disliked the bourgeoisie, idealised the aristocracy [and] . . . recognised frivolity as the most insolent refinement of satire'.[30] It is to that darker, satirical Beaton that we should now turn.

VI *The Comedian*

Very often – more often than we might wish to believe – Beaton arranged his representations of the great, the good, the noble and the beautiful as satirical grotesques, encased in a fictional theatre of display. His line of caricatured celebrities perhaps ended with that of Lord Goodman, 1968, in which the sitter is seen head-on and boxed-in within the space formed by the ends of Beaton's bed at his London home in Pelham Place. The frame betrays Beaton's fascination with Francis Bacon's painting in the fifties, and his staging of grotesques in well-furnished, luxuriously-coloured surroundings. As a vengeful dandy (and as a photographer), he schooled himself in a kind of caricatural Modernism that had become a major tendency in the last hundred years of British art, from Max Beerbohm, Aubrey Beardsley and Walter Sickert, through to Francis Bacon. As a system of representation in Beaton's work, this grotesque mode was identified in his first exhibition. There it perturbed critics who, through Beaton's strategies, were offered insecure positions from which to view (and review) *Miss Nelson As Seen By Her Dog* or *The Madonna Enthroned*. The latter, reported the *Morning Post*, 'is on the comic side and so is in questionable taste', while *Mother and Daughter* was 'cruel'.[1] This last picture could well have been linked to an interview with Beaton the following month, when he set up his usual pose of the wilful and fastidious dandy who turned away commissions, saying, 'I refuse to "take" any dull fat mother with her schoolgirl of sixteen.'[2]

A Baconesque Framed Eminence
S10 *Lord Goodman*, 1968 (Sotheby's, London)

Terminal Poser in the Twilight of Bohemia
H18 *Augustus John*, c. 1940 (Sotheby's London)

This was the other, angrier, face to Beaton's pursuit of fictions of the celebrated. It was a side which was only acknowledged occasionally or else was subsumed in the act of consigning Beaton's productions to the status of visual gossip. *Time*, in 1931, discussed 'The Beaton Method', which seemed to amount to another set of two-faced representations of adoration *and* loathing for the 'Beauties' that Beaton had to 'take'. '[He] make[s] a highly flattering photograph of a lovely lady in an exotic attitude . . . To this is added a not nearly so flattering drawing and a slightly malicious essay,'[3] commented *Time*. Beverley Nichols, the author, was one of Beaton's cult heroes of youthful success in that celebrity universe of journalism which Beaton set out to conquer, and which Nichols had charted in his early autobiography, *25* (1925), a handbook to the possibilities of fame which Beaton read avidly. Later, in the fifties, Nichols was to analyse Beaton as a satirist, describing his 'curious spidery sketches of Society beauties glimpsed through razor sharp eyes',[4] a picture which confirmed *Time*'s earlier account of Beaton's masked aggression, and his misogynism.

On the other hand, Beaton was part of a larger graphic discourse which surrounded caricature. In late-twenties London there was a definite fashion in society, for caricature a 'fad' which was being reported as 'The Craze For Caricature'[5] in women's magazines intended for lower-middle-class readership, and was even suggested as a desirable social accomplishment. There was also a major Daumier exhibition in 1927, at which Beaton was interviewed with Osbert Sitwell for the evening papers.[6] But Beaton had been preparing a specifically satiric persona since Cambridge University, where he had portrayed himself reading a highly visible copy of the tenth volume of Juvenal's *Satires*. He adopted comedy as a mode for his diaries and journalistic writing from his earliest years: irony, pastiche, satire and caricature become his great narrative devices.[7] Beaton's diaries move towards a comic resolution of reported setbacks, social embarrassments and family tensions, which are paraded with a ceaseless egoism. This egoism is their great theme: it is 'Beaton's Progress', an epic which is constantly and comically traced over the terrain of society and High Bohemia which he pitted himself against in mock-heroic fashion. Hayden White has described this kind of narrative as a comic dream, 'the triumph of the protagonist over the society which blocks his progression to this goal . . . [this] kind of comic emplotment may be called the Comedy of Desire'.[8] In such a comedy narrative, 'my greatest triumph' is his successful courtship of Greta Garbo, the photocratic star, the enigma, and the beautiful woman in the picture.[9]

By the forties and fifties, Beaton's gestures of comic caricature were being made in an ageing universe of once Bright Young People – stars, photocrats and artists. Death is surely coming for Walter Sickert and for Augustus John in the pictures he took of them in the early 1940s; these are portraits of the ruination of the lionized painter-photocrats. In his portrait of John in 1940, house curtains became baroque drapery, and with John's help, candelabrum in hand, a romantic Bohemia in decline was staged, pre-figuring the mad, piratical portrait which Beaton was to make of John at the end of the fifties. Osbert Sitwell detected Beaton's adept use of the grotesque in 1930, when he wrote of Beaton's photograph of the ageing comedienne Nelly Wallace, shown at the second Cooling Galleries' exhibition: 'The grotesque style which she affects is portrayed with consumate mastery; each of these photographs is as beautiful and as strange a thing as an etching by Callot or Della Bella.'[10] The citation of these seventeenth-century Baroque artists by Sitwell, acting as a connoisseur of the grotesque, is crucial in re-assembling two paradoxical structures of feeling in 'Beaton's Progress' – the 'beautiful' and the 'grotesque', or as Sitwell described it, the 'strange'. In his portraits of Nelly Wallace and Lady Alexander, there is one of Beaton's motifs, the figure of an elderly, tattered, painted and overstaged monster, read paradoxically as astonishing, or 'beauti-

'The Merry Widow' modernized as a Hollywood Star
F20 *Marlene Dietrich, New York*, 1937 (Sotheby's, London)

ful'. Another motif, less caricatural but still related to this satiric mode, is the sinister 'fatal' woman, like that found in his 1935 portrait series of Marlene Dietrich. Melodramatic, enigmatic, independent, dressed in the 1904 clothes of *The Merry Widow* musical comedy, Dietrich appears threatening, or rather mock-threatening, for Beaton is playing with the clothes and signs of the *femme fatale*. These signs are used ironically, scavenged from his childhood archives of musical comedy theatre productions, and then gathered together in his albums.

Dietrich in 1935 resembled Beaton's drawing eight years earlier of the 'sinister "Rose Queen" . . . a Victorian lady . . . with a . . . menacing air',[11] based on Queen Alexandra. An immense phantasy of Beaton's revolved primarily around the figure of his beloved imaginary matriarchs of the Edwardian period. Yet, in his sarcastic portraits of Lady Oxford and Lady Lavery in the twenties and thirties, and in his later portraits of Mae Murray and Elsa Maxwell in the fifties, this phantasy was visibly decomposing as Beaton's sadistic aggression caricatured his previous love objects.[12] Mae Murray was placed behind a lace barrier, resembling the apparition of Diane Arbus's *Woman with a Veil, Fifth Avenue, New York* (1968); other ageing stars of stage and screen were defaced, just as Robert Aldrich was to do in *Whatever Happened to Baby Jane?* (1962). Lady Oxford, as early as 1930, was described by Beaton as having 'powdered hair, brittle arrogance and witch-like delicacy' in his *Book of Beauty*. Ten years later, he photographed her like a Daumier caricature, *profil perdu*, but her head like a dead turkey's – literally an 'old-bird', in Beaton's conflicted misogyny.[13]

[29]

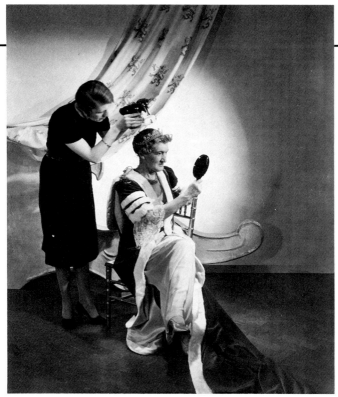

The Toilette of a Gossip Column Queen
Lady Oxford, 1937 (Sotheby's, London)

These women were portrayed by Beaton as spectacular and elderly female wrecks. Among his grotesques, he was most fascinated by the millionaire's widow, Mrs Mosscockle, whose fantastic appearance gave him the occasion to write extensive baroque passages about her that were published in his revised 1926 diary. She is represented by him as a failed copy of Queen Alexandra, a shambling version of the Edwardian hostess, but nevertheless, to the connoisseur of the grotesque, a collectable counterfeit to be pursued as a derelict, abysmal sign of a sign. She was multiplied over and over again in his photographs and photomontages, 'A travesty to end all travesties',[14] as Beaton wrote in his diary. Beaton narrated his visit to her as a dramatized comedy in a series of acts, complete with stage directions, a pastiche of a Wildeian comedy. At the outset, he confessed to the wish which had led to his surveillance of this battered effigy of Edwardianism: 'it was my penchant for the grotesque that made Mrs Mosscockle fascinating to me.'[15] It was the *inauthenticity* of Mrs Mosscockle which fascinated him, since she passed as an ironic icon of 'nobility', compared to the authentic appearance of Queen Alexandra, whom he had actually spied upon in July 1924. At that time, watching Queen Alexandra, Beaton's phantasies of vision, photography, and frame were mapped onto the royal figure herself, but were qualified by the massive sentiment of romantic Royalism. 'I even peered [at Sandringham] through one of the ground floor windows, and caught a glimpse of the Old Queen pottering about the sitting room. Stopping at a crowded table she picked up a silver framed photograph of the Duke and Duchess of York taken by Bertram Park, in soft focus.'[16] From his gaze upon her glance, the latter portrait became for him a Proustian 'sentimental acquisition', a beloved Royal object, collected in the allegorical act of collecting precious photographs.

The framing of the noble face in frame or mirror also reminded Beaton of those childhood memories of his mother at her toilette, seated in front of her dressing-table, her face (and perhaps his too) reflected in the mirror in which he photographed her in the mid twenties. The play of mirrors, and the spectacle of the woman 'making-up', became for him a mightily invested and recurrent topic; as late as the sixties, Margot Fonteyn was shown reflected in large room-sized mirrors, and also in the mirror of her powder-compact. Using the same motif, Beaton photographed the actress Martita Hunt on the set of David Lean's *Great Expectations* (1946),[17] portraying her as the elderly, disintegrating Miss Havisham, gazing at her cobwebbed dressing-table, and catching there a glimpse of the face of her young ward, Estella. This *grand guignol* portrait brought together Beaton's powerful mythology of the superior matriarch, a sadistic voyeurism, and the theme of the mirrored subject's narcissistic gaze.

This motif of the mirrored matriarch formed the extraordinary introduction to the novel by painter and writer Percy Wyndham Lewis, *The Apes of God* (1930), a long fictional critique of High Bohemian mentality in the London of the twenties and the tastes and habits of the Sitwell family in particular. Lewis opened with a prologue which had the Beatonesque title, 'The Toilette of a Veteran Gossip Star', and went on to anatomize the elderly Lady Fredigonde Follet (who was, like Lady Asquith, a 'Gossip Column Star') as she was being made-up, 'her formidable image framed by a cheval glass'.[18] But more than this, Lewis used the notion of decay to allegorize a far larger topic – the British cultural climate, where the decadence of the High Bohemian micro-culture indicated a wider, encroaching decadence for the nation, the state and the Empire. *The Apes of God* was set in 1926 against the background of the General Strike, a premonition of Britain's decline and fall; Beaton's first exhibition in 1927 was taken by some as a similar portent of political collapse. The reviewer in *Apollo* magazine, January 1928, re-told Osbert Sitwell's comic description of Beaton toppling onto the Sitwells' bodies from the top of the ladder from which he was taking high-angle pictures, seeing

The Child's Glance at the Mother's Look:
the Dressing-Table Madonna
A20 *Mrs Beaton Reflected*, *c.* 1925 (Sotheby's, London)

A Controlling Matriarch – Snobbery and Decay
K18 *Still from 'Great Expectations'*, 1946
(Private Collection)

in it a political metaphor: 'there you have a description of a modern Götterdammerung . . . and as it not only happened once, but perhaps is not unlikely to happen again on a far bigger stage. There was a kind of *après nous le déluge* about this innocent and pleasing little show – a portent that the deluge is not far off, and that when it comes it will be a rather risible anti-climax.'[19] The Empire and Beaton would tumble one day, but it would be of no consequence, for comedy was the master of Beatonesque history.

British culture was thus perceived as entering into a decline, a fallen, ironic 'iron-age' where only caricature and satire could adequately signify. This was also to be the opinion of Peter Quennell when he began his commentary to Beaton's scrap-album compendium of his photographs, *Time Exposure* (1941). Set opposite the sentiment and trauma of Beaton's portrait of *Eileen Dunne* (a blitz victim, framed head-on in her hospital bed, just as Lord Goodman was to be thirty years later), Quennell's introduction makes an apocalyptic reading of Beaton's photographs as belonging to 'a period . . . as catastrophic as the epoch that preceded the fall of the Roman Empire'.[20] His mode of address resembled Lincoln Kirstein's ironic commentary to Walker Evans's *American Photographs* (1938), which he saw as being records of an age before 'imminent collapse'. Certainly, some consciousness of living in an iron-age – living on after the high point of Western civilization – haunts and inflects Beaton's thoughts. For him, the high point was, of course, the Edwardian era before the Great War, which was followed by the great fall and an immeasurable alteration. To restore a plenitude to existence, Beaton could appeal only to some historically lost authority, one based in his mother's time and in the epoch of his own childhood; a matriarchal authority, perhaps of the *ancien régime*. This was constructed for Beaton out of that group of society hostesses which he adored (and hated) – Sybil Colefax, Emerald Cunard, Elsie de Wolfe, Elsa Maxwell and Lady Oxford. It followed closely the example of Lytton Strachey's writings of the 1910s and 1920s where he described a Utopian eighteenth-century world, presided over by a matriarchy of Salon hostesses – Madame de Sévigné, Madame de Lieven, Madame du Deffand and Mademoiselle de Lespinasse.[21]

Behind the Edwardian *ancien régime*, there stood also in Beaton's imagination the reference point of the eighteenth-century *ancien régime*. A sculpted head of Marie Antoinette surmounted the overmantel at Reddish, signifier of the eighteenth century, its pictorial iconography composed of bowers, gardens, ruins and *fête champêtre* groups. This was an intimate imaginary world of correspondents, hunters of erotic souvenirs, diarists and guitar players, which Beaton had transferred to his private photographs of Ashcombe in the thirties, and to his fashion and portrait photographs well into the seventies. He organized period-revival sets for his portrait photography by arranging complex scenographies, sometimes based on porcelain figures or collected objects, whether Rococo chairs or Edwardian props. Borrowing pictorial paradigms direct from Watteau, Fragonard, Gainsborough and Piranesi, he enlarged them as scenery backdrops that acted, in that iron-age of the thirties, as sentimental fragments of another, lost civilization, one which was phantasized as being noble, aristocratic, and matriarchal. Thus, in July 1939, he could write: 'pictures were taken of the Queen [HM Queen Elizabeth] against my old Piranesi and Fragonard backgrounds'.[22]

In Beaton's first published diaries, with their evocative eighteenth-century title *The Wandering Years* (1961), a title associated with the historical rhetoric of youth's sentimental progress, he gave the title 'The Last Summer' to his account of the summer of 1939; another year, like 1914, of closure, of threatened loss, and interruption to the 'beautiful' stream of phantasmic portraits of society ladies. He had already described his experience of such a loss when he remembered his childhood from the vantage point of 1930 in *The Book of Beauty*. There he described his toy theatre stage, full of pictures of actresses and nobility which he had cut from the weekly glossy magazines: 'then – oh horror! the war came and *The Sketch* and *Tatler* stopped for a week, after which a very thin ghost of these magazines appeared filled with photographs of – soldiers. But I prayed very hard, and soon the photographs I wanted reappeared.'[23] This was the infantilist language of J. M. Barrie's *Peter Pan*, but it was also an obsessively egoistic version of history as comedy, where pleasure could be renewed through the consoling apparition of the 'beautiful' photograph.

——— VII *Penitence, War and Orientalism* ———

Beaton organized, and was organized by, the spectacle of the Second World War. He re-wrote his own story, which was likewise re-written by others, until the outlines of another Beaton emerge, one who renounced frivolity and was engaged in recording martial activity. The war is figured by Beaton, and by those who wrote about him, as some kind of transfiguring purgation, a rhetoric which continued to structure accounts of Beaton for nearly forty years.[1] There was a redemptive programme to the representation of Beaton during these war years, and a kind of puritan and purgatorial narrative was utilized by Raymond Mortimer and Peter Quennell in their wartime writings about him. A confessant, repentant Beaton was ventriloquized by Quennell in *Time Exposure* (1941), a Beaton who once, in the thirties, 'had a passion – a perverse passion he now considers – for the romantic quality of the artificial and the charm of the second rate'.[2] Thus, recalling the previous decade, the dead walk before Quennell as they walked before Beaton when he wrote his diary in the Western Desert in 1942. There, relics of vanity were remembered, together with a ritual loathing for the inter-war period – 'a period when, trusting in Baldwin, we went to fancy dress parties, did imitations, danced the Lindy Hop and carted heavy luggage over the face of the globe',[3] – a protracted *mea culpa* for his involvement in the culture of appeasement and his casual anti-semitism.

But redemption, of a kind, was accomplished; and a film still by Beaton, reproduced on the cover of *The Sketch* in 1941, is metaphoric for this moment in Beaton's career. It shows an actress, Valerie Hobson, standing fashionably dressed in the ruins of a bombed building, playing the main role in *Unpublished Story* (1942), 'a fashion journalist turned war reporter',[4] casting modishness aside and austere of countenance – in short, transfigured by her new wartime identity. This sort of transformation was being ascribed to Beaton as well, and his career was brought into alignment with the changed political circumstances, which had shifted from appeasement in the thirties to the heroic wartime collectivity of the forties. In 1943 the book reviewer Henry Saville, writing in *The News Review*, said that 'as far as any one man typifies any one thing, Cecil Beaton can be considered today to symbolize the revolution the war has wrought in Britain'.[5] In the thirties, observed Saville, he was 'amusing, mostly clever', but in the last three years had been transformed by serious 'reporting'. Saville concluded that 'it needed a war to make Beaton write and illustrate so good a book as *Near East*'.[6] Thus, Beaton was represented as fulfilling the imperatives of war, a renascent Briton discovering new and sober skills that were suited to the prioritized style of documentary realism, which could depict Britain at war. In 1940–41, Beaton's work appeared in that exemplary magazine of photo-stories and documentary realist style, *Picture Post*. Soon, however, the functional demands of his tasks as an official Ministry of Information photographer began to put a strain on his dandy-photographer persona, exempt from 'trade'. As he wrote to Francis Rose in 1941, 'I am really very overworked . . . I've done such a lot of photography but it isn't really funny any more. It is just like being a press photographer.'[7]

Yet, although Beaton tried to accommodate himself to the new photographic language of heroic documentary propaganda, his repertory of devices – irony, theatrical framing, the grotesque, the use of mirrors and an open display of fiction – were still operative, working against the grain of the dominant codes of documentary style. Sometimes they coincided, as in his long assignment to record the RAF in 1941, where Beaton adapted and represented the mythic pathos of the 'Few' from Fighter Command and Bomber crews. Even here, Beaton lapsed into his brilliant juggling act with 'star' fictions. In his portrait on the cover of *The Sketch* in October 1941, an anonymous fighter pilot, DFC and Bar, is shown standing backlit in fine de Meyer-style profile, before banks of studio arc lights with their barn doors open, like a relaxing film star in uniform.[8] This was a recollection by Beaton of his cunning and reflexive Hollywood photographs of the early thirties, when he portrayed stars such as Gary Cooper, Buster Keaton and William Powell on film sets, among the fictions of the backdrops, with the cameras and arc lights of the film studio openly visible. This was a development of the Hollywood 'star' photography of Anton Bruehl and James Abbé, and Beaton's display of the means and fictions of the studio had been hailed in American film-fan magazines as 'Hollywood Debunked';[9] but the fighter pilot, in 1941, was represented as an entirely mythical, heroic being.

A Star Incarnation for 'The Few':
Film Studio Glamourisation for the RAF
H13 'An English Fighter Pilot, DFC and Bar',
The Sketch, October 1941

If Hollywood's fictions were still active in his wartime photographic language, Beaton was also involved in manufacturing British fictions to be sent to America. His portrait of Churchill in the Cabinet Room was first used in major British daily newspapers on 23 December 1940, with captions reminding the reader that Churchill would speak to Britain and the Empire that night on the radio. The photograph then appeared full page in *Life* magazine, with a text commenting on Churchill's 'great Bulldog jaw and penetrating stare . . . He inspires an Empire in its hour of need.'[10] Beaton's iconography of Churchill for the American market had already been established by his photo essay published in *Life* in October 1940, called 'Churchill, England'.[11] This essay was centred not upon the Premier's physiognomy and his symbolic, bulky power, but instead upon the village of Churchill in Dorset – a pastoral personification of Churchill the man, now redoubled as chief symbol of Britain. Beaton portrayed a cross-section of members of this village in a documentary style. But his choice did not reflect any heroic documentary typology of Britons at all. The group that he picked for *Life* was a bizarre and caricatural collection of eccentrics – exceptions all of them: a local millionaire; an odd-job man recruited from the local workhouse; and an aristocratic lady in reduced circumstances – a comedy of pecuniary status. This was a village England that had been collected from the extreme margins, a kind of musical-comedy-Tory England, just as Churchill, in his role as British Premier, came from the same political margins of nostalgic Toryism.

At this point, *Life* began to take up Beaton's reportage work, after carrying his portrait of the bomb victim, Eileen Dunne, in her hospital bed on its cover in September 1940. It, too, signalled the implied transition in Beaton's career from frivolity to implications of heroism: '*Life* received from Cecil Beaton, England's crack Society photographer, the pictures of a North England bombing.'[12] Eileen Dunne was twice framed, once by the edge of the picture and again by the bed-frame itself, just as the towers of St Paul's are framed in his Blitz photographs by a bombed arch, like a rusticated screen. To photograph the war, Beaton turned it into a framed spectacle, with similar ornamental screens and sub-frames to seal in the picturesque ruins. He did this most conspicuously, perhaps, with his abyss of empty frames made from wrecked tank turrets, up-ended as circular metal forms at Halfaya Pass in the Western Desert in 1942. *Vogue* printed this picture as *Desert Design* in November of that year with a caption that once more mobilized Beaton's aesthetic of the grotesque, stating that 'he found these macabre and beautiful forms'.[13] It was a fundamentally decorative and ornamental landscape of war that he represented in his commissions, war continually supplemented by found theatrical, scenographic and *parergonal* devices,[14] a photographic strategy already clearly under way in the 1930s in his portrait and fashion photography, which relied heavily upon the use of screens and frames.

Photographing the Photographer
on an Oriental Stage
16 '*Souvenir*' *of the Dome of the Rock*, Jerusalem, 1942
(Sotheby's, London)

Beaton's war was a staged war, a static war behind doorways, windows and screens. An example of this can be found in the Chinese police detachment that he photographed at Chengtu in head-on stasis, as if they were presenting themselves for applause to an imaginary theatre audience, with a cut-out circle for a proscenium arch, and flats behind and around them. Everywhere in Beaton's war photographs, officers, soldiers and civilians are spread horizontally to make informal chorus lines in these theatres of war. Beaton's choice of code was well made, for he knew that he could not possibly compete with the kind of visceral combat photography that had been developed in the late thirties by Robert Capa, whose pictures of the bombing of Hankow, published in *Life*, had been collected by Beaton for inclusion in his 1938 *Miscellaneous Scrapbook*. Beaton's framed, distanced and ornamental world removed itself from the Capaesque, photo-journalist ethic of involvement and immediacy. In the introduction to *Near East* in 1943, he announced that 'this book has no news value',[15] demonstrating his aversion to that dreaded, routinized, workaday role of the 'news-photographer'. By his calligraphy and autography, writ large on the cover and binding, Beaton managed to customize his production of *Near East* into a kind of wartime travel book and album that seemed unique in an age of austerity regulations and standards, a luxury item of exotica.

[35]

All Beaton's visual metaphors of the theatre, his collections of grotesque detail, his doubling and mirroring served, in the context of India, Egypt and Palestine in the early and mid-forties, to declare secretly the essentially comic organization of the East and of the Empire in decline. In New Delhi in 1944, Beaton photographed William Henderson, a British officer in ceremonial uniform, his helmet removed, indolently posed with one foot leaning on a plinth, gazing up at the back of an enormous, over-life-size statue of Queen Alexandra, which he captioned 'Imperial Delhi'.[16] This gesture, which appears near the beginning of his book *Far East* (1945), was one of ironic nostalgia, a nostalgia for the Edwardian High Noon of Empire symbolized by the effigy of Queen Alexandra. This is a nostalgia which Beaton felt keenly, but nevertheless he admitted to himself and to his readers in *Far East* that it was an absurdity, a comic gesture of hopeless affirmation in British power. New Delhi, Beaton wrote, was 'a city built for an exhibition',[17] a symptom of Imperial rule which had 'no roots to develop a future'.[18] Beaton was left instead with a melancholy vista of the Orient as pure display, of a Beatonesque exhibition from the Imperial Centre; for he had arrived, as he knew, too late. (But also too early, at a different moment and with a different role to, say, Henri Cartier-Bresson, who only a few years later was to record the close of Colonial rule in the East.) In the stasis of history, Beaton could only ironize. He continually juxtaposed the signs and debris of Western technology, advertising and entertainment with their oriental setting, showing the Orient to be contaminated with the West and with the display of British styles and signs, rather than being an immaculate Oriental spectacle. In the Western Desert of Egypt, he found Western writing everywhere: autographs cut into cacti by the troops, and graffiti on the tail planes of RAF Liberators. Eastern calligraphy abutted Western signs: he photographed an elderly musical comedy star, Alice Delysia, against Islamic decoration in Cairo, while in other examples a British soldier drinks tea in front of a wall covered with Islamic script, and Egyptians in *jellabas* pass before a film poster of MGM stars Hedy Lamarr, Lana Turner and Judy Garland in the film *Ziegfeld Girls* (1941).[19] These ironic cultural superimpositions are still ornamental and decorative, but also bizarre and deconstructive.

Beaton's Orient was comically unstable. But then it could never be unified or intact because it could never reproduce the Orientalist fiction of the East that he had first seen in the London theatre of his childhood. It could never correspond, as he wished, to those stage panoramas of *The Garden of Allah* in Drury Lane (1920), or to Lovat Fraser's designs for Lord Dunsany's play *If* (1921), or to the great musical comedy fictions about the East that were performed at Daly's Theatre in Leicester Square, such as *The Geisha*, *San Toy* and *The Cingalee*. The Orientalist mentality, which has been

Superimposition of East and West
Cairo Patterns, Near East, 1943 (Sotheby's, London)

systematically examined by Edward Said in literary forms,[20] was also well sedimented iconographically in that part of the British theatrical imagination in which Beaton was well schooled. With his first Orientalist photographs taken in a brothel in Morocco as far back as 1933, Beaton had returned to that model of the Orient that he had first identified on stage in *The Garden of Allah*, and also in those Royal Academy paintings that he was so versed in from the early twenties, like Glyn Philpot's *L'Après-midi Tunisien* (1921): exotic and erotic spectacles of staged Oriental 'otherness'. Besides being theatre-based, this Orient – Beaton's Orient – was also a patterned, decorated, imaginary place like the mirrored temple walls at Jaipur and Calcutta which Beaton was to photograph.

In China Beaton pushed his constructions of photographic space into a flatter, more planified world. With increasing frequency, he presented portraits in front of façades or walls, with enormous ideograms or Chinese decorative motifs painted or worked upon them. These were Rococo, Sitwellian representations, where the faces were just one more emblem that could be floated off, leaving a purely decorative sign, just as he did with the cover for *Chinese Album*, which Beaton derived from his portraits of Chinese gatekeepers. In Chengtu, Szechuan Province, he photographed the façades of shops – frames within frames, and apertures within apertures once more.[21] He paid special attention to the flagmaker of Chengtu, with his festoons of American and Chinese Nationalist flags: a celebratory ornament in the visual economy of cornucopian excess that held sway over Beaton's decorated text, where all stuffs and materials elaborated themselves in agitated display.

The 'feminine' superfluity of tulle, which so fascinated Beaton in the twenties and thirties was to him a quintessentially Edwardian material, one with which he had protectively wrapped his Kodak. His love of transparency reappeared with the use of other translucent materials, particularly cottons, and with the camouflage netting, blinds and screens that he found in the props of the East at war. To Beaton, Egypt and India were netted and curtained places, sites shaded against the sun for soldiers, natives, and grand colonial and enthroned Imperial rulers. In his visual imagination, these were places which entertained an intertextual relationship with Noël Coward's words from his song for the review, *Words and Music* (1932), entitled *Mad Dogs and Englishmen*: 'In the Philippines, there are lovely screens/to protect you from the sun'.[22] If New Delhi was to Beaton an 'exhibition' city, then the entire Empire was similarly a scenographic and emphatically nostalgic spectacle, which was lit by dappled, shuttered and screened light just like that at Daly's Theatre. Beaton attempted to match the pictorial and theatrical schemata of Orientalism with the great, half-Westernized, shambling and recalcitrant sites which constantly betrayed his phantasies. In Teheran, in 1942, he was despatched to photograph the Shah of Persia and his wife, hoping 'to photograph the Queen looking like the Persian miniatures that were made during the golden age of Shah Abbas'.[23] His ploy failed; Beaton related comically that Queen Fawzieh was wearing 'vulgar' Shaftesbury Avenue clothes and that the Palace was 'as new as any Hollywood Picture Palace'.[24] Ironically, he regretted that he could not find a pristine Orient, and that the division between West and East was closing. He admitted that his romantic nostalgic project was ruined: 'It was my mistake. How unwise to try to link the past with the present.'[25] Beaton painfully discovered that the East was not in another primitive age; it was modernized, ruled, co-ordinated and organized by British administrators and their nominees. At least, this is the evidence of his portraits, where maps dominate offices and officers, and an 'Englishman of the East', Glubb Pasha, 'an expert-adventurer-eccentric'[26] modestly shoulders his task as an Imperial agent, altogether dominated by the instrumental telephone shown in abrupt close-up on his desk.

VIII *The Romantic Royalist*

For Beaton, the dream of the past – his conserving mission – acquired such priority that it effectively structured one of his most significant achievements, the renovation of Royal portraiture from the late thirties to the fifties. The determining factors of the style and iconography with which he chose to represent the Royal family can be discovered back in the twenties, in his insistence on romantic femininity and a return to an Edwardian, or even Victorian, imagination of 'feminine' ornamentation, to tulle and to gauze. That it was a definite image of a woman, aristocratic and radiant, that was at stake can be seen in his childhood and adolescent cult for Queen Alexandra. Beaton placed her, as the only coloured reproduction and the frontispiece to his *Book of Beauty*, with a crown floating above the picture frame, around which he drew exclamatory rays. The long continuity of British monarchy, signified by the intricately-decorated pastiche painting of Queen Alexandra, worked to safeguard the notion of modern 'Beauty' around which Beaton had written his book. 'Beauty' was theorized as virtually a sacred remnant from the recent (Edwardian and Victorian) past in Beaton's introduction, a remnant connected with aristocracy, nobility and the stage, which was under siege from modernizing elements in the world. Earlier, he had contrasted two versions of *The Merry Widow*, his favourite, talismanic childhood musical comedy, in a 1924 caricature for *Granta*, the Cambridge University magazine.[1] One version was titled 'As she was', with a huge hat, Edwardian ballgown, jewels, pearls and gloves, all signifying a past order of supplemented femininity from his mother's era; the other, 'As she is, Alas', was an anonymous, thin 'Flapper-Girl', boyish in a tube dress.[1] Thus was established a remembered Utopia of gender, where a Firbankian 'Artificial Princess' stood over the emancipated, post-Great War woman.

OCTOBER 24, 1924   THE GRANTA   37

THE MERRY WIDOW

By Cecil Beaton.

As she was and as we would always see her.   As she is, alas.

The Edwardian Preference
The Merry Widow, from *Granta*, 24 October 1924

Faced with an interview on the topic of 'Woman of the Future' in 1928, the year of the extension of female suffrage, Beaton readily predicted a reaction against 'the rather harsh "sex equality" business. This "woman doing all the work" nonsense, this driving the car . . . "running a job", is wearying. So there is now a tendency among women to Lavender picking in old-world gardens.'[2] Like a figure from an Augustus John painting of before the Great War, Beaton held his phantasy of 'old-world' femininity as a counter-balance to another, but equally phantastic, threat from the sexual metaphors of what he called 'a race of Robot women, uncaring and unreal'.[3] Beaton had already prescribed a kind of ban on contemporary dress in his portraits of women, thereby following in the steps of a tradition among portrait painters especially prevalent in the eighteenth and nineteenth centuries – 'As far as possible I avoid allowing modern clothes to appear in a photograph . . . I try to get my sitters to wear some kind of costume that has withstood the criticism of time',[4] – that was located amidst a decor of 'rosebuds, chiffons and turtle-doves'.[5] A genre of whimsical revivalism was clearly at work, just as it was in the paintings of his friend Rex Whistler, or in Beaton's favourite novels by David Garnett. Through whimsy it seemed possible to neutralize the present by fancy dress, supplemented with an ornamentalism that might even attempt, in Beaton's words, 'to decorate a machine with dog roses'.[6] The threat of mechanized Modernism was also related to the shadow of Bolshevism, and by association, in Beaton's imagination, to that traumatic break in his images of 'Beauty' that had been occasioned by the beginning of the Great War. In his early scrapbooks, he had collected a press cutting of 'The Murder of the Czar's Daughters'[7] where, appallingly, female nobility was doomed and beautiful royalty was under threat. Bolshevism was undoubtedly a great cultural terror for the British middle classes during Beaton's formative years, and it also looms as an apocalypse on the horizon of High Bohemia and society in Wyndham Lewis's *The Apes of God*. Beaton feared that it would entail an end to 'Beauty', and this knowledge was confirmed and reinforced through his friendships with those White Russian emigrés whom he knew in the thirties – Pavel Tchelitchew and Baron Hoyningen-Huene – and also in the brilliant evidence of the exiled Ballets Russes from Soviet Russia.

There was a major change in British consciousness of the Royal Family in the twenties. While George V was the secure father of the nation, Europe was left bereft of its royalty by the revolutions of 1917–19. (Beaton's *My Royal Past* [1939] was a comic essay about the nostalgia for those lost European institutions and pageantry, a nostalgia which had arisen in the inter-war period.) The historian David Cannadine has identified the innovative way in which British royalty was represented in the twenties, particularly with the advent of outside radio broadcasts for state ceremonials and weddings. These began with the wedding of the Duke of York in 1923, and soon developed, under the Director-General of the BBC, Lord Reith, into 'audible pageants' which addressed the bulk of the British public through a new mass medium, drawing them into 'a sense of participation in ceremonial'.[8]

It was of great importance that Beaton came to maturity in this new mass-media, Royalist era and was eventually to take his first pictures of HM Queen Elizabeth (now the Queen Mother) in July 1939, signifying a further change in the diffusion and meaning of the British monarchy's image in an era of mass communication. Like Lord Reith, Beaton also effected 'The Invention of Tradition'.[9] This was not so much in terms of technical form as in style and connotation, through a strongly romantic representation of a 'fairy book' queen,[10] which was circulated to an extent that few royal portraits had been before. This transformed the symbolic meaning of the monarchy after the trauma of Edward VIII, inflecting it strongly towards a sweet nostalgia for the Edwardian and Georgian periods. The official caption, typed and stuck on the back of one of the July 1939 portraits, underwrote this new, post-abdication rhetoric of maternal continuity and 'Beauty' rather than that fatal modernity which had surrounded the iconography of Edward VIII: 'the serenity of this beautiful photograph well portrays the sweetness and dignity of HM The Queen'.[11]

Beaton's own recital of that July 1939 sitting at Buckingham Palace was narrated as an adoring piece of rococo fiction, a staging for his diary of an eighteenth-century *fête champêtre* in the present day, populated solely, blissfully, by himself and his fairy queen monarch, and visually coded by the nebulosities of Watteau and Pater, with the omnipresent, magical material, tulle, and the atmospherics of the regally sacred. It was a brief, idyllic episode in the still Imperial centre of the metropolis, framed by 'my old Piranesi and Fragonard backgrounds',[12] as well as the mighty doorways and pillars of the Palace. His portrait of Her Majesty in profile, by a sofa with sunlight from windows behind her, had its prototype in the Baron de Meyer's photographs[13] from the circle of Edward VII, with Lady de Grey and that last, lost world of grand quarters and deliquescent light, displaying a courtly elegance. Another group of portraits, taken in the grounds with parasol and white ball dress, referred directly to the paintings of de Meyer's friend, the artist Charles Conder, who depicted loose, light-filled fantasias populated by white-clad leisured ladies. These were all Edwardian schemata, which Beaton the romantic-conservative now invoked for this occasion. But the central signifier in them all was light, irridescent and nebulous. A repeated Beatonesque association of light and monarchy, which he had first indicated by the rays emitted from Queen Alexandra's crown, characterizes these photographs; they are royal *auras*. Beaton was later to write: 'It has caught her radiance . . . that elusive quality of light and fairybook charm surrounding her.'[14]

Reproductions of his photographs of the Queen and her daughters as heroines of a transfigured, neo-romantic monarchy, were ubiquitous in the forties and fifties and were applied, emblematically, to book and magazine covers, and addressed all sections of the British and Imperial public from *The Girls' Own Paper* in April 1943, to *The Queen's Book of The Red Cross* (1939), or *The Times of India* in 1944. Because of their cultural currency, they were used for a multitude of other functions, and a version of his portrait of HM Queen Elizabeth was given as a Christmas postcard to all men and women serving in the British armed forces in December 1949. They entered countless scrapbooks as royal souvenirs. The great wave of monarchist sentiment in Britain in the first half of the forties was part of the mental restructuring of the 'Churchillian renaissance', a culture in which Beaton flourished. In 1943, Nigel Dennis drew together the different strands of the emergent cultural con-figuration of romantic Toryism, including the wartime novels of Evelyn Waugh, and even the quix-otic, exceptionalist statements of Salvador Dali. 'In exchange for puritanism', Nigel Dennis wondered, 'are we to have, as Dali suggests, "an individualist tradition . . . aristocratic and probably monarchic"?'[15] Although deprived of its political base through Churchill's loss of power at the 1945 election, this cultural drift continued and intensified as a reaction to the egalitarian policies of the post-war Labour government and its austere stance. As a political Conservative as well as a cultural one, Beaton resisted socialist restrictiveness, writing bitterly in his scrapbook for 1947, beneath a cutting of Sir Stafford Cripps, the Labour Chancellor, who had been photographed puritanically refusing champagne at dinner: 'What England came to after the Great Victory'. A few pages away, Beaton had included a photograph from the *Illustrated London News* of the Union Jack being hauled down at Lucknow after Lord Louis Mountbatten's negotiation of Indian independence.[16] The end of Empire had arrived, and the floating fictions of British ascendancy, which Beaton had depicted in 1944, were now utterly detached.

Beaton redoubled his gestures of nostalgia, and almost exiled himself to America where he toured in a revival of Wilde's comedy, *Lady Windermere's Fan*. His resistance to change was reflected in his performance in, and designs for, a group of flamboyant theatre and film productions, which re-staged the *fin de siècle* and the Edwardian era. They should be seen, at least initially, as anti-austerity compen-sations, beginning with *Lady Windermere's Fan* (1945–46), then continuing with Korda's production of *An Ideal Husband* (1947). As a genre, these designs reached forward into the fifties and sixties with sets and costumes for *Gigi* (1957) and *My Fair Lady* (1955 and 1963). His works of the late forties were the scenic counterparts to the arrival and success of Christian Dior's 'New Look', in a shared cultural field of revivalism and nostalgia for that world before the modern era, before 1914.

Colour was, perhaps, the chief element in this late forties strategy, whether in his fashion photo-graphy, interior decoration or theatre design. During the war and immediately afterwards, Beaton

The Faerie Queen
HM Queen Elizabeth, 1939 (Private Collection)

had constructed his photography as a kind of *grisaille*, producing a grey, even-toned world of melancholy that was in such a marked contrast to Bill Brandt's chiaroscuro, and which provided Irving Penn with a decisive point of departure; 'the deliberate cultivation of soft grey colours',[17] as one of Beaton's English *Vogue* superiors described it. But in 1946, at the moment of his extended visit to America, Beaton began to experiment with colour, not only in an anti-naturalistic register, but also in a code rooted in his remembrance of colours from late childhood and adolescence. He returned, among other things, to the high artificial colouring of the costumes from *The Beggar's Opera* (1920), especially the 'ice-cream pink' that Lovat Fraser had employed in his designs. For Lady Windermere's costume, Beaton designed a gown in apricot, 'a romantic colour which has been neglected for nearly three decades'.[18] Colour was for him a proof of artifice, and the difference (and identity) between woman and photograph: all those things that he described as having been first imprinted on his memory by his glimpse of the pink tinting on Lily Elsie's postcard. Colour was bound to infancy, to childhood and to adolescence and its world, elements that were all reconstituted in his plays and photographs. Beaton probably put colour most fully at the service of spectacle (before *Gigi*, that is) in his sets for Korda's film production of *An Ideal Husband* (1947). Korda, an intimate of Churchill and, like Beaton, a flamboyant conservative and romantic royalist, was driven to manufacture florid productions which, he hoped, would colonize the American market with romantic British pictures, a project not unlike Beaton's aim on first going to America in 1928. Beaton's colour was the most remarked upon aspect of the film – 'puce, purple and pink walls',[19] and 'pastelled technicolour',[20] to the extent that American critics complained of its artificiality and its loss of storyline, since it appeared to move towards 'a series of living, moving tableaux'.[21]

Kordaesque lavishness and hot colouring were then displaced into Beaton's royal portraits at the end of the forties. 'He introduces a touch of crimson into every room',[22] wrote an American critic of Beaton's interior decorations in 1947, attributing Beaton's debt specifically to the taste of Lady de Grey, 'a friend of Queen Alexandra and Diaghilev'.[23] That luxurious red – an heraldic, not Socialist, red – that was in evidence in several parts of his portrait of HM Queen Elizabeth in 1949, lay encased in the extraordinary set constructed partly of real drapery, and partly of painted curtains, that was built by his assistant, Martin Battersby, and then erected by Beaton in the Music Room of Buckingham Palace. There, in painted fiction, was the idyllic garden, 'not a real garden'.[24]

Beaton was back, refusing austerity and embedded in the painted backcloth world of those Edwardian portraitists (and before them, of the Victorian, Camille Silvy) whose work he had craved, admired, and wished to emulate and collect. As the headline in the socialist *Daily Herald* read, 'I wanted it to look Victorian Beaton'. In an interview with Dudley Barker, he was reported as saying, 'I wanted to make it look like a painting by Winterhalter',[25] and clearly his project was to write himself into that certain tradition of royal portraiture, just as he had some years before when, for *Vogue* magazine,[26] he had photomontaged one of his own photographs of HM Queen Elizabeth, from 1939, onto a set of reproductions of previous oil paintings of British royalty. All had heavily opulent frames drawn by Beaton, and included Van Dyck's *Queen Henrietta Maria*, Edmund Brooks's *Duchess of York and the Princess*, Zoffany's *George III and His Family*, and finally Winterhalter's *The First of May* – a predominantly female collection of gendered royal signs. Placing himself amongst them, he entered the lineage of Royal portraitists and there, in the presence of maternal authority, began again his restless, endless allusions, his nostalgias and revivals, his re-stagings and re-framings far from mother's bed, and all along the radiant, eccentric lines of British culture in this century.

PART I

1 Cecil Beaton, *Photobiography*, p. 13.
2 *Ibid.*, p. 14.
3 Salvador Dali, *The Secret Life of Salvador Dali*, New York, 1943.
4 Max Ernst, *Beyond Painting*, New York, 1948.
5 Cecil Beaton, 'The Story of an Exception', *Photography as a Career*, ed. A. Kraszna-Krausz, London 1944, pp. 28–32.
6 'If Fetishism exists it is not a fetishism of the signified, a fetishism of substances and value . . . it is a fetishism of the signifier. That is to say that the subject is trapped in the factitious, differential, encoded, systematised aspect of the object. It is not the passion for substances which speak in fetishisms, it is the passion for the code.' J. Baudrillard, 'Fetishism and Ideology: The Semiological Reduction', *For a Critique of the Political, Economy of the Sign*, St. Louis, USA, 1981, p. 92, pp. 108–10.
7 Ed. A. Kraszna-Krausz, *op. cit.*, pp. 28–32.
8 The display of framed portraits in Coward's plays, and stage discussions which originate with them, is very much a phenomenon of his dramas at this time. Walter Sickert's new identity as Richard Walter Sickert denotes his interest in photo-generated painting, which began in the latter half of the 1920s.
9 *The Sphere*, 6 December 1930, p. 456.
10 cf. Roland Barthes's gloss on Edgar Morin's *Le Cinema ou L'homme imaginaire*, Paris, 1956, in his essay 'The Photographic Message', *Image/Music/Text*, ed. S. Heath, 1978, p. 23.
11 *Illustrated*, 3 March 1951, p. 18.
12 Cecil Beaton, *The Wandering Years*, pp. 20, 277, 316.
13 *Ibid.*, p. 316.
14 *Tatler*, 30 November 1927.
15 Cecil Beaton, 'Scrap Albums', *Vogue*, n.d.; *Cuttings Books*, vol. XIV.

PART II

1 Cecil Beaton, *The Wandering Years*, p. 86.
2 Osbert Sitwell, 'Appreciation', Cooling Galleries exhibition catalogue, November 1927.
3 *The Sunday Herald*, 27 November 1927.
4 *Everybody's Weekly*, 14 January 1928.
5 *Ibid.*
6 Unidentified press cuttings from Cecil Beaton, *Cuttings Books*, vol. I.
7 Text by Salvador Dali in *The Metamorphosis of Narcissus*, 1937, unpaginated.
8 Cecil Beaton, *The Wandering Years*, p. 81.
9 See *Tatler*, 19 January 1927, cover.
10 My argument here, as elsewhere, is greatly indebted to Jean Sagne's introduction to *Cecil Beaton*, Paris, 1984. For Sagne, Beaton's doubling is '*thème centrale de sa production*'.

11 For a discussion of the significance of mirror representation, adapted from the writings of Jacques Lacan, see Christian Metz, *The Imaginary Signifier*, 1982, p. 82.
12 Evelyn Waugh, *Decline and Fall*, 1974, p. 128.
13 Elsie de Wolfe, *After All*, 1935, pp. 84–5.
14 Louise Burchill, 'Either/or', *Seduced and Abandoned*, ed. A. Frankovitz, 1984, pp. 28–44.
15 Hugo Vickers, *Cecil Beaton*, London, 1985, p. 290. For an important examination of Mountbatten which raises the central issues of publicity, theatricality, Empire and representations of authority within British culture, see David Cannadine, 'Masterpiece Theatre', *New York Review of Books*, 9 May 1985, pp. 6–9.
16 *The Sketch*, 13 June 1945, p. 329. The photograph is no. IB.2355 in the Imperial War Museum collection of photographs, London.
17 'Beaton Plays with Effects', *The Sketch*, 22 February 1943.

PART III

1 Miles F. Shore, 'Biography in the Eighties: A Psychoanalytic Perspective', *The New History*, ed. T. K. Rabb and R. I. Rothberg, New Jersey, 1982, pp. 89–113.
2 Quentin Bell, *Bloomsbury*, 1968, p. 96.
3 See the arguments of Martin Green on generational revolt and conflict among the young dandies (including Beaton) of the 1920s in *Children of the Sun*, 1978.
4 Cecil Beaton, *The Parting Years*, p. 45.
5 Virginia Woolf, *Orlando*, 1928, p. 312.
6 Hugo Vickers, *Cecil Beaton*, London, 1985, p. 45.
7 *The Bystander*, 15 July 1931.
8 Hugo Vickers, *op. cit.*, p. 350.
9 Virginia Woolf, *op. cit.*, 'Orlando on her return to England', facing p. 158.
10 Virginia Woolf, *op. cit.*, 'Orlando about the year 1840', facing p. 246.
11 Virginia Woolf, *op. cit.*, 'Orlando at the present time', facing p. 318.
12 *The Graphic*, 14 June 1924, p. 113.
13. Luigi Pirandello, *Henry IV*, ed. E. Martin Brown, 1962, p. 246.
14 *Ibid.*, p. 207.
15 *Ibid.*, p. 176.
16 *Truth*, 7 September, 1930.

PART IV

1 Cecil Beaton, 'The Story of an Exception', *Photography as a Career*, ed. A. Kraszna-Krausz, London, 1944, pp. 28–31.
2 Osbert Sitwell, 'Appreciation', Cooling Galleries exhibition catalogue, November 1927.

3 *Ibid.*

4 Hugh Cecil, 'Society Portraiture New Style', *The Graphic*, 14 June 1922.

5 Ed. A. Kraszna-Krausz, *op. cit.*, p. 30.

6 *Ibid.*, p. 31.

7 Cecil Beaton, 'A Remembrance of Things Proust', British *Vogue*, February 1972, pp. 78–83.

8 Cecil Beaton, *The Wandering Years*, p. 81.

9 *Ibid.*

10 Osbert Sitwell, *op. cit.*

11 See the author's 'Picturing the End of Empire', *Creative Camera*, January 1982, pp. 359–63.

12 *The Morning Post*, 23 November 1927.

13 *The Star*, 22 November 1927.

14 'Review', *The British Journal of Photography*, 21 November, 1927.

15 See 'Les Morts', *Photographies*, Avril 1984, no. 4, pp. 74–8. *The Portrait* by Valentine Hugo (1931) is reproduced on p. 77.

16 *Tatler*, 14 December 1927, p. 493.

17 *The Standard*, 22 November 1927.

18 *Ibid.*

19 Cecil Beaton, *Cuttings Books*, vol. I.

PART V

1 'The New Photography', British *Vogue*, 14 December 1927.

2 Osbert Sitwell, 'Appreciation', Cooling Galleries exhibition catalogue, November 1927.

3 Cecil Beaton, *Cuttings Books*, vol. I

4 cf. Cecil Beaton, *The Wandering Years*, p. 147.

5 'Review', *The British Journal of Photography*, 21 November 1927.

6 cf. Cecil Beaton, *The Wandering Years*, p. 94, and also Cecil Beaton, *Cuttings Books*, vols. II and III.

7 See catalogue of the *Internationale Austelling des Deutschen Werkbunds 1929*, Stuttgart entries 104–11.

8 *Münchner Illustrierte Press 1929*, no. 41.

9 See Cecil Beaton, *Cuttings Books*, vols. II and III.

10 Baron, *Baron by Baron*, London, 1957, p. 204.

11 'The Review', *The British Journal of Photography*, 21 November 1927.

12 'Fantasy in Photography', *World's Press News*, 5 June 1930, p. 18.

13 Cecil Beaton, *The Face of the World*, pp. 114–16.

14 *World's Press News*, *op. cit.*

15 Cecil Beaton, *British Photographers*, p. 36.

16 Osbert Sitwell, *op. cit.*

17 *World's Press News*, *op. cit.*

18 *Ibid.*, p. 38.

19 Cecil Beaton, *The Face of the World*, pp. 114–16.

20 'Portraiture With a Simple Kodak', *The Kodak Magazine*, 1 January 1928, p. 39.

21 Hugo Vickers, *Cecil Beaton*, London, 1985, pp. 126–7.

22 'Far Above Beauty', *New York City Journal*, 18 November 1929.

23 *The British Journal of Photography*, 2 December 1927.

24 Cecil Beaton, *Cuttings Books*, vol. I.

25 P. Wyndham Lewis, *The Apes of God*, London, 1930, p. 387.

26 *The Graphic*, 23 June 1928, p. 466. The article also reproduces a photograph of the last pre-First World War Ascot, one of Beaton's favourite topoi.

27 *Ibid.*

28 Francis Steegmuller, *Cocteau*, London, 1970, pp. 139–40.

29 David Bailey in conversation with David Mellor, April 1983.

30 Cyril Connolly, *Enemies of Promise*, London, 1938, p. 45.

PART VI

1 Cecil Beaton, *Cuttings Books*, vols. I and II.

2 *The Evening News*, 7 December 1927.

3 'Too, Too, Vomitous', *Time*, 2 February 1931.

4 Beverley Nichols, *The Sweet and Twenties*, London, 1958, p. 212.

5 *Woman's Life*, 31 March 1928, p. 4.

6 Cecil Beaton, *Cuttings Books*, vol. I.

7 'The Book of Beauty', *Library Review*, Summer, 1931.

8 Hayden White, *Metahistory*, London, 1973, p. 90.

9 Hugo Vickers, *Cecil Beaton*, London, 1985, p. 312.

10 Osbert Sitwell, 'Appreciation', Cooling Galleries exhibition catalogue, New York, 1931.

11 Ella Hepworth Dixon, *The Westminster Gazette*, 30 November 1927.

12 See J. Lacan, 'Desire and the Interpretation of Desire', *Psychoanalysis and Literature*, ed. S. Felman, Baltimore, USA, 1982, pp. 11–52.

13 Cecil Beaton, *The Book of Beauty*, p. 8.

14 Cecil Beaton, *The Wandering Years*, p. 106.

15 *Ibid.*

16 *Ibid.*, p. 48.

17 *The Sketch*, 3 April 1946, p. 185.

18 P. Wyndham Lewis, *The Apes of God*, London, 1930, p. 11.

19 'Review', *Apollo*, January, 1928.

20 Cecil Beaton and Peter Quennell, *Time Exposure*, p. 3.

21 See Lytton Strachey, *Biographical Essays*, London, 1960.

22 Cecil Beaton, *The Wandering Years*, p. 375.

23 Cecil Beaton, *The Book of Beauty*, p. 2.

PART VII

1 See James Danziger, *Beaton*, London, 1980, pp. 39–43, and Gail Buckland, *Cecil Beaton War Photographs 1939–1945*, London, 1981.

2 Cecil Beaton and Peter Quennell, *Time Exposure*, p. 4.

3 Cecil Beaton, *Near East*, p. 43.

4 *The Sketch*, 3 December 1941.

5 Henry Saville, 'Books of the Week', *News Review*, 12 August 1943.
6 *Ibid.*
7 Hugo Vickers, *Cecil Beaton*, London, 1985, p. 149.
8 *The Sketch*, 22 October, cover.
9 Cecil Beaton, *Cuttings Books*, vol. x.
10 *Life*, January 1941, p. 59.
11 'Churchill, England', *Life*, October 1940.
12 *Life*, 23 September 1940, cover and pp. 26–7.
13 British *Vogue*, November 1942, p. 42.
14 See Jacques Derrida, 'The Parergon', *October*, 1979, no. 9, p. 26.
15 Cecil Beaton, *Near East*, p. vii.
16 Cecil Beaton, *Far East*, facing p. 8.
17 *Ibid.*, p. 8.
18 *Ibid.*, p. 9.
19 See Cecil Beaton, *Near East*, facing p. 27 ('Cairo Patterns').
20 Edward Said, *Orientalism*, London, 1980.
21 For an example of Beaton's *mise-en-âbyme* visual strategy see Cecil Beaton, 'Hat Check Girl', *Cecil Beaton's New York*, facing p. 208.
22 Noël Coward, *Play Parade*, London, 1939, vol. II, p. 118.
23 Cecil Beaton, *Near East*, p. 100.
24 *Ibid.*, p. 101.
25 *Ibid.*
26 Edward Said, *op. cit.*, p. 246.

PART VIII

1 *Granta*, 24 October 1924, p. 37.
2 *Evening News*, 22 February 1928.
3 *Ibid.*
4 *The Daily Chronicle*, 8 January 1926.
5 *Evening News*, *op. cit.*
6 Cecil Beaton, *The Book of Beauty*, p. 9.
7 See Cecil Beaton, *Miscellaneous Scrapbook 1908–20*; source *Tatler*, 1 September 1920.
8 David Cannadine, 'The Context, Performance and Meaning of Ritual; The British Monarchy' and the 'Invention of Tradition *c*. 1820–1977', *The Invention of Tradition*, ed. E. Hobsbawm and T. Ranger, London, 1984, pp. 101–65.
9 *Ibid.*
10 *Illustrated*, 4 November 1950, p. 39.
11 I am indebted to Eileen Hose for this detail.
12 Cecil Beaton, *The Wandering Years*, p. 375.
13 See *Portrait of a Man* reproduced in *Pictorial Photography in Britain 1900–20*, Arts Council of Great Britain, 1978, illustration no. 38.
14 *Illustrated, op. cit.*
15 Nigel Dennis, 'Evelyn Waugh, The Pillar of Anchorage House', *Partisan Review*, July/August 1943, p. 350.
16 *The Blue Scrap Book*, 1947; source *Illustrated London News*, 23 August 1947.
17 H. W. Yoxall, 'Fashion Photography', *Penrose Annual 1949*, pp. 68–70.
18 'Beaton's Color Palette' US *House and Garden*, February 1947, p. 75.
19 *Daily Express*, 4 November 1947. For the significance of the colour pink within a scheme of sexual poetics, see Jane Gallop, 'Annie Leclerc Writing a Letter, with Vermeer', *October*, Summer 1985, no. 33, pp. 103–118: 'Pink then becomes *the* color of sexual difference . . . sexual difference itself becomes feminine', p. 104.
20 *The New York Post*, 15 January 1948.
21 *Ibid.*
22 US *House and Garden, op. cit.*
23 *Ibid.*
24 Cecil Beaton, *Cuttings Book*, vol. xxx.
25 *Ibid.*
26 *Ibid.*

CHRONOLOGY

❧ SNAPSHOTS IN TIME: A WORKING LIFE ☙

Terence Pepper

A2 *Family Group: Cecil (far left) with his mother Etty and brother Reggie, c.* 1908 (Private Collection)

[1904]
14 January: Cecil Walter Hardy Beaton is born at 21 Langland Gardens, Hampstead, the first of four children born to Esther 'Etty' Beaton (née Sisson; 1872–1962) and Ernest Walter Hardy Beaton (1867–1936), a timber merchant. His brother Reginald is born in April 1905 and his sisters Nancy and Barbara ('Baba') are born in 1909 and 1912.

[1911]
The Beaton family move to Temple Court, Templewood Avenue, a neo-Georgian mansion close to Hampstead Heath.

[1913]
June: Alice Louise Collard (known as 'Ninnie') is engaged as nanny to the Beaton children. A keen amateur photographer and gardener, she inspires and encourages Beaton's early efforts with a Box Brownie and subsequently helps with lighting as well as printing, developing and enlarging film for his later portrait sessions.

[1912–1915]
Attends Heath Preparatory School as a day boy with his brother Reggie. Bullied by his contemporary Evelyn Waugh, who becomes a life-long adversary and later, in *Decline and Fall* (1928), bases the character of the photographer David Lennox on Beaton.

[1916]
Sent as a boarder with Reggie to St Cyprian's at Eastbourne; Cyril Connolly and George Orwell are contemporary pupils, both of whom later write accounts of the deprivations endured there.

[1918]
January: enters Harrow where his talent for painting and drawing is encouraged by the art master, W. Egerton Hine. Sells his first drawing, a picture of Pavlova, for 10s 6d and twice wins the Lady Bourchier Reading Prize. Enjoys amateur school theatricals, a recreation in which his father played an active part before his marriage in 1903.

[1922]

4 October: enrols at St John's College, Cambridge. Concentrates most of his time on theatrical enterprises and photography. Begins the first of 38 diaries written whilst at Cambridge. Appears in ADC (Amateur Dramatic Company) production of Thackeray's *The Rose and the Ring* as Princess Angelica and designs dresses and scenery for their production of *The Gyp's Princess* (1923).

[1924]

Appears as the Marchioness Matilda Spina in ADC production of Pirandello's *Henry IV*. His designs and scenery are praised in *The Spectator* by Humbert Wolfe, who suggests Beaton might be 'a legitimate successor to Lovat Fraser'. Designs subsequently shown at 1928 Venice Biennale. His photographs of Marlowe Society's production of *The Duchess of Malfi* are his first photographs to appear in *Vogue* (Early April issue).

Page from *The Gentlewoman*, 1 August 1925

A14 *Baba Beaton with Cecil Beaton in Mirror, c.* 1917 (Sotheby's, London)

[1925]

In his last term at Cambridge, Beaton designs sets and costumes for the Footlights revue *All the Vogue*, in which he also appears. He leaves Cambridge without a degree. Some of his theatre designs are included in the International Theatre Exhibition, Wembley, and are published in *The Studio*. Several theatrical caricatures are published in *Granta* (1924–5). Meets London's youngest professional photographer Paul Tanqueray (b. 1905) at a theatrical garden party and subsequently visits him often for technical advice and to make use of his darkroom and studio. Failing to earn a regular salary, he starts work in his father's office, but this lasts only eight working days.

[1926]

February: the Beaton family move to 61 Sussex Gardens, London w2, where Beaton supervises elaborate redecoration schemes which include the purchase of a four-poster bed and the painting of lilies on peppermint-green walls. April–July: works in the office of a Mr Schmiegelow which he does not enjoy. Visits many publishers with his portfolio and receives first commission for a book cover design from Longmans for Robert Herring's novel *The President's Hat*. Makes unsuccessful trip to Venice, meets Diaghilev but secures no commissions. Attempts to write a play but has more success photographing some of the Bright Young People in specially improvised settings. 7 December: breaks into a new world by photographing Edith Sitwell as a medieval tomb sculpture between carved cherubs on a black and white linoleum floor. Becomes a friend of Stephen Tennant.

B25 *Edith Sitwell Receiving Breakfast in Bed at Renishaw*, 1930 (Sotheby's, London)

D10 *Ashcombe: Circus Bedroom*, 1932 (Sotheby's, London)

[1927]

Designs costumes for two charity matinées organized by Olga Lynn: *The China Shop* at the Savoy and *A Pageant of Great Lovers* at the New Theatre. Appears himself as Apollo in the former and Lucien Bonaparte in the latter. Visits the Sitwells at Renishaw which leads to several collaborations: designs settings for play by Osbert and Sacheverell called *All at Sea* at the Arts Theatre, and also the cover for their book of the same name. Osbert Sitwell writes introduction to the catalogue of Beaton's November exhibition of photographs and drawings at the Cooling Galleries, which establishes him as a major photographic figure. From the Early August issue, Beaton becomes a leading contributor to *Vogue* of articles, caricatures, illustrations and photographs.

[1928]

Designs clothes for Dream of Fair Women Ball at Claridges, including a jump suit for the 'Bride of 1940', and also for Olga Lynn's charity matinée at Daly's Theatre, *A Pageant of Hyde Park 1765–1928*. Travels to New York in November and begins work for American *Vogue*. Fortune Press publish Shane Leslie's translation of Pierre Louÿs's *The Twilight of the Nymphs* with Beaton illustrations published in collotype.

[1929]

May–June: Beaton is only British photographer represented at Stuttgart *Film und Photo* exhibition. Holds exhibitions at the Elsie de Wolfe Gallery in New York and at the Everglades Club in Palm Beach before returning to London after four months in America, with a secure contract with Condé Nast. Photographs Lily Elsie, his childhood heroine and star of *The Merry Widow*, and visits Paris to photograph Colette. November: returns to New York with Anita Loos and is commissioned by *Vanity Fair* (*Vogue*'s sister magazine) to travel to Hollywood and photograph stars such as Gary Cooper and Alice White, on condition that he acquires a camera that takes technically superior 10×8 in. negatives. Celebrates the New Year at William Randolph Hearst's mansion, San Simeon.

[1930]

Meets Peter Watson in Vienna, and later, in Venice, begins a largely unhappy four-year love affair with him. July: he acquires the lease of Ashcombe, a house set in idyllic Wiltshire countryside, which provides the location for many entertainments. November: Duckworth publish Beaton's first book, *The Book of Beauty*, and he holds his second exhibition at the Cooling Galleries. He also designs costumes for a mannequin parade in *Charlot's Masquerade*, a revue with Beatrice Lillie at the Cambridge Theatre. 10 June: with Oliver Messel and Michael Weight, Beaton is responsible for designing costumes for Living Posters Ball in aid of the Elizabeth Garrett Anderson Hospital. His photograph of three of the participants for a Lever Brothers poster is exhibited as *Soap Suds* at the London Salon of Photography.

Snapshot album page: Oliver Messel, Peter Watson and Cecil Beaton in Venice; scenes at Ashcombe
with Edith Olivier and Beaton, September 1930 (Private Collection)

C1 *Fred and Adèle Astaire*, 1930 (Sotheby's, London)

Soap Suds, 1930 (Sotheby's, London)

c15 *Self-portrait with Anita Loos*, 1930 (Sotheby's, London)

c28 *Gary Cooper*, 1931 (Sotheby's, London)

[1931]
Returns to New York for an exhibition at the Delphic Studios and photographs more film stars in Hollywood including Fay Wray and Loretta Young, often amidst the set scaffolding. November: attends a charity performance in Chicago of a series of *tableaux vivants* based on the costumes and poses of the subjects in *The Book of Beauty* – the four-headed multiple exposure of Lady Lavery is played by four women while Mrs Adlai Stevenson impersonates Anna May Wong.

[1932]
January: makes third visit to Hollywood to take glamorous photographs of a garlanded Dolores del Rio and near-naked Tarzan – Johnny Weissmuller – as well as the Marx Brothers, Jackie Cooper and Marlene Dietrich. After several attempts, meets Greta Garbo, who gives him a yellow rose which he keeps until his death.

[1933]
18 January: masterminds a lavish wedding for his sister Nancy, who marries Sir Hugh Smiley, Bt. at St Margaret's, Westminster, complete with six bridesmaids and a Constance Spry floral display. Photographs Prince George (later Duke of Kent). In America Beaton's fashion photographs of model Mary Taylor are highly acclaimed. Visits Paris and meets Jean Cocteau, Pavel Tchelitchew and Christian ('Bébé') Bérard, all of whom have an important influence on his work. Visits North Africa with George Hoyningen-Huene who persuades Beaton to use a Rolleiflex. October: brother Reggie, on leave from the RAF kills himself by jumping in front of a tube train at Piccadilly.

[1934]
Completes 26 costume designs for a black production of *Romeo and Juliet* in New York. Commissioned by C. B. Cochran to design his revue *Streamline*. Becomes staunch friend of Bérard in Paris and is painted by Tchelitchew. November: his younger sister Baba marries Alec Hambro.

[1935]
Takes famous photograph of Marlene Dietrich in black-feathered hat and jewelled dog collar in New York, watches Silver Jubilee celebrations in London, and dresses up as Charles I in the Pembrokes' pageant at Wilton. Takes part in amateur film at Ashcombe called *The Sailor's Return*, based on David Garnett's book set in the 1880s. Beaton plays the sailor and John Sutro, a director of London Film Productions, organizes the cameramen. Begins décor and costume designs for Frederick Ashton's ballet *The First Shoot* (music by William Walton, written by Osbert Sitwell) which forms part of Cochran's revue *Follow the Sun*, premièred in Manchester before a London showing in 1936.

Lord Berners, in costume for the Ashcombe *fête champêtre*,
1937 (Sotheby's, London)

[1936]

Travels to Mexico and covers maiden voyage of *RMS Queen Mary* for *Vogue*. Designs for Boris Kochno's production of *Le Pavillon* with the Ballets Russes de Monte Carlo, and for Ashton's Old Vic-Sadlers Wells production of *Apparitions* with Margot Fonteyn and Robert Helpmann. November: exhibition at Redfern Gallery, *Design for Three Ballets*. 20 November: photographs and sketches Mrs Wallis Simpson preceding abdication crisis. Beaton's father dies aged 68.

Cecil Beaton and John Betjeman during the filming of
The Sailor's Return, 1935 (Private Collection)

[1937]

January: New York exhibition at the Carroll Carstairs Gallery attended by Gala and Salvador Dali. Inclusion

Preparing for the publication of *Cecil Beaton's Scrapbook*,
1937 (Weidenfeld & Nicolson Archive)

of Mrs Simpson portrait attracts crowds. Photographs Duchess of Kent and many peeresses for Coronation issue of *Vogue*. Pays two visits to Mrs Simpson in France and takes her wedding portraits at the Château de Candé. July: organizes an elaborate *fête champêtre* at Ashcombe with Michael Duff, which includes a fully-costumed Restoration Comedy. September: after a two-year search for a publisher, Beaton persuades Batsford to publish *Cecil Beaton's Scrapbook*, a collection of essays, photographs and drawings suggested as a publication by Bébé Bérard. The book is designed by Brian Cook (later Sir Brian Batsford) with a very elaborate jacket and wallpaper endpapers. An exhibition of the original artwork is held in London, and later New York where Beaton designs Tallulah Bankhead's costumes for a Broadway production of *Antony and Cleopatra*.

[1939]
Invited by Alexander Korda to design costumes for his wife Merle Oberon in a proposed film of *Manon Lescault* (later abandoned). Summoned to Buckingham Palace to photograph Queen Elizabeth. Takes series of highly romanticized portraits pronounced by the press as 'best ever' royal photographs, which are released shortly after outbreak of war. Also publishes spoof royal memoirs entitled *My Royal Past* (Batsford). Joins ARP unit at Wilton.

[1940]
With John Sutro, Beaton writes amateur production of *Heil Cinderella*, in which Beaton and Olga Lynn play the roles of the Ugly Sisters. The production is in aid of the *Daily Sketch* War Relief Fund and travels on from Wilton to Brighton and Bournemouth and a short London run. He photographs war leaders including Winston Churchill, and tours the North for the Ministry of Information, taking his famous photograph of the bandaged three-year-old Eileen Dunne, clutching a toy in a bleak hospital bed. The photograph appears on the cover of 23 September issue of *Life* and is used as an American fund-raising poster. This picture, and those of the Queen, persuade *Vogue* to re-employ Beaton. His photographs of bomb-damaged buildings in London are published in *History under Fire* (Batsford) with text by James Pope-Hennessy.

New York Sidewalk, 1938 (Sotheby's, London)

[1938]
The February issue of American *Vogue* features Beaton drawings that contain microscopic anti-semitic doodlings. He is promptly asked to resign. Prevented from working in America, he travels extensively in Europe and the Mediterranean, and Bérard paints his portrait. Researches and writes *Cecil Beaton's New York* for Charles Fry at Batsford.

Drug Store Service, New York, 1937 (Sotheby's, London)

Duke and Duchess of Windsor, Château de Candé, 1937
(Sotheby's, London)

Winston Churchill, Prime Minster, 1940
(Cecil Beaton's *Cuttings Book*, vol. XXVII)

G18 *HM Queen Elizabeth*, 1939 (Private Collection)

[1941]

Becomes involved in various films, including H. G. Wells's *Kipps* for Carol Reed, which recreates a period setting of 1906 and stars Diana Wynyard and Michael Redgrave. Also designs for Gabriel Pascal's film of the Shaw play *Major Barbara* with Deborah Kerr, and produces 14 dresses for Sally Gray in Brian Desmond Hurst's film *Dangerous Moonlight*. For the war effort he visits numerous RAF stations and produces two well-received books – *Air of Glory* (HMSO) and *Winged Squadrons* (Hutchinson). *Time Exposure*, an anthology of all of his work with a commentary by Peter Quennell, is published by Batsford. For the Victoria Palace Theatre Beaton designs a 1912 Brighton Pier set with costumes as part of *Black Vanities*, a George Black revue. Takes stills and designs costumes for *The Young Mr Pitt*, another Carol Reed film starring Robert Donat and Robert Morley, which is released the following year.

N8 *HRH Princess Elizabeth in her Uniform of Honorary Colonel of the Grenadier Guards*, 1942 (Private Collection)

H8 *Eileen Dunne, Life* cover, 23 September 1940 (Sotheby's, London)

[1942]

Flies to Cairo to take photographs for the Air Ministry and sees Canal Zone and desert. Visits Iran, Iraq, Palestine, Transjordan and Syria before returning home via neutral Portugal, where he photographs the President, General Carmona, his Cabinet and other local celebrities which results in an exhibition of 56 photographs held at the Estudio do SPN in Lisbon in December. In London Beaton photographs Mrs Roosevelt, the American President's wife, at Buckingham Palace and Batsford publishes *Near East*, a selection of Eastern photographs with text by Beaton. *Vogue* commissions portraits of Cecil Day-Lewis, Cyril Connolly, Eddy Sackville-West, Raymond Mortimer, Rebecca West and Noël Coward. Photographs Princess Elizabeth at Buckingham Palace.

[1943]

Wings on her Shoulders, with Beaton's photographs of the WAAFs, is published by Hutchinson. Designs sets for Binkie Beaumont's revival of Shaw's *Heartbreak House*, and costumes for Edith Evans. Setting off for India, Beaton's plane crashes at Land's End, but undaunted he sets off again on next available flight.

[1944]

In India Beaton stays first at the Viceroy's House, Delhi, where he photographs Lord Wavell and Lord Louis Mountbatten before making extensive survey photographs of war effort and social services for the Ministry of Information. Travels on to Chungking and tours China for more photography. Returns to civilian life via New York. Stays in Paris at British Embassy with Duff Cooper (then Ambassador) and Lady Diana, and stages an exhibition of war photographs before returning to London. Collins publish Beaton's *British Photographers* in their 'Britain in Pictures' series, a well-received first history of British photography to date. For the theatre he designs sets and costumes for John Gielgud's production of the Eric Linklater play *Crisis in Heaven*, and also costumes for the film of Frederick Lonsdale's play *On Approval*.

[1945]

Further books of wartime work are published: *Far East* (Batsford); *India* (Thacker & Co.); *Indian Album* (Batsford), dedicated to Lord Wavell; and *Chinese Album* (Batsford), dedicated to Clarissa Churchill. Designs overtly gothic sets for touring production of Pinero's *Dandy Dick* and begins work on Gielgud's lavish production of Wilde's play *Lady Windermere's Fan* at the Haymarket Theatre. *Vogue* commissions include portrait of Quintin Hogg, which Irving Penn later credits as a major influence on his own work.

Picasso and American GIs in Liberated Paris, 1944
(Sotheby's, London)

Cecil Beaton in RAF Official Photographer's Uniform, 1942
(Sotheby's, London)

J23 *General Carton de Wiart*, 1944
(Sotheby's, London)

[1946]

Revisits New York and meets Greta Garbo again; proposes marriage. Takes a series of 'passport' photographs of her but falls out of favour when Garbo decides, too late, that they should not be published in *Vogue*. Beaton is asked to play the part of Cecil Graham in San Francisco production of *Lady Windermere's Fan* which he also designs; his performance is praised enthusiastically both there and in New York, its subsequent venue. He designs the Royal Opera House production of *Les Sirènes* in London, also Ivor Novello's production of Somerset Maugham's play *Our Betters*, and costumes for Maurice Elvey's film *Beware of Pity*.

Cecil Beaton as Cecil Graham on the Set of
'Lady Windermere's Fan', 1946 (Sotheby's, London)

[1947]

Buys Reddish House at Broadchalke, Wiltshire, having been evicted from Ashcombe on expiry of lease. *Ashcombe: The Story of a Fifteen-Year Lease* is published by Batsford two years later (1949). Under contract to Alexander

07 *The Hon. Mrs Reginald Fellowes at the Beistegui Ball,*
Venice, 1951 (Sotheby's, London)

Korda, Beaton begins work on designs and costumes for *An Ideal Husband* starring Paulette Goddard, and *Anna Karenina* starring Vivien Leigh and Ralph Richardson. Both are filmed simultaneously on adjoining sets and are released the following year.

[1948]

Starts friendship with Lucian Freud and the young Truman Capote. Designs *The Return of the Prodigal* with John Gielgud and Sybil Thorndike. 14 December: takes first official photographs of the one-month-old Prince Charles.

[1949]

Photographs the Windsors in Paris and stays with Somerset Maugham at Cap Ferrat. In Paris, designs Kochno's ballet production of *Devoirs de Vacances* with Leslie Caron and Les Ballets de Champs Elysées. The Old Vic production of *The School for Scandal* with Beaton designs is premièred at the New Theatre.

[1950]

In New York Beaton redecorates an apartment at the Sherry-Netherlands Hotel which he uses as setting for subsequent photographic sittings. Designs rococo sets and period costumes for the play *Cry of the Peacock* at the Mansfield Theatre, New York. *Les Illuminations*, a Beaton-designed ballet by Frederick Ashton with music by Benjamin Britten, is premièred by the New York City Ballet (later revived in 1981 at Covent Garden as tribute to Beaton). In London he takes first photographs of Princess Anne and designs production of Pinero's *The Second Mrs Tanqueray* with Gladys Cooper, Eileen Herlie and Leslie Banks. *Fonteyn: Impressions of a Ballerina* by William Chappell is published with 40 photographs by Beaton.

[1951]

Visits Florida, Jamaica and Miami and publishes his autobiography, *Photobiography* (Odhams). Anticipates start of new career in the theatre with his first play *The Gainsborough Girls*. At its Brighton opening at Theatre Royal, play receives disastrous notices. Designs *Our Lady's Tumbler* by Ronald Duncan for its performance in Salisbury Cathedral, and designs jacket cover for his book *The Blue Fox. Ballet*, published by Allen Wingate, contains over 100 photographs, line drawings and text reflecting Beaton's personal impressions and influences. Designs Ashton's *Casse-Noisette* for Royal Opera House, Covent Garden, and a one-act version of *Swan Lake* for the New York City Ballet. Irving Penn's portrait of Beaton, taken the previous year, is published in British *Vogue* to accompany article by Beaton celebrating the Festival of Britain. Attends and photographs the Beistegui Ball in Venice as a French *curé*.

N28 *HM Queen Elizabeth II, Coronation Day*, 1953
(Private Collection)

[1952]

In New York Beaton designs for American production of Ashton's ballet *Picnic at Tintagel* and Truman Capote's play *The Grass Harp*. In London he designs for the Lunts' production of the Noël Coward play *Quadrille* at the Phoenix Theatre.

[1953]

Undertakes the first of two American lecture tours, later to form the basis of his book *It Gives Me Great Pleasure* (1956; Weidenfeld & Nicolson). Takes official Coronation portraits and makes sketches of ceremony in Westminster Abbey. Publishes *Persona Grata* (Weidenfeld & Nicolson) with text by Kenneth Tynan, an alphabetical series of profiles with Beaton portraits. Designs *Aren't We All* by Frederick Lonsdale for Binkie Beaumont. October: enlists at the Slade to improve his painting and draughtsmanship.

N27 *HM Queen Elizabeth, the Queen Mother, with HRH Prince Charles and HRH Princess Anne, Coronation Day*, 1953
(Private Collection)

[1954]

The Glass of Fashion, a personal anthology of his own tastes and interests, and designers who influenced him, is published in England (Weidenfeld & Nicolson) with other editions published in France, Japan and America. October: he works on designs for Old Vic production of *Love's Labour's Lost* and designs for New York production of *Portrait of a Lady* with Jennifer Jones.

[1955]

Work on Enid Bagnold's *The Chalk Garden* in New York ends acrimoniously and Beaton gains more satisfaction from working on the American stage version of *My Fair Lady*.

[1956]

My Fair Lady opens in New Haven and then in New York. Having parted company with *Vogue* the previous year, Beaton begins work for *Harper's Bazaar* and takes an important series of portraits including those of Marilyn Monroe, Joan Crawford, Carson McCullers, Hermione Gingold and Grace Kelly. Receives Nieman-Marcus fashion award in Dallas for *My Fair Lady* dresses. November: has another exhibition of theatrical drawings at the Sagittarius Gallery. Photographs Maria Callas.

Q13   *Leslie Caron on the set of 'Gigi'*, 1957
(Sotheby's, London)

[1957]

Receives a CBE in the New Year's Honours List and travels to Japan with Truman Capote, which results in another book, *Japanese* (1959), published by Weidenfeld & Nicolson, who also publish Beaton's *Face of the World*, a scrapbook of his work of the forties and fifties designed by Mark Boxer. Begins work on sets and costumes for film musical of Colette's *Gigi*, set in the Belle Epoque and filmed partly on location in Paris, for which Beaton wins his first Oscar for best costume designs. Sits for a Francis Bacon portrait which is never completed.

[1958]

March: designs Edwardian bedroom at Ideal Home Exhibition which provokes much comment. April: exhibition at Redfern Gallery to coincide with opening of *My Fair Lady* in London. October: earns 6,000 dollars for one morning's work at Londonderry House in London for Modess advertisements. Designs costumes for film *The Truth About Women*, directed by Sydney and Muriel Box, and the opera *Vanessa* for the Metropolitan Opera Company.

[1959]

The Gainsborough Girls is restaged as *Landscape with Figures* with Donald Wolfit as Gainsborough, and tours Dublin, Newcastle and Brighton before finally closing in Wolverhampton. In New York he designs costumes for Howard Keel in *Saratoga* and scenery for Noël Coward's *Look After Lulu*. In England he designs costumes for Anthony Asquith's film of Shaw's *The Doctor Dilemma* with Leslie Caron and Dirk Bogarde.

022   *Marilyn Monroe*, 1956 (Sotheby's, London)

[1960]

Takes official wedding photographs of Antony Armstrong-Jones (later Lord Snowdon) and Princess Margaret, and the first photographs of Prince Andrew. Decorates Royal Opera House, Covent Garden, with 25,000 pink carnations and 600 yards of silk for a gala performance attended by President de Gaulle, and is appointed a Chevalier of the Legion of Honour. Sits to Augustus John for a portrait which is never finished. Illustrates Folio Society's edition of *The Importance of Being Earnest*, and designs sets and costumes for the Hal Prince musical about brothel life, *Tenderloin*, and also costumes for *Dear Liar*, a touring dramatization of correspondence between Ellen Terry and George Bernard Shaw.

R19 *Cecil Beaton with Audrey Hepburn, 'My Fair Lady' (film version)*, 1963 (Sotheby's, London)

[1961]

Designs sets and 400 costumes for Metropolitan Opera House production of *Turandot*. Publishes the first volume of his diaries, *The Wandering Years 1922–1939* (Weidenfeld & Nicolson), which, after two years of editing, receives a very favourable reception.

[1962]

Appears engagingly on John Freeman's searching interview programme on BBC TV, *Face to Face*, which is broadcast on 18 February, four days before his mother dies at the age of 89. Becomes the first Englishman for three centuries to be invited by the Comédie Française to design a production – Sheridan's *The School for Scandal*. In America he photographs Robert Kennedy's family, and in Denmark he takes pictures of the dying Isak Dinesen (Baroness Blixen). Meets Edith Sitwell several times and photographs her again for her 75th birthday.

[1963]

Spends ten months in Hollywood on the film production of *My Fair Lady*. Enjoys photographing Audrey Hepburn in a multitude of costumes he created for the film but has several unpleasant exchanges with George Cukor, the director, who tries to ban Beaton from the set. Beaton's designs for Ashton's ballet, *Marguerite and Armand*, starring Margot Fonteyn and Rudolph Nureyev, are seen at the Royal Opera House, London.

[1964]

My Fair Lady is released and wins Beaton two Oscars. Exhibitions of his designs are held in America at the Rex Evans Gallery in Los Angeles, and his diary of the making of the film – *Cecil Beaton's Fair Lady* – is published (Weidenfeld & Nicolson). November: 190 costume designs are exhibited at the Redfern Gallery, London.

[1965]

Visits Picasso at Mougins, where he paints and photographs the artist. Publishes the second volume of his diaries, *The Years Between 1939–1944* (Weidenfeld & Nicolson). David Bailey's *Box of Pin Ups* includes portrait of Beaton with Nureyev.

[1966]

Holds exhibition at Lefevre Gallery of large-scale portrait paintings including that of *The Times* art critic John Russell, David Warner, Picasso, Alec Guinness and Mick Jagger (based on a Bailey photograph). Designs costumes for Metropolitan Opera's production of La Traviata.

[1967]

Visits Morocco and makes friends with the Rolling Stones, photographing Mick Jagger extensively. In Venice Beaton decorates the Palazzo Rezzonico Ball in red, white and gold, its theme being seventeenth-century Venice. At Pelham Place he photographs Twiggy for *Vogue*.

Twiggy at 8 Pelham Place, 1967 (Sotheby's, London)

[1968]

Filmed by Lord Snowdon for a documentary about old age and geriatrics entitled *Don't Count The Candles* and is enraged when he sees it. Invited by Roy Strong, director of the National Portrait Gallery, to stage a retrospective exhibition. Designed by Richard Buckle, it is opened by the Queen Mother and includes new photographs of the Queen and Prince Charles specially taken for the event. Other exhibitions of his drawings are held at the Wright Hepburn Gallery, London, and Palm Beach Gallery, Miami. Commissioned to take on-set photographs of Mick Jagger, Anita Pallenberg and James Fox in Nicholas Roeg's film, *Performance*. *Best of Beaton* is published (Weidenfeld & Nicolson) with introduction by Truman Capote.

s15 *Mick Jagger on the set of 'Performance'*, 1968
(Sotheby's, London)

[1969]

1 May: *600 Faces*, his retrospective photographic exhibition, opens at the Museum of the City of New York. Beaton begins work on Vincente Minelli's film *On a Clear Day You Can See Forever*, designing costumes for Barbra Streisand. On Broadway he designs costumes and sets for the musical *Coco* with Katharine Hepburn playing the part of Chanel. Sits to David Hockney for a portrait drawing commissioned by *Vogue*.

s6 *David Warner*, 1965 (Sotheby's, London)

[1970]

Flies to Hollywood to photograph Mae West and paints additional portraits in Miami for exhibition at Palm Beach Gallery. Takes the official 70th birthday photographs of the Queen Mother at Royal Lodge. April: is awarded a Tony for his *Coco* designs. Visits South America and does research work for biography of his Aunt Jessie, which is published the following year as *My Bolivian Aunt* (Weidenfeld & Nicolson). David Bailey begins work on a television documentary *Beaton by Bailey*.

[1971]

Fashion – An Anthology opens at the Victoria and Albert Museum, made up of dresses collected by Beaton from 1969 to 1971 from private owners of clothes by the world's greatest designers. Attends the Rothschild Ball, held to celebrate the centenary of Proust's birth, dressed as Nadar the photographer, and photographs many of the guests for *Vogue* including Leslie Caron, Elizabeth Taylor and Richard Burton, Jane Birkin and Serge Gainsbourg, as well as Marisa Berenson. Photographs Gabriele d'Annunzio's house on Lake Garda and holidays in Spetsai where he makes sketches.

[1972]

Receives knighthood and attends investiture at Buckingham Palace. June: third volume of his diaries are published, *The Happy Years 1944–1948* (Weidenfeld & Nicolson), which discloses his affair with Greta Garbo. Holds another exhibition in Miami at the Palm Beach Gallery. Attends the funeral of Duke of Windsor at St George's Chapel, Windsor. Visits Egypt.

[1973]

Collaborates with Gail Buckland on an important history of photography, *The Magic Image*, and publishes the fourth volume of diaries, *The Strenuous Years 1948–1955* (both Weidenfeld & Nicolson).

[1974]

Visits Mexico and Guatemala. His 70th birthday is marked with an exhibition at Kodak's Gallery in High Holborn. At Peter Quennell's 69th birthday party he is punched and knocked down on leaving by Robert Heber-Percy, still smarting from criticism in Beaton's diaries, *The*

Happy Years. July: he suffers a severe stroke which paralyses his right arm. Gradually he begins to recover, teaching himself to paint with his left hand.

[1975]

Pelham Place, his London home, is sold and he now lives at Reddish. June: *The Magic Image* is published (Weidenfeld & Nicolson).

[1976]

Beaton sells his photographic archive, with the exception of his Royal portraits, to Sotheby's. The fifth volume of diaries, *The Restless Years 1955–63*, is published (Weidenfeld & Nicolson). First retrospective exhibition of Beaton's watercolours, costume designs, book designs, portraits and caricatures held at Parkin Gallery, London.

[1977]

Beaton begins to accept photographic work again. November: studio sale is held at Sotheby's and portrait of Edith Sitwell fetches £750. Visits New York and takes portraits of Diana Vreeland, Louise Nevelson, Anita Loos and Joe Papp, which were published in the *Sunday Telegraph* the following year.

[1978]

Photographs Lesley-Anne Down at Reddish for fashion feature commissioned by *The Daily Telegraph*. Publishes his final volume of diaries *The Parting Years 1963–1974* (Weidenfeld & Nicolson).

[1979]

Covers Paris Collections for March issue of French *Vogue*. In London he photographs Ralph Richardson, Princess Michael of Kent, Patrick Procktor, the actress Diana Quick and Zandra Rhodes. *Self Portrait with Friends*, the composite volume of his diaries edited by Richard Buckle, is published (Weidenfeld & Nicolson). Hugo Vickers is appointed biographer (*Cecil Beaton* is published in 1985 by Weidenfeld & Nicolson).

[1980]

Cecil Beaton dies four days after his 76th birthday, and is buried at Reddish. June: the house and its contents are sold by Christie's.

01 *Self-portrait*, 1951 (Sotheby's, London)

A Fly in Amber

❧ BEATON AS DIARIST ❧

Hugo Vickers

Cecil Beaton described his role as a diarist as one who sought 'to preserve the fleeting moment like a fly in amber'.[1] He began this mission, which went hand in hand with a dozen other careers, while still at Harrow. Evidently the nature of what he then recorded was best left unread, for in a moment of panic (recorded in a later diary) the Harrow notes were consigned to oblivion. Beaton's surviving day-by-day diaries begin in the autumn of 1922 when, aged eighteen, he entered Cambridge University. Over a period of some fifty years he amassed a total of 145 volumes. Of these the first 56 volumes cover his Cambridge years and his emergence into the life of the 'Bright Young Things'. By 1927, after his breakthrough into high society, life had become too busy and exciting to leave much energy for the chronicling of it. However, when Beaton set off on a new adventure, such as his first visit to New York in 1928, or his trip to Hollywood in 1929, it is possible, once again, to track his daily progress. This kind of diary recurred at various times throughout his life, but especially when he was travelling. There were several reasons for this: first, he had more time to himself; and second, part of his life was financed by writing accounts of his travels. Therefore in a sense the diary was his way of keeping notes. When abroad, his awareness of new excitement and new places visited was naturally more acute, and for Beaton to have set off without a diary to hand would have been as unthinkable as travelling without a good book or an alarm clock.

At other times the diary served as Beaton's confessional. Here he confided his private thoughts, his ambitions and fears, details of intimate experiences (such as his love affair with Greta Garbo) and the pains and illnesses that dogged his later years. Unlike other famous diarists, he seemed to delight in writing statements which reflected badly on him. Yet in so doing he revealed behind his façade of fantasy a touching honesty and a sense of realism.

Beaton also performed what the Countess of Avon described as 'living autopsies'[2] on his friends. Preoccupied with the plight of a colleague, obsessed by a sparring partner with whom he was collaborating, or intrigued by the behaviour of a friend, he would occasionally sit down and relieve himself of several pages concerning their lifestyle, their motives and their past history. For example his account of a day in the life of Lady Diana Cooper included such intimate details as how she applied her make-up before going out; and of Clarissa Eden, newly married to the Foreign Secretary, he noted an unaccustomed formality – instead of wandering unannounced into Beaton's garden, she now rang the front door bell.

Beaton's love of theatre was another vital ingredient of his diaries. The recorded gestures and dialogue of his friends served another purpose, for Beaton was to use them one day in his own various plays. His diaries are peppered with phrases under the heading 'How the Rich Live'. He loved to note the sayings of those who were isolated by position or money. For example, Princess Marina once asked him: 'How do you get to Ascot if you don't come down the course in a carriage?'[3] He relished the Duke of Devonshire's comment of 'Privilege after Ability',[4] on stepping aside for Beaton as they entered the dining-room. The same keen eye was turned on activities at Vice-Regal Lodge in Delhi, where Beaton was posted by the Ministry of Information in 1944, and a summer in Tangiers with David Herbert in 1949 seems to have been spent amassing every detail possible on local characters such as Ada and Feridah Green, a rich treasure trove for anyone writing a study of that murky, musky town. Unfortunately his talents as a playwright never found favour with critics or theatre managers. Although he could create a beautiful set and dress the cast in a stunning series of costumes, when they came on stage he was unable to bring them to life. Their dialogue was too mannered and led nowhere. It was a failure which caused him much heartache.

Above all, Cecil Beaton was a visual man. His caricatures and sketches of politicians and other figures in public life show a keen eye for detail, but it is questionable how much attention he paid to what they said. Beaton's perceptive friend Stephen Tennant put his finger on this trait when he said: 'You may think Cecil is listening intently to what you say. He isn't. He's counting the hairs in your nostrils as you speak.'[5]

Beaton's diaries reflect this visual discernment. His record of the trial of John Christie at the Old Bailey in 1953 is a telling example. Accused of the murder of his wife and three other women, all found plastered into the wall of 10 Rillington Place, Christie was found guilty, and later hanged. Beaton had attended the trial out of curiosity, later describing him aptly in his diary as a man whose pained expressions were those of an actor giving a brilliantly spontaneous performance. Similarly, when in New York, Beaton occasionally left his artistic world for an afternoon at the United Nations building. It is enlightening to learn his view of Krushchev, whom he saw as a great Russian bear. Beaton did not record what the interpreters related, but noticed that Krushchev, having interrupted Harold Macmillan's speech to the assembly, 'turned round to Tito to continue his vilification of England – suddenly [he] gave the sharpest wink I've ever seen – the wink of a pig'.[6]

There was a public face to Beaton's recorded impressions of historical events, as well as a private one. He felt the keeping of such records to be something of a duty, confessing that his main reason for attending the Duke of Windsor's funeral, which entailed deserting his painting in the country, was to write about it for posterity. Yet, characteristically, from several pages of original manuscript on this event, he published only three brief paragraphs in *The Parting Years*,[7] one of six diaries edited by Beaton and published in his lifetime.

One of the differences between Beaton's unpublished and published diaries is well illustrated by his treatment of the death of Princess Marina. In *The Parting Years* he quoted from his *Sunday Times* tribute, a polished piece of writing which the Princess's family and friends appreciated. But in the unpublished version Cecil recorded his problems in striking the right note when writing of someone whose life had, to a large extent, lost its point. As the author of Beaton's authorized biography, it was my privilege to have access to all his unpublished diaries. This revealed the extent to which Beaton doctored his published manuscripts to present yet another extension of the Beaton image. It was especially rewarding to have copies of his notes on Egypt, Kenya and Turkey with me when travelling in those countries and to compare my own experiences with his. It was a great joy (and almost a relief) to find Beaton relishing the Winter Palace at Luxor, where the Edwardians spent their winters, with the same enthusiasm as the Valley of the Kings, and to have the benefit of his

Extract from Beaton's diary, Tunis trip, December 1933

recorded conversation with Peter, the Copt guide, who was present when Lord Carnarvon discovered the tomb of Tutankhamen. One passage from these travel notes merits re-quoting here. Written in the Egyptian desert during the Second World War in 1942, it is a spontaneous and uncorrected piece of prose:

I wondered how on earth warfare could be carried out in this desert. The distances so appalling. The picture of warfare became impossibly confused. No lines could be held. Little pockets of men would become small isolated pinpricks on this vast terrain: we followed along by the sea and in the evening light everything soon became very beautiful, the sea the colour of those Brazilian butterflies wings. I have never seen the sea so blue before. Then when the pall of light sank behind the horizon we were treated to a show of magic beauty. The sunset was something unimaginable, more transient than a flower, more brilliant than any jewel, more fluid than any architectures, more varied than any landscape was the landscape in the sky, with islands of gold and silver, peninsulas of apricot and rose against a background of many shades of turquoise and azure. The activity of the sky, changing so quickly yet apparently motionless, made the earth look even more barren and forlornly ugly.

So this is the desert, a very different desert from the Sahara, dust desert that I had imagined it to be . . .[8]

It was of this piece that Richard Buckle, the editor of the composite volume of Beaton's diaries entitled *Self Portrait with Friends*, wrote: 'There is a description by him of a desert sunset, exact without being "purple", of which Maugham or Waugh would have been incapable.'[9]

Perhaps, in time, a fuller version of Beaton's diaries will be published containing those passages which make them inappropriate for publication while friends and family survive. This is not because they are of a scandalous nature, but because Beaton was in a position to know secrets, and invariably recorded them. By virtue of his contact with royalty, film-stars, actors, directors, politicians, war leaders, society figures, and even the protagonists of the sixties, historians will turn to him again and again for a quick and illuminating flashlit cameo.

Beaton is thus assured a place alongside the other celebrated diarists of the twentieth century. Foremost among these was Harold Nicolson, a key source on literary and social London, and life in the House of Commons. By typing notes daily after breakfast he produced a diary of some three million words. Anthony Powell judges Evelyn Waugh a better diarist than Beaton, though he believes that Beaton was better than Nöel Coward. There are some who say that Waugh's diaries should not have been published, that they were in essence the working notebooks of a novelist or travel writer. Malcolm Muggeridge thought them 'an elaborate joke', while Frances Donaldson denounced them as 'little but the angry jottings of an introvert'.

Nöel Coward wrote his diary every Sunday morning, recording his reactions to the reception of his own works, brief resumés of whom he had seen in the past week and his opinions on the plays he had attended. Though valuable, Coward's diaries are disappointing compared to his other writings. Reviewing them in the *Sunday Times*, Adam Mars-Jones described Coward as: 'a diarist who would rather be dull than vulgar, and for whom self-analysis was always an indiscretion'.[10]

'Chips' Channon is already established as a kind of Pepys, intensely interested in politics and social life. His account of the abdication alone ensures him a place in history and few twentieth-century biographies are written that do not draw from him.

Sir Robert Bruce Lockhart's two volumes are too often neglected. He was a diplomat who knew Trotsky well and was an intimate friend of many important British politicians. He was also a journalist whom Beaverbrook appointed to write the 'Londoners' Diary'. While he was cautious in print, he was completely uninhibited in his private diaries. Kenneth Young, who edited the diaries, wrote that he was 'much more business-like, less literary' than Harold Nicolson, while 'far less superficial' than 'Chips' Channon 'and wider in scope.

Another diarist, Sir Alexander Cadogan, caused a different kind of stir, particularly in the diplomatic world. A staunchly upright man, whom his colleagues could have been forgiven for judging something of a dullard, he concealed behind a dispassionate public face a dry, acerbic wit. A recent addition to the list is Sir John Colville, whose diaries give invaluable insight into the life of Sir Winston Churchill. James Lees-Milne also has a dedicated following as he plies his way through the great houses of England in connection with his work for the National Trust. It was he who wrote of the diaries of Beaton and Eddy Sackville-West: 'We could not be hoisted to posterity on two spikier spikes'.[11]

Perhaps the most important contributing factor to Cecil Beaton's success as a diarist is that he was not born into the world whose activities he chronicled so faithfully. As a child, Beaton romanticized his home life. He thought his mother was a society lady (though in fact she was the daughter of a blacksmith); he was aware of and very impressed by his Aunt Jessie's diplomatic and theatrical connections (while somewhat exaggerating their importance in his mind); he resented the poverty of his father's life and business, and his loyalty to a host of dreary Beaton uncles, cousins and old business acquaintances. (Incidentally, despite Beaton's disparaging account of his old father in his diary, Mr Beaton emerges as a delightful if somewhat bewildered character.) At Harrow and Cambridge, and during his early years in London, Beaton observed a very different social milieu to which he was greatly attracted. His rise to join them inevitably sounds contrived and he emerges as nothing less than ruthless in the machinations he employed to become part of their world. Each step, whether progressive or retrogressive, was recorded in his diary. There is a case for saying he needed to adjust his surroundings to suit his temperament and his talents. For he found his family staid and middle-class, hardly a suitable environment in which to develop a career as stage designer and photographer. He had much to offer his new-found friends. He glamorized them in portrait photographs and caricatured them in *Vogue*. That he was so readily accepted in an exclusive world hostile to outsiders is testimony to the pleasure his friends gained from his company. And he, too, was stimulated by the quick-fire imaginations of Stephen Tennant, Brian Howard and others. Had Beaton belonged to this world by right, he would have been considerably less observant. As it was, his eyes eagerly devoured every detail, while his pen committed them to paper. Yet Beaton all his life suffered from a lack of self-confidence and never really felt a part of his adopted social circle, despite the insouciant air he often assumed.

Never is Cecil Beaton's diary parochial. As Richard Buckle states in the introduction to *Self Portrait with Friends*, published in 1979 shortly before Beaton's death:

> Beaton stands alone. Neither Sévigné, nor Pepys, nor Walpole, nor Greville, nor Nicolson, nor Channon met – and photographed – such a diversity of men and women, travelled in five continents during a world war, or spent a year in Hollywood designing the most successful musical film of all time.[12]

Beaton had the knack of being in the right place at the right time, and over a period of fifty years he had the foresight and energy to record all that he saw. The sharp focus of his ever-curious mind, and the shrewd astuteness with which he viewed an era which he himself helped to shape, will ensure that his career as a diarist will rank high in importance alongside his other remarkable achievements.

1 Cecil Beaton, *The Wandering Years*, introduction.
2 *Daily Telegraph*, 19 January 1980.
3 Cecil Beaton's unpublished diary, June 1962.
4 *Ibid*.
5 Stephen Tennant to Hugo Vickers, 1 March 1981.
6 Cecil Beaton, *The Restless Years*, pp. 119–120.
7 Cecil Beaton, *The Parting Years*, p. 147.

8 Cecil Beaton's unpublished diary, 29 April 1942.
9 *The Sunday Times*, 28 July 1985.
10 *The Sunday Times*, September 1982.
11 James Lees-Milne, *Ancestral Voices*, London 1977, p. 217.
12 *Self Portrait with Friends*, ed. Richard Buckle, London, 1979, introduction, pp. ix–x.

E14 *Mary Taylor in a Dress of Cloque Rayon by Molyneux,*
1935 (Sotheby's, London)

An Instinct for Style

THE FASHION PHOTOGRAPHY OF CECIL BEATON

Philippe Garner

—— *Impressions Received* ——

Cecil Beaton's infancy coincided with the earliest phases of a new discipline within the commercial applications of photography. Fashion photography, a complex weave of idealized beauty, artifice, artistry, technical dexterity and commercial dictats, had its origins in the Edwardian era, into which Beaton was born on 14 January 1904. Crucial to this evolution were the developments in printing which enabled fashion journals to exploit photographic illustrations as easily as line drawing illustrations. The refinement of half tone printing and the possibility of reproducing photographic images in full colour gave a new dimension to fashion magazines and marked the beginning of a boom in this area of publishing. The pioneering French magazines, *Les Modes*, *Femina* and *Le Figaro Modes*, were soon to be eclipsed by a revitalized *Vogue*, published by the American, Condé Nast (the British edition of which was first published in 1916), and by its great rival, *Harper's Bazaar*.

The earliest professional fashion studios were the Paris establishments of Reutlinger, Félix and Talbot where, in the tradition of nineteenth-century portrait studios, conventionalized poses before painted backdrops were the norm. The profession of fashion model did not then exist, and models were often drawn from the world of the theatre. In Britain the stars of the Edwardian musical comedy were the popular idols of their day, and their exaggerated dress was perhaps the strongest influence on fashion. The young Beaton's fascination with these glamorous stage stars, foremost amongst them Lily Elsie, and their elegant, elaborately stylized costumes, led to a lasting passion for the worlds of fashion and theatre. The interplay of these two influences became an essential ingredient of Beaton's aesthetic. Characteristically, when designing his *My Fair Lady* costumes he drew extensively on the illustrations in the Edwardian theatrical journal *The Play Pictorial*, and frequently throughout his career as a fashion photographer his work made allusion to the world of the stage.

Amongst the photographers whose work defined beauty in the eyes of the young Beaton were the West End portraitists such as Lallie Charles and Rita Martin, who enjoyed success as flatterers of Edwardian society and stage subjects . The first fashion photographer whose work impressed and influenced Beaton was Baron de Meyer, whose shimmering light effects and stylish poses Beaton has described in rapturous prose using musical metaphors.[1] Beaton acknowledged another, perhaps less obvious but equally fascinating influence in the work of Francis Bruguière, a photographer who, 'By using lights on strips of metal and paper . . . created an abstract world . . . The results were a marriage of the camera and the essence of light.'[2] Beaton's artistry as a fashion photographer developed from the lessons of early practitioners whose task was to idealize their subjects. He enriched this function with a painterly eye for the effects of light, space and imagery.

[69]

4825 B ROTARY PHOTO E.C.   MISS LILY ELSIE.   FOULSHAM & BANFIELD

above left *Modes Drécoll*, photographed by Reutlinger, Paris, *c.* 1903 (Private Collection).

above right *Lady Ripon*, photographed by Baron de Meyer, *c.* 1911, platinum print formerly in the collection of Cecil Beaton (National Portrait Gallery, London).

below left *Constance Drever as Rosalinda in 'Nightbirds'*, Lyric Theatre, Shaftesbury Avenue, London (production opened 30 December 1911), published in *The Play Pictorial*, vol. XIX, no. 115 (John Culme).

below right *Lily Elsie as Sonia in 'The Merry Widow'*, Daly's Theatre, Leicester Square, London (production opened 8 June 1907), photographed by Foulsham & Banfield, published as a postcard by the Rotary Photographic Co. (John Culme).

Beaton's scope and sensibility as a fashion photographer can only have benefited from his unique additional roles as a chronicler of twentieth-century fashion and as a photographic historian whose distinguished written contributions to these subjects include most notably *The Glass of Fashion*, published in 1954, and *The Magic Image*, published in 1975.

Introductions Made

Beaton's career as a fashion photographer grew naturally out of his work as a society portraitist and flourished under the patronage of *Vogue*, first in London and then in New York and Paris. H. W. Yoxall, studio manager of *Vogue* in London, recalled, 'One of my chief claims to fame [is] that, in 1927, I signed [*Vogue's*] first contract with Cecil Beaton, just down from Cambridge – though I can't bespeak the credit of discovering him. That was done by our then editor Alison Settle. Cecil was first engaged as a social cartoonist, but his photographic talent soon emerged.'[3]

Beaton recalled his introduction to American *Vogue*.

> On one of her yearly visits to England in search of talent, Mrs Chase, the American editor-in-chief of *Vogue* magazine, had seen some of my drawings. Mrs Chase considers she showed considerable perception in feeling that they showed promise and that they would one day be useful to her magazine. When she was told that I also took photographs, I was summoned to her office to submit my work . . . the pictures were obviously amateur work . . . But Mrs Chase was not entirely put off. 'If you come to New York you must do something for us.'[4]

Mrs Chase wrote of this first meeting, 'I remember the day Cecil first came into my London office – tall, slender, swaying like a reed, blond, and very young. The aura emanating from him was an odd combination of airiness and assurance.'[5]

In 1928 Beaton made his first trip to New York. He recorded: 'I showed my latest photographs to Mrs Chase,[6] who considered that, although they might be poor technically, they had the merit of being unlike the pictures of any other photographer. I was soon taken into the *Vogue* fold, and commissioned to photograph beautiful women up at the Condé Nast's fabulous apartment on Park Avenue.'[7] He returned from his New York trip with a 'contract with the Condé Nast Publications to take photographs exclusively for them for several thousands pounds a year for several years to come'.[8]

A return visit to New York during the winter of 1929–30 established what was to become a regular pattern of work on both sides of the Atlantic. It was on this trip that Condé Nast, who 'took an avuncular interest in [Beaton and his] photography',[9] encouraged a greater professionalism in his protégé. He insisted that 'It's all very well for you to take pictures with a snapshot camera; but you've got to grow up!',[10] and demanded that Beaton put aside his 3A Kodak in favour of a 10 × 8 inch plate camera. Beaton tried out the new camera in Hollywood, and from 1930 this large format gave added quality to his fashion photographs and other work.

Beaton's earliest published fashion studies are tentative essays, for the most part less self-assured than his contemporaneous portrait work; often somewhat stiff, they followed a stereotyped formula of a model in an interior setting, gaze to one side, with her hand resting on a table, chair back or mantel. He seemed more in his element with 'celebrity' models such as the Marquise de Casa Maury, a favourite of Beaton's at this time,[11] and achieved polished results when collaborating with such sleek thoroughbreds as top New York model Marion Moorehouse.[12]

The Reckless Years

Beaton rapidly achieved a reputation as one of the foremost talents in international fashion photography. He was in great demand and was to fill countless pages of *Vogue* with his inimitable blend of wit, invention and high style. 'Until the arrival of Cecil Beaton and Norman Parkinson', recalled H. W. Yoxall, 'our London studio was lamentably short of native aptitude; and even when they had arrived they were constantly being whisked off to Paris and New York.'[13]

Amongst his most able contemporaries were the American Edward Steichen and the Paris-based George Hoyningen-Huene. Beaton's comments on their work and his reaction to it reveal much as to his own aims and approach. Of Steichen he wrote:

Nathalie Paley, photographed by George Hoyningen-Huene, 1933

[He] was the Almighty Photographer at this time [*c.* 1927]. His rich and meticulous studies . . . so full of light and shade, were now covering the pages of *Vanity Fair* and *Vogue*. But much as I admired Steichen's work . . . I knew that it would be hopeless for me ever to try to work in his vein. My work was the opposite end of the photographic pole . . . Whereas Steichen's pictures were taken with an uncompromising frankness of viewpoint, against a plain background, perhaps half-black, half-white, my sitters were more likely to be somewhat hazily discovered in a bower or grotto of silvery blossom or in some Hades of polka dots.[14]

Beaton's reaction to the style of his other distinguished contemporary, however, was quite different:

Later I came under the influence of the work of Hoyningen-Huene, *Vogue's* star photographer in Paris. Huene in turn had been under the spell of the great Steichen, but he brought more elaboration and extravagance to his photographs than the American master. Whereas Steichen seldom approached his subjects with humour, there was something almost frivolous in the way Huene brought a whole new collection of properties to his studios . . . Huene's violent activities in the pages of *Vogue* gave me my greatest incentive to rival his eccentricities.[15]

The thirties saw Beaton creating with eclectic abandon a vernacular of novel imagery which drew on a wide variety of sources, not least the influence of the many artists with whom he came into contact. There were surrealistic settings and props inspired by Dali and de Chirico, neo-romantic flourishes with a debt to Christian Bérard or Pavel Tchelitchew, baroque *mises-en-scène* in the manner of the most whimsical interior decorators of the day, and endless idyllic, dramatic and witty variations on the fashion theme.

Years later Beaton wrote:

In the thirties the fashion photographers came into their own. As one of them, I must confess to having indulged myself in the generally prevailing recklessness of style. My pictures became more and more rococo and surrealist. Society women as well as mannequins were photographed in the most flamboyant Greek-tragedy poses, in ecstatic or highly mystical states, sometimes with the melodramatic air of a Lady Macbeth caught up in a cocoon of tulle . . . ladies of the upper crust were to be seen in *Vogue* photographs fighting their way out of a hat box or breaking through a huge sheet of white paper or torn screen . . . Princesses were posed trying frantically to be seen through a plate-glass window that had been daubed with whitewash . . . Backgrounds were equally exaggerated and often tasteless. Badly carved cupids from junk shops on Third Avenue would be wrapped in argentine cloth or cellophane. Driftwood was supposed to bring an air of neo-romanticism to a matter-of-fact subject. Christmas paper chains were garlanded around the model's shoulders, and wooden doves, enormous paper flowers from Mexico, Chinese lanterns, doilies or cutlet frills, fly whisks, sporrans, egg beaters, or stars of all shapes found their way into our hysterical and highly ridiculous pictures.[16]

Beneath the fanciful trappings, other ideas were explored in a more purely photographic idiom – the play of projected shadows, silhouettes and patterns of light through cut-out paper, the latter especially calling to mind Beaton's reference to Bruguière. Beaton's passion for the theatre, meanwhile, provided specific inspiration for various fashion shots, including his 'puppet-theatre'[17] series, and studies in the wings of unidentified productions[18] or amidst back-stage clutter.

Beaton's favourite models of this era included Mary Taylor, whose distinctive beauty he might be said to have invented, Princess Nathalie Paley and Helen Bennett, whom he posed on one occasion in a studio filled with giant ice-blocks for a feature entitled 'How to keep cool' (see Cat. L 20).[19]

Abstraction by Francis Bruguière, 1920s

L16 *Pierre Balmain Chinese Brown Woollen Coat with Trousers*, 1945 (Sotheby's, London)

AN INSTINCT FOR STYLE

The New Realism

By 1936 a reaction had set in against the surfeit of romantic and extravagant indulgence which had marked Beaton's early work. This led him to explore new directions, and, once again, he became an innovator in his search for the ingredients of a new realism. One afternoon in 1936, he wrote:

> I was about to photograph a number of sports suits when suddenly I felt I could no longer portray them languishing in the usual attitudes of so-called elegance. I made them put on dark glasses and stand in angular poses . . . I was called in for a special conference. What did I mean by making my models look so unladylike? . . . I retorted that, for me at any rate, the days of simpering were over . . . In my photographs the models had given up pretence. They were young and fresh, and, to my mind, infinitely more alluring; they lent realism.[20]

In the previous year Beaton had surprised Bettina Ballard, the fashion editor with whom he was working, with his change of style. She recorded: 'We were on our way to a sitting of street clothes in Paris one day when we passed by some offices that were being replastered. Beaton looked at the mess and said, "How divine – exactly the background we need for these little costumes."'[21] And so the photographs were taken amidst the builders' debris.[22] Beaton was a pioneer in exploiting the seemingly incongruous realism of such locations as a setting for stylish clothes, a device he also employed in his portraits made around the same date in Paris, in which he used a destroyed and derelict railway station as a backdrop. In these photographs Beaton had created, albeit unwittingly, a precursor for his celebrated war-time image of a model in a Digby Morton suit, seen against the rubble of a bomb-damaged London building.[23]

Beaton's growing disenchantment with the canons of elegance associated with *Vogue* led to conflict with the editorial staff and with the American art director, Dr Agha. An unrelated dispute in February 1938[24] caused the termination of his American contract and a substantial reduction, until after the Second World War, in his fashion output. Beaton persisted in his endeavours to inject an element of realism into his work. Looking back on his career in 1968 he identified a distinct shift in mood demanding a fresh, less rarefied, though nonetheless stage-managed repertoire of poses, expressions and locations. He wrote:

> The posed, static hands with the pointed index finger and arched wrist acquired an overnight vulgarity; the celestial expression in the eyes suddenly became a joke shared by everyone except the sitter. The earlier pictures appeared over re-touched and altogether too artificial with ladies with forced rosebud simpers and impossibly golden curls.
>
> Likewise, the locales for fashion photography changed from the boudoir, with its Louis Seize clichés, to places where the angelic Aunt Edna Woolman Chase would fear to tread. Instead of being caught nonchalantly arranging a vase of flowers with a satin shoe pointing to the full-blown rose on the Aubusson, sitters were seen in lowlier surroundings at humbler tasks: sewing, drinking from a cup, or feeling for rain. The results of my experiments in this genre of photography were considered to prove that I had at last grown up, and had acquired a new sense of reality. 'Reality' was taken up by editors as the 'new thing'.[25]

Beaton's 1945 study of a wistful young model in a plain jacket and trousers by Balmain is a masterpiece of this new realism. The antithesis of the high fashion mannequin, she is seen against a rough wall in a Paris courtyard with 'the lighting of a Corot'.[26]

L24 *Charles James Evening Dresses*, 1948 (Sotheby's, London)

Return to High Style

The dramatic revitalization of Paris couture after the war, heralded by Christian Dior's 'New Look' collection launched in February 1947, swept Beaton towards a new phase in his work. Ever sensitive to, and ever prescient of, shifts in the mood of fashion, he evolved a high style appropriate to the new grandiose elegance of haute couture as exemplified by Dior, Balmain, Fath and Balenciaga in Paris or by Charles James, Beaton's contemporary at Harrow, now the star of New York couture.

Beaton's best work of this period was often seemingly straightforward, his models posed in grand interior settings or even against plain backdrops, without the contrivance of his work of the thirties. More fluid and altogether more seductive than his first attempts at interior shots in the late twenties, the epitome of this genre is the 1948 group of eight models in pastel silk satin evening gowns by Charles James, posed in a rich neo-classical salon (Cat. L 24).[27] Beaton captured the haughty elegance of a new generation of models including Jean Patchett, Dorian Leigh and Dovima. Accepted back into the fold of American *Vogue* at the end of the war he was again in regular demand in London, Paris and New York.

[76]

Exciting new talents, however, were bringing fresh ideas to fashion photography from around 1950. The mercurial young Richard Avedon was filling page after page of *Harper's Bazaar* with inspired location work, while, at *Vogue*, Irving Penn breathed a noble serenity into studio work, and his daylight studies against a neutral backdrop gave a new stature to the medium. By the mid to late fifties new photographers, including William Klein and Frank Horvat, were creating snappy, witty 'street-wise' images which blended fashion stylishness with documentary vitality. Beaton's formulae, however elegant, were starting to look somewhat predictable and in 1955 his contractual links with *Vogue* were terminated.

Changing Times

Through the late fifties and the sixties, until his last sitting for British *Vogue* in 1973, Beaton made fashion photographs on a regular freelance basis for *Vogue*, often, in the latter years, as a 'star' guest, which left him free to work for other magazines. At *Vogue* he found favour with the eccentric, exuberant New York editor-in-chief, Diana Vreeland, though her dismissal in 1972 at a time of financial crisis marked the end of an era in which free rein was given to the whims of editors and photographers.

Model in Dior Dress, photographed by Irving Penn, published in *Vogue*,
French edition, October 1950, p. 73 (Condé Nast)

By 1970 Beaton was clearly the scion of a different era with different aesthetic criteria to those of the aggressive young photographers in the mould of the hero of Antonioni's 1966 film *Blow Up*. Fascinated though he may have been by the young heroes of the sixties, he found it difficult to relate to their tastes. 'I find', he wrote in his diary in February 1974, 'that, accepting the inevitable, and "being my age"' . . . the young seem so different, so beautiful, so energetic. They are like creatures from another planet and are as difficult to understand as young fowls or other animals.'[28]

In these later years Beaton was at his best when working in his established vein, in sophisticated interiors with models whose innate elegance conformed to his norms of high style. But he was arguably less successful in producing distinguished results when working with models such as Twiggy, whom he posed rather awkwardly in his Pelham Place home in 1967 for British *Vogue*;[29] by contrast, he was in his element with Baroness Fiona Thyssen as model, photographing the Paris couture autumn collections in 1966 for the *Weekend Telegraph*.[30] Her aristocratic poise and the splendid interiors in which she was posed combined in Beaton's lens to produce results worthy of him. A variety of stylish settings, both traditional and avant-garde, together with celebrity 'extras' provided the context for some of his most interesting late work – a series called 'The Great Indoors' for British *Vogue* in 1968 (Cat. s46).[31]

His *Vogue* session with Tina Chow in February 1973[32] (see Cat. T11) was to be his last before his incapacitating stroke. In 1979, however, he was invited by French *Vogue* to photograph the spring collections.[33] This was to be his final fashion assignment and it proved to be a distinguished curtain call in his grand style – celebrity models and haute couture exploited with flair and self-assurance in a series of photographs which serve to underline the elements of Beaton's sensibilities as a photographer of fashion.

In Conclusion

Beaton's contribution to the history of fashion photography, during a career which spanned half a century, was a considerable one. His was a unique talent. It has been said of Beaton that he was not a photographer's photographer, a suggestion which could be explained by his professed technical ignorance and seemingly dilettante approach to the medium. He played the role of the gentleman amateur but in fact 'was a remarkably hard-working professional, sharply attentive to the smallest detail of every image his camera produced'.[34] It was integral to his working methods, however, to be, in the words of Bettina Ballard, 'forever improvising. It bored him to plan photographs and he was too confident of his ability to give them much thought. He was quite right, as something amusing always came out of his last-minute inspiration.'[35]

Irving Penn acknowledged Beaton's skill in creating with such apparent facility the images of beauty which he pursued. 'He could take a store girl from Texas or New York and transform her. Photography is projection. He projected them. Sometimes Cecil would come into the studio, giving the impression that he'd had too much wine at lunch. He'd seem not to have thought about it all very much. He'd tear a bit of paper on one side, he'd talk to the model. He'd go behind the camera. Out would come the Cecil Beaton woman.'[36]

Beaton's fecundity was confirmed by Dr Agha, who, despite their numerous battles over the years, graciously conceded in a letter to him that 'practically all of the devices, trends and techniques that make today's photography (or at least fashion photography) what it is were originated or first used by you'.[37]

[78]

Successful fashion images depend on a sure instinct to creat a sense of mood, beauty and sometimes place which, at its best, defies analysis. Beaton defined fashion photography as 'an insidious profession. In art, it is what sex-appeal is to love. Artifice can be a dangerous thing; when misapplied the results are vulgar and tawdry. Its correct use depends on instinct. It is up to the fashion photographer to create an illusion. In doing so, he is not behaving with dishonesty, but when properly invoked, the result is not merely an illusion; rather, it makes the observer see what he *should* see.'[38] 'The fashion photographer's job', he wrote on another occasion, 'is to stage an apotheosis'.[39]

Truman Capote considered Beaton 'a recorder of fantasy. He added that 'through the years [Beaton had] documented and illuminated the exact attitude of the moment'.[40] The juxtaposition of notions of fantasy and documentation is in some ways paradoxical, yet in Beaton's work invention and reality are indeed brought together. The world of high fashion which Beaton presents was for him a very real world. It was the world in which he chose to live, and to which his many-faceted professional activities were the ideal passport.

Beaton was an impresario who used fashion to colour the scenario of the play that he made of his life, and in which he himself starred as production photographer and principal player. He had written in 1929, 'I would like to live in scenery'.[41] In 1968 his feature series 'The Great Indoors' was introduced with the words 'Consider a house to be a theatre, every room a stage and every girl a player.'[42] Beaton's friend Stephen Tennant commented aptly, 'In Cecil Beaton's art it is always the birthday morning – the eve of the Ball, the rise of the curtain.'[43]

1 For example: Cecil Beaton, *Photobiography*, pp. 26–8; Cecil Beaton and Gail Buckland, *The Magic Image*, 1975, p. 106.
2 Cecil Beaton, *Photobiography*, p. 38.
3 H. W. Yoxall, *A Fashion of Life*, 1966, p. 105.
4 Cecil Beaton, *op. cit.*, p. 45.
5 Edna Woolman Chase and Ilka Chase, *Always in Vogue*, 1954, p. 10.
6 On 10 November 1928.
7 Cecil Beaton, *op. cit.*, p. 53.
8 *Ibid.*, p. 56.
9 *Ibid.*, p. 60.
10 *Ibid.*, p. 60.
11 British *Vogue*, 22 February 1928, p. 41.
12 See Cecil Beaton, *op. cit.*, p. 176.
13 H. W. Yoxall, *op. cit.*, p. 103.
14 Cecil Beaton, *op. cit.*, p. 53.
15 *Ibid.* p. 38.
16 Cecil Beaton, *The Glass of Fashion*, p. 191.
17 American *Vogue*, 15 June 1936, p. 63.
18 For example: British *Vogue*, 14 October 1936, pp. 92–3.
19 See Cecil Beaton, *Photobiography*, p. 71.
20 *Ibid.*, p. 72.
21 Bettina Ballard, *In My Fashion*, 1960, p. 46.
22 American *Vogue*, 1 January 1936, pp. 66–7; French *Vogue*, March 1936, pp. 15, 28–9.

23 'Fashion is indestructible', British *Vogue*, September 1941, p. 32.
24 The 'all the damn kikes in town' dispute, detailed in Hugo Vickers, *Cecil Beaton*, 1985, p. 207 ff.
25 Cecil Beaton, *The Best of Beaton*, p. 113.
26 American *Vogue*, 15 December 1945, p. 59; British *Vogue*, November 1945, p. 53.
27 American *Vogue*, June 1948, pp. 112–13.
28 Quoted: Hugo Vickers, *Cecil Beaton*, p. 570.
29 British *Vogue*, October 1967, pp. 112–17.
30 'Beaton and the Baroness', *Weekened Telegraph*, 2 September 1966, pp. 32–7, 39.
31 British *Vogue*, December 1968, pp. 90–97.
32 British *Vogue*, 15 April 1973, pp. 74–7.
33 French *Vogue*, March 1979, pp. 245–91.
34 Gail Buckland, *Cecil Beaton War Photographs, 1939–45*, 1981, p. 7.
35 Bettina Ballard, *In My Fashion*, p. 46.
36 Hugo Vickers, *Cecil Beaton*, pp. 347–48.
37 Cecil Beaton, *op. cit.*, p. 163.
38 Cecil Beaton and Gail Buckland, *The Magic Image*, p. 280.
39 Cecil Beaton, *op. cit.*, p. 74.
40 *Ibid.*, p. 164.
41 Beaton's diary, 20 December 1929, quoted: Hugo Vickers, *Cecil Beaton*, p. 251.
42 British *Vogue*, December 1968, p. 91.
43 *Horizon*, September 1941, vol. IV, no. 21, pp. 213–14.

D13 *Family Group under the Ilex*, Cecil Beaton with his sisters Nancy and Baba, *c.* 1935 (Private Collection)

LANDSCAPE, NATION AND IDEOLOGY

∾ THE ROLE OF THE GARDEN IN CECIL BEATON'S ART ∾

Ian Jeffrey

'He had a good instinct for gardens'.[1] 'His garden was his joy'.[2] John Morris Smallpeice thought highly of his employer. Brought up in Surrey, where his father worked at Wisley Gardens, Smallpeice moved to Bapton Manor in the Wylye Valley in Wiltshire in the 1950s, and thence to Reddish, Sir Cecil Beaton's house at Broadchalke, where he remained until his retirement. The garden at Broadchalke was a showpiece: Mr Carpenter, the Sutton's representative from Reading, said that it had 'the best lawn in the West Country'.[3] The garden was opened to the public twice a year, and endless pains were taken to see that it was in prime condition. Altogether there were five acres of land, although only two of these constituted the principal garden. The rest, on the other side of the road, had been wild originally, but Beaton did not care for the stinging nettles, and had it dug out to form a lake, while a stream was diverted to constitute a water garden with irises and primulas. A bridge covered with wisteria completed the transformation. A great deal of work was involved in this restructuring, but Beaton was a good man to work for, 'a kind man',[4] endlessly attentive and appreciative, always impatient to get back from Salisbury Station to see how the garden looked. And when he walked around the garden he was able to see what others could not. As an employer he came with the highest possible recommendations.

It was a difficult garden to put to rights, for in the area around the house there was very little top soil – only around six inches – and if roses were to grow, the ground had to be excavated and good soil brought in as a base. At first Beaton wanted to grow too much in the space available, but that phase soon passed. He was fond of white flowers; the daisies growing along railway embankments always caught his eye, and he liked Cow Parsley and Queen Anne's Lace, although for the most part he preferred broad-petalled flowers. Californian poppies were favourites, as were Icelandic poppies and tree peonies. Of the cottage flowers, he liked delphiniums and hollyhocks, and he also grew lilies (in particular *Lilium candidum*), amaryllis and agapanthus in pots, which were later transferred to frames for overwintering. Red geraniums were kept in tubs by the garage wall, and were replaced by tulip bulbs during the winter. In the winter garden itself, behind the house, winter jasmine grew, while passion flowers covered a trellis. Hellebores were planted in the shadier borders to flower in the spring, and in the orchard Beaton grew white daffodils – 'Mt Hood', for example (he preferred daffodils of the narcissus type). Carnations were forced in a greenhouse for indoor use, as were azaleas.

Roses were Beaton's special love. He preferred the softer colours of the old-fashioned roses to the modern sort, of which the only variety he favoured was the pink, scented 'Constance Spry'. The

M20 Cecil Beaton with John M. Smallpeice: Reddish House Garden, *c.* 1965
(Sotheby's, London)

yellow rose 'Lawrence Johnson' was the first to flower in the garden. 'Wedding Day', with its sprays of delicate white flowers, clambered through apple trees in the orchard, while the orange-pink, scented 'Gloire de Dijon' climbed up the walls of the house. Near the terrace grew the carmine-pink Bourbon rose 'Zéphirine Drouhin' and a white clematis. He kept a bed of 'Iceberg' roses, with their palish-pink buds and a tinge of green to the white of the petals, and then there was the musk rose 'Penelope', with flowers that turned from salmon-pink to white. The end of the terrace was occupied

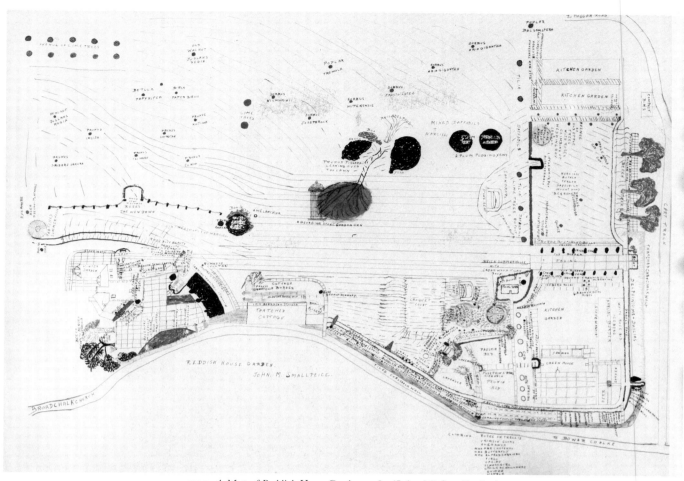

M39 *A Map of Reddish House Garden*, 1985 (John M. Smallpeice)

Tree, Ashcombe, 1930s (Sotheby's London)

Roses on the Wall, Reddish, c. 1950 (Sotheby's, London)

by 'Fantin Latour' and the 'Queen of Denmark', the first a Provence rose in delicate pink, the second a warm, rich pink, said to be one of the most perfect of the 'Old Roses'. He bought his plants from Miss Murrell's nursery in Shrewsbury, and was an interested reader of many nursery catalogues. Beaton numbered among his friends such reputable gardeners as Lady Salisbury, Lady Tree and Mr Michael Tree of Donhead St. Andrew, Lady Avon who lived at Alvediston, Lady Head at Bishopstone and Mrs Betty Somerset of Woodleigh Hall.

He was an attentive gardener who knew how to achieve certain effects. John Morris Smallpeice remembers an instruction to resite a maroon-crimson 'Tuscany' rose behind a white-flowered plant so that the red of the rose might show through and not be wasted as a mere background feature. And he had ideas about planting, like the placing of day lilies under fruit trees – ideas which not every gardener would regard as acceptable practice. He was gifted as an amateur gardener, but no authority. Compare him, for instance, to Eden Phillpotts, the novelist, who wrote well about his own garden (*My Garden*, Country Life, 1906). Phillpotts knew the names of all his plants and was capable of the finest assessments: 'The plant is worth growing, but not worth fussing about',[5] he wrote, *a propos* the commelina in his all-white rockery. Phillpotts was in control, a gardener with a magnifying glass who was aware that this or that plant came from the Cape, or Yunnan or the slopes of Mt Fuji, and aware of the year in which it was discovered and the name of the botanist who brought it back to England. In these terms, Beaton seems more exuberant than professional.

One of the remarkable features of Beaton's gardening career is that it began relatively late in life. His first love affair with the English countryside is recounted in *Ashcombe: The Story of a Fifteen-Year Lease*, published in 1949 (B. T. Batsford Ltd). Ashcombe was the Wiltshire house in which Beaton lived from 1930 to 1945. Little in that book gives the impression that he was an expert gardener. He presents himself as a tyro and a failure: 'The greatest disadvantage to overcome was the downland soil, so poor, shallow and chalky. It was not surprising therefore that the bulbs and plants that I ordered in such extravagant quantities should not thrive as I had seen them illustrated in the catalogues. The chalk soon robbed the colour from the most hardy survivors of our daffodils and croci, and the nettles grew with appalling tenacity.'[6] A self-confessed ignoramus, in fact, and frivolous: 'I enjoyed doing a little superficial weeding.'[7]

The Ashcombe confession touches on major questions of English ethics. To be a bad gardener is despicable. To confess to having been one shows candour and hints at an authentic re-birth into the true culture of these islands. Gardening was a test of authenticity, and a test which was mostly failed. The greatest of English gardening writers, S. Reynolds Hole, Dean of Rochester and author of *A Book about Roses* (innumerable editions were published from 1869 onwards), emphasized the relationship between gardening and character. Gardening found out the *nouveaux riches* and the heedless. This is his imagined reply, in *A Book about Roses*, to a moneyed interlocutor who had been half-hearted in following his advice: 'You have taken no trouble which deserves the name; and as to expense, permit me to observe that your fifty Rose-trees cost you £4, and your sealskin jacket £20. You don't deserve beautiful Roses, and you won't have any until you love them more.'[8] He adds, over the page: 'Not a *soupçon* of sympathy can I ever feel for the discomfiture of those Rose-growers who trust to riches.'[9] His concern is for those people who 'really love'[10] the rose, and he finds them in all sections of society, especially among the poor (notably Nottingham artisans). In a later book, *Our Gardens*, published in 1899 (J. M. Dent), he cast a wider net, damning those who did not fully appreciate the joys of the garden: pedants preoccupied by research; middle-aged nymphs infatuated by the intangible; Forsytes grateful for green peas and new potatoes; chatterboxes, garden specialists

Fête Champêtre Decoration, Ashcombe, 1937 (Private Collection)

and intent competitors; and Oxford undergraduates who thought of the garden as a place for lawn tennis and cigarettes. Finally, he discovers an elect of true gardeners drawn from all walks of life, each member easily able to recognize another: 'Sometimes that hand [of friendship] was huge, and hard, and discoloured: sometimes it was small and white.'[11]

Ashcombe, which might be subtitled *The Making of an Englishman,* records Beaton's gradual enlightenment, mirrored by his attitude towards gardening. 'The cuttings of Caroline Testout, given me by neighbours, were flourishing in truest musical-comedy vein, and our *lilium candidum* were surely unequalled in horticultural history.'[12] This is the writer having fun at his own expense, for 'Caroline Testout', a pink-flowered sort of a hybrid tea rose, is a ready grower and hardly in the same class as the 'Queen of Denmark', later grown at Reddish; and *L. candidum,* although prone to botrytis, is a survivor among the lilies. The Reddish Beaton could look back on the Ashcombe Beaton as a *guignol* gardener, dependent on neighbours and good luck.

While the early part of *Ashcombe* is presided over by Rex Whistler, who stands for the sociable and fashionable side of English life, the latter is under the spell of the Doves, young and old, and their country values. Beaton found a gamekeeper, Betteridge, in residence when he first bought Ashcombe. Betteridge, 'in leggings and a green hat',[13] stayed on with his family, 'all as unspoilt and contented as Le Nain peasants'.[14] He describes them as tutelary spirits: 'they seemed to me to be as much part of the place as the bricks and weeping ilex trees'.[15] But their contentment was extravagant, and the resultant neglect of the property was more than Beaton could stand on his return from long periods away. They were replaced, and his account of that replacement is told

[85]

as a turning point. At first there was a 'series of Shakespearean comics from Tollard Royal',[16] and then Providence intervened in the shape of 'an elderly man in leggings from the village with his son'.[17] Old Dove is the spirit of England incarnate. Father and son 'possessed that unruffled calm and quiet assurance which is seldom found today',[18] and he added that 'they brought to Ashcombe some of the special qualities of the place itself'.[19] Mysteriously, by force or quality of character, they set the place to rights and 'the flowers that had failed us before, now decided to blossom into glorious life'.[20] Dove is described as a mythic, autochthonous figure: 'His face contained the goodness of the earth itself. His clothes were, by their elaborate cut and fashion, obviously made in Queen Victoria's reign, and had grown by now, as lichen becomes part of a stone or the bark of a tree, to become part of his trim body.'[21]

Walter Sickert and his Wife, Thérèse Lessore, in their Garden, 1942 (Sotheby's, London)

Lady Diana Cooper Gathering Daisies, c. 1943 (Sotheby's, London)

For Beaton, Dove was a symbol of England and of redemption. The story of Ashcombe opens with a *fête champêtre*, peopled by Lady Ottoline Morrell, the Marchesa Casati and Margaret Drummond Hay who came from 'over the hill with a group of Valkyries on horseback'.[22] Then the sounds of abdication and of the occupation of the Rhineland gradually intrude, and as the crisis deepens Dove is invoked and delivered. Putting his age-old knowledge to use in the garden, he is invaluable during the Ashcombe years, and his death during the course of the war is told symbolically: flights of warplanes passed overhead, while the clouds on his funeral day were those of Constable. 'Yet even during the great upheaval of war, one wondered if by the loss of a man of such grace, intuitive knowledge and simplicity of purpose, another valuable link had not been broken with a vanishing England.'[23] Beaton then ended that section of the book with a cryptic remark from young Dove, in relation to clematis, on new roots and the smallest tendrils.

Ashcombe had been built as an establishment, a big house with stables and attendant buildings. All this is recorded and mapped in a painting of the mid-eighteenth century bought by Beaton from Sir Gerald Grove of Shaftesbury: 'The picture ever since has been my favourite possession.'[24] Beaton wrote at length on the history of Ashcombe, and was clearly able to imagine it as a place with a past. His account is in the style of the famous 'Highway and Byways' series of guidebooks, published by Macmillan and Co. around 1900, in which Britain is presented as a land with a rich local history, rather than as a landscape fit for consumption. Reddish House at Broadchalke also had a history; at least, there were traces of cockfighting apparatus in the attic, and that was the sort of detailing which attracted the guidebook writers of 1900.

Ashcombe, originally envisaged by Beaton as a site fit for re-styling in the Rococo manner, caught the imagination of the artist-photographer and reclaimed him for England. His vision, which began with a plethora of Cuvilliés and stucco cherubs, ended with the funeral of Dove. Ashcombe had its equivalents elsewhere in British art and letters: Capel-y-ffin, Piggotts, Rock Hall, Charleston, Rodmell – all country refuges of the 1920s. In Virginia Woolf's letters from Rodmell during that period, the country is portrayed as obdurate and archaic; dogs bark, wood is sawn, apples stolen and scandal received phlegmatically. 'Place' asserts itself in the face of an increasingly mobile society. The England imagined by artists and writers from the 1890s up to the Second World War is an England of localities, of particular street corners, river frontages, parks and villages. The country of James Whistler, Walter Sickert, William Nicholson and Théodore Roussel is made up of named places, streets in Chelsea and pubs in Parson's Green, under this light and in that weather. And 'place' is one of the themes of Galsworthy's *Forsyte Saga*, published in 1921; for that author, 'place' is a difficult concept not to be treated lightly; a paradise like the fatal Robin Hill is a test and a drawer-out of character. Ashcombe made such searching enquiries of Beaton, and, with the expiry of the fifteen-year lease, consolidated his views on British values.

Ashcombe is both a collection of sketches of a country idyll and a fable telling of the artist's coming to maturity. On a heroic level Dove intervenes, *ex cathedra*, as an agent of the national will. He might have opened the artist's eyes, and returned to him his vision of England, yet there is no necessary connection between the autochthonous Dove and the sharp-eyed enthusiast of Reddish. Dove may have made the desert bloom, but he did not pass on his skills. Beaton's true precursor at Ashcombe was his own mother, described as able and attentive: 'In the summer evenings she would wander about the garden accompanied by Suzie, her small dog, noticing so many things that would escape me. "Those iris – look how the bulbs have come up to the top of the ground. We need a lot of earth putting around them; and that lilac, look how it is pulling away from the elder tree. We must get Dove to cut down those elders, they are very unhealthy things and you never get anything to grow near them. That rose needs pruning; that shoot has too many leaves – a rose should always have five leaves, its strength goes if it has more."'[25] That sounds more like the careful gardener described by John Morris Smallpeice.

The Master of Reddish stood on an equal footing with the other great gardeners of the locality. He, too, like an exemplary country gentleman, exhibited in the local horticultural show and won prizes for roses, not unexpectedly. A history of the village horticultural society in Britain might open all sorts of doors. When were they founded? The new railway system made it possible for serious growers, gentlemen with glasshouses, to exhibit far and wide in the late-nineteenth century and to win medals in serious competition. Specialist rose growers exhibited in the big cities, and Dean Hole describes himself as a visiting judge at one of these events in the 1860s. But village horticultural shows were either founded or re-established in the 1940s, when they were managed by professionals and artisans, and local countrymen exhibited their produce – although specialist growers of dahlias and chrysanthemums might have come from the suburbs and council estates. The village horticultural show brought together, and still brings together, people from all walks of life, and suggests a unified society in which ploughmen and lawyers can find a common identity. It was in such a village show at Broadchalke that Beaton loved to exhibit, his main rivals being the local cottage gardeners. Again, it was a question of involving himself in the matter of England, in an idea of the culture as a whole.

At Reddish, flowers were picked constantly to the point where there were almost more blooms inside the house than out, and they were arranged to look natural. Beaton photographed across speckled poppies in the orchard, like an invention by Monet; features were picked out through gaps in the shrubbery or at the end of vistas; the house itself served as a backdrop to particular blooms – the white of a Japanese anemone set against the faded pink brickwork. But the garden was more than an available plot of land or stage-set. Paul Fussell, in his rich account of *The Great War and Modern Memory*,[26] quotes Siegfried Sassoon writing in *Siegfried's Journey* about an encounter with Winston Churchill at the Ministry of Munitions. The pacificist Sassoon (who was to live at Heytesbury, thus becoming a neighbour of Beaton's at Ashcombe) remembered Churchill expounding, 'War is the normal occupation of man. War – and gardening!' 'These are the poles,' Fussell adds, as though gardening was a necessarily Arcadian practice. It was never so; more a rigorous test of character. From another point of view it might be said that gardening was, to Dean Hole and his successors, a quasi-surreal practice through which Providence and The Infinite might be invoked. To be 'green fingered' was to be gifted; it was a sign of belonging, of being of the place – autochthonous. It was through his gardens at Ashcombe and then at Reddish that the artist atoned for his cosmopolitanism, and found a way back from the bizarre and the eccentric where he had first started. Beaton opens his book on Ashcombe by looking back on 1930: 'Since this time my taste has passed through an almost complete cycle and to-day I collect the very things against which I once inveighed.'[27]

1 John Morris Smallpeice, in an interview with Ian Jeffrey and David Mellor, Salisbury, 21 July 1985.
2 Interview, as above.
3 Interview, as above.
4 Interview, as above.
5 Eden Phillpotts, 'My Garden', *Country Life*, 1906, p. 109.
6 Cecil Beaton, *Ashcombe*, London, 1949, p. 17.
7 S. Reynolds Hole, *A Book About Roses*, J. M. Dent, 1869. This book was frequently republished.
8 *Ibid.*, 1st edition, p. 9.
9 *Ibid.*, p. 10.
10 *Ibid.*, p. 11.
11 S. Reynolds Hole, *Our Gardens*, London, 1899. These remarks are drawn from Hole's introduction, 'Enjoyments of a Garden', pp. 3–20, in the 4th edition, 1901, with illustrations by Arthur Rackham and photogravures by F. H. Evans.
12 Cecil Beaton, *Ashcombe*, p. 49.
13 *Ibid.*, p. 13.
14 *Ibid.*
15 *Ibid.*, p. 14.
16 *Ibid.*, p. 71.
17 *Ibid.*
18 *Ibid.*
19 *Ibid.*
20 *Ibid.*
21 *Ibid.*, p. 94.
22 *Ibid.*, p. 33.
23 *Ibid.*, p. 99.
24 *Ibid.*, p. 25.
25 *Ibid.*, p. 91.
26 Paul Fussell, *The Great War and Modern Memory*, Oxford 1975, p. 234.
27 *Ashcombe*, p. 10.

Jacket Design for 'Cecil Beaton's New York', 1938

Eggie's Pupil

❧ BEATON AS ARTIST ❧

Michael Parkin

'Inside Cecil Beaton', said Alan Jay Lerner, 'there was another Cecil Beaton sending out lots of little Cecils into the world. One did the sets, another did the costumes. A third took the photographs. Another put the sketches in an exhibition, then into magazines, then in a book . . . He was the only designer whose sketches were stunningly beautiful and outrageously funny at the same time.'[1]

What characterized Beaton the artist, or for that matter Beaton the designer or Beaton the photographer, was his aptitude for sheer hard work, his determination to succeed, and his unflagging energy. Throughout his career he remained resolutely a professional. Beaton the artist was never content; intolerant of imperfection, he was always trying to improve and learn from others. His keen observation made him a born satirist and a brilliant caricaturist, capable of achieving an astonishing likeness with a few strokes. Long after an event, or a visit to a new place, he could recall accurately the minutest details – a talent that was later to be of great assistance to him in designing for the stage and film. Beaton's love of drawing and painting spanned his entire lifetime, and his output was impressive: on his death he left a studio so full as to represent another life's work, quite apart from his photographs and countless other achievements.

Beaton's artistic interests were awakened at an early age. When barely three years old, he climbed into his mother's bed one morning and noticed a picture postcard of the actress Lily Elsie on the counterpane. It was this image that sparked off an enduring fascination with the theatre, photography and drawing. Later, he was to pore over weekly magazines illustrating Edwardian theatrical beauties, and if it was not Miss Elsie, it was Gaby Deslys, Gertrude Millar or Florence Smithson. These magazines were to have a life-long influence on Beaton, and time and time again he was to find inspiration in the Edwardian era. 'Heroes of childhood remain heroes for life',[2] wrote Sir Roy Strong, remembering Beaton's first set designs and costumes for *The Second Mrs Tanqueray*. Beaton's father had in his youth been an enthusiastic amateur actor, and had kept an album of newspaper cuttings on current theatrical productions. It gave him, as Beaton said, 'an aura of romance'.[3]

The earliest drawing by Cecil Beaton that has been exhibited dates from 1909, when he was five years old, and undoubtedly there were earlier efforts. His first studies display an understandable innocence, whilst indicating an early sense of form. He drew and attended art classes while at Heath Mount School and St Cyprian's, and at Harrow he enjoyed painting under the tuition of the white-haired W. Egerton Hine, affectionately known as 'Eggie'. 'I learnt to paint watercolours of bluebell woods in exactly the same manner as my master',[4] wrote Beaton, who became Hine's most promising

B55 *Five Bacchantes from 'Twilight of the Nymphs'*, 1928 (Michael Parkin Fine Art Ltd)

A33 *Judgement of Paris*, 1927 (Private Collection)

pupil, winning prizes in both 1919 and 1920, his work being dubbed 'prolific and clever'.[5] An outing to see Pavlova dance resulted in endless drawings of the ballerina, one of which he sold for 10s 6d – his first sale. Another school visit to the Royal Academy inspired in Beaton the ambition to become a Royal Academician. In a high-ceilinged, oak-panelled studio he would paint society portraits in the manner of Luke Fildes or De Laszlo. But it was not to be. Instead, it was Edward 'Boy' Le Bas, his best friend at Harrow and Cambridge, who became the exhibitor at the Royal Academy. Their schoolmates – 'Hodgypot' and 'Jeffpot' – were also destined for artistic careers: the former became the artist Eliot Hodgkin, and the latter the art dealer Arthur Jeffress. Beaton's discovery of the Renaissance led to a love of paintings by Botticelli and Filippo Lippi; the linear quality of works by the Pre-Raphaelites and Aubrey Beardsley was another revelation, as was the Ballets Russes with its vibrant designs by Picasso, Marie Laurencin and Bakst.

Cecil Beaton left Harrow for Cambridge as a prize art student with a fascination for stage design and a flair for caricature, and it was at this point that his drawing started to acquire a style that was essentially his own. At Cambridge he became a whole-hearted aesthete, joining the theatre clubs (the ADC and the Marlowe Society), designing costumes and scenery, and acting. Many ambitious productions were attempted including *The Rose and the Ring* (ADC, 1922) and *Volpone* (Marlowe Society, 1923), and his final designs at Cambridge for the 1925 Footlights revue, *All the Vogue*, displayed the now unmistakable Beaton stamp.

After Cambridge, Beaton launched himself as a photographer – the main talent by which he earned his living and built his reputation. But he had many other talents which merged rainbow-like into each other. His photographer's eye for capturing character led him to paint portraits, while his merciless wit revealed itself in biting caricatures. As a satirist and caricaturist, Beaton often delighted in revealing his subjects' less attractive features: his portrayal of Violet Trefusis shows a large-bosomed, pig-faced figure under which appears the caption, 'Violet always had a delightfully insouciant way of putting her cigarette out in a pat of butter.' Understandably, this gift was hardly acclaimed during his lifetime. *Vogue* published kinder examples before the Second World War, but one or two private collections have more telling parodies. His talent for portraiture is acknowledged by Richard Buckle, who recalled the astounding likenesses of Kenneth Clark and Irene Worth achieved in seconds by Beaton while he watched them on television. His exceptional gift for encapsulating the very essence of his subject is apparent even in his costume designs, which always manage to convey the character of the role being played.

832 *Violet Trefusis in Later Life, c.* 1960 (Private Collection)

c32 *Self-portrait*, 1928 (Terence Pepper)

Beaton constantly strove to develop his own style. Apart from childhood memories of the stars of Edwardian theatre, and the Ballets Russes, his vision was also shaped by the splendour of royalty and the aristocracy, and his Arcadian vision of country life, epitomized by Ashcombe, his home in Wiltshire. In common with most creative people Beaton was influenced by others. Like Jean Cocteau he was a *bricoleur* or *fregoli* – literally a quick-change artist – who had to be surrounded by equally talented minds. It was Cocteau's versatility Beaton admired and strove to emulate. He saw himself as a sensitive talent that needed to be encouraged and stimulated in order to achieve full potential. His drawings of the mid-twenties reflect the effect of meeting a new world of intellectual and bright young people, including the Sitwells, Stephen Tennant, Rex Whistler, Edith Olivier and Peter Watson. Beaton enjoyed these years and made connections with such influential figures as Mrs Edna Chase, the editor of American *Vogue*. The very idea of New York was a stimulant, and towards the end of the decade Beaton arrived in Manhattan. He met, photographed and drew personalities like Fred and Adèle Astaire, Alfred Lunt, Lynn Fontanne, the interior designer Elsie de Wolfe and Noël Coward. On his return from America he published *The Book of Beauty*, which consisted of photographs and illustrations of the well-known beauties of the day. His simple line drawings were thought to accentuate the beauty of his sitters, and the book was an immediate success.

For Beaton the thirties meant Paris and the start of his friendships with Tchelitchew, Bérard, Cocteau, Gertrude Stein and Alice B. Toklas. Beaton said of Tchelitchew: '[he] cast an almost hypnotic influence over me',[6] and of Bérard, 'from the moment we met Bébé gave me his open hand.'[7] Beaton, whom Cocteau christened 'Malice in Wonderland', was nonetheless intrigued and fascinated when Cocteau began to take him seriously. They explored New York and cruised the Mediterranean together. Beaton's drawings in Malta of Alex Mavromati's puppet show reflect Cocteau's influence in their admirable economy of line. On his travels in Spain with Tchelitchew, Beaton was introduced to the work of El Greco for the first time. 'Here was something that one had only dreamt of, each a whirlwind, a vision, muscular, sensitive [and] tumbling with vitality.'[8] The artist Sir Francis Rose was another influence at this point in Beaton's career – probably an adverse one. Beaton, who thought he resembled Toulouse-Lautrec in appearance, believed that, after Bérard, Rose was the 'greatest painter of today'.[9] Others, however, including Tchelitchew, thought differently.

Wartime service with the RAF and travel through five continents brought Beaton few opportunities for drawing or designing. However, after the war, when he had settled down at Reddish, his new home at Broadchalke in Wiltshire, he realized that in order to develop he must 'allow time to start painting seriously'.[10] Despite accolades in the fields of photography and design – he was appointed Official Photographer at the Coronation, awarded the CBE and then a Knighthood, and won Oscars for *Gigi* and *My Fair Lady* – Beaton was not satisfied. His constant desire to learn led him, at the age of fifty, to enrol at the Slade School of Art. He took this decision because of what he felt to be a lack of tuition in draughtsmanship, and because he wished to learn the use of oil paint. He wanted to become proficient as a painter and was now set on course, setting up his easel in a studio amidst far younger men and women. But his time at the Slade brought home to him 'with appalling cruelty, the difference between the quality of the work I have been doing and that which it will be necessary for me to do if I am to succeed by serious standards'.[11] William Coldstream (Slade Professor of Fine Art) asked if he was beginning to see the results he had hoped for. Beaton felt that perhaps he was not, but 'nevertheless, the big rousing shock has been to realise what a serious business it is! There was no alibi and even if one thinks it possible to avoid a hurdle one is soon found out trying to by-pass it.'[12] He concluded: 'I have perhaps gleaned a bit through my ears, but not enough through my eyes or with my mind.'[13]

Beaton's attendance at the Slade, an endearing act of humility, had a curious effect. His technique certainly improved, but the personal idiosyncrasy of his drawing vanished. Subsequent portraits in oil seemed to be lit by the afterglow of a Tchelitchew, whom he so admired, while his drawings

Peter Watson, early 1930s (Michael Parkin Fine Art Ltd)

With the sixties Beaton had felt he was entering an epoch that was more in sympathy with his own inclinations. He always kept abreast of the times and formed new friendships with the young, drawing and painting Mick Jagger, David Bailey, Christopher Gibbs and Julian Ormsby-Gore. By the seventies, however, Beaton was finding difficulty in keeping pace with modern trends, and started worrying about his eyesight. In 1974, at the age of seventy, Beaton suffered a severe stroke which left his right side paralysed. With sheer will-power and determination he managed to walk again unaided, showing enormous inner strength. He measured up to the problem and resolved to continue his life as fully as possible, learning to write, draw and paint with his left hand. He would sit for hours at Reddish, either inside or out, drawing the study, the library, the hall or the garden, and always trying to

resembled those of the also revered Augustus John. John had drawn his portrait in 1952, and Beaton, who always had a clear image of how he wished to look, found the work pleasing. As with Cocteau, it was John's confident linear dexterity that he attempted to emulate, later being influenced by the same quality in David Hockney's work. When Hockney came to stay at Reddish, Beaton found him 'funny, full of laughter, unspoilt, enchanting, young and colt-ish and carelessly beautiful'.[14] Patrick Procktor, whom he also met during the sixties and described as 'a fellow painter (a chap with hair worn like a Renaissance nobleman)',[15] was in turn to exert a similar influence his graphic style. In 1965 Beaton went to Mougins to draw and photograph Picasso, who flattered him that he had the 'eyes of a painter'.[16] He advised Beaton to 'do what Degas did and and have pages that are transparent so that you can turn over and trace the good bits and ignore the bad'.[17]

c36 *Joan Crawford*, 1932 (Michael Parkin Fine Art Ltd)

improve on his previous effort. These drawings and watercolours, produced against all odds, have a style which is almost naïve. Their strong bold colours reflect his admiration of Bérard, while their innocence recalls his early drawings at Harrow as a prodigy of 'Eggie' Hine.

For Beaton graphic art was an important facet of his many-sided life. Drawing, like writing his diaries, provided a release from often pent-up feelings and offered a means of relaxation. It is said he was not a happy man – those for whom fame is an ambition rarely are. But fame he achieved, and one cannot but admire the ceaseless energy and industry he put into his life and work. He loved art and other artists, and his written impressions of first encounters are full of enthusiasm and admiration. Augustus John he found 'a giant . . . a great polar bear [who] likes to hug and kiss playfully almost anyone he finds sympathetic and congenial'.[18] He listened to John's views on Graham Sutherland: 'He seems to pay little attention to the classical requirements of draughtsman-ship.'[19] But Beaton thought differently, shortly afterwards buying two small Sutherland paintings from the Leicester Galleries for £16. Henry Moore, too, became a friend, and Beaton rejoiced in his enthusiasm when he said in his North Country voice, 'I just adore going out into my studio and, taking my chisel and hammer, going bang, bang, bang!'[20] When he met Francis Bacon, Beaton felt 'immediate rapport',[21] although the portrait Bacon painted of him was not a success and was destroyed. But he enjoyed Bacon's company and wisdom: 'With Francis the air is mountain fresh; one feels invigorated.'[22] Bacon considered the Bérard portrait of Beaton very good and thought he was not fully appreciated either for his vision, or the quality of his paint. Beaton agreed. Rex Whistler, whom Beaton met shortly after Cambridge, became one of his greatest friends, and his early death distressed Beaton a great deal. Whistler's inspiration stemmed not from contemporary sources, but from the eighteenth century, and for Beaton he had 'an eternal fountain of creative talent . . . His gifts were winning, many-sided and brilliant.'[23]

The influence of fellow artists, and Beaton's stylistic flexibility are vital considerations in making a critical appraisal of Cecil Beaton's graphic art. Although at times imagination is lacking or bor-rowed, Beaton's drawings remain bright, witty, succinct and inventive. His best drawings, which most clearly display his personal, idiosyncratic style, are those completed in America during the thirties, and the numerous line sketches in *The Book of Beauty, Cecil Beaton's Scrapbook* and the diaries. These have a simplicity of line and an immediacy that is lost in the mass of detail in many of his set designs and later work. Always humorously critical of himself (and others), he achieved his results through constant practice, industry and sheer professionalism. Stephen Tennant was right when he said that Beaton was 'the best "grown-up child" in painting . . . his vibrant vivid works evoke a smile (is he a Dufy?), a joy that is pure and unrestrained.'[24] But although Tennant thought him 'a self created genius',[25] he questioned his merits as a great artist. Beaton himself hated the idea of the 'commercial' in him superseding the role of the 'artist'. Yet all his work bore the distinctive Beaton touch, from his set and costume designs, in which his style changed totally from one produc-tion to the next, to his memorable caricatures, drawings and watercolours, which display an uncom-mon gift still demonstrated even in the work executed with his left hand.

Without doubt, in future years historians and critics will come to give greater consideration to Sir Cecil Beaton the artist. At the sales of his stage and costume designs, portraits and landscapes held at Christie's in 1984, and the exhibitions entitled *Memorial* (1983) and *Cecil Beaton and Friends* (1985) held at the Parkin Gallery, the public demonstrated how eagerly Beaton's drawings and watercolours are sought. Throughout his life he remained open to new ideas, and was constantly refining his work in the field of graphic design. He will be remembered.

K25 *Set Design for 'Our Betters'*, 1946 (Private Collection)

1 A. J. Lerner to Hugo Vickers in Hugo Vickers, *Cecil Beaton*, London, 1985, introduction, p. xxv.

2 Roy Strong to Michael Parkin, *Hommage to Beaton*, Parkin Gallery exhibition catalogue, London, 1976.

3 Charles Spencer, *Cecil Beaton : Stage and Film Designs*, London, 1975, p. 7.

4 Cecil Beaton, *The Strenuous Years*, p. 175.

5 *The Harrovian*, Summer Term, 1919.

6 Cecil Beaton, *The Wandering Years*, p. 226.

7 *Ibid.*, p. 228.

8 Hugo Vickers, *op. cit.*, diary entry for Summer 1934, p. 176.

9 Hugo Vickers, *op. cit.*, diary entry for April 1938, p. 218.

10 Ed. Richard Buckle, *Self Portrait with Friends*, diary entry for April 1948, p. 213.

11 Hugo Vickers, *op. cit.*, diary entry for 14 January 1954, p. 370.

12 Ed. Richard Buckle, *op. cit.*, diary entry for 13 December 1953, p. 277.

13 Cecil Beaton, *The Strenuous Years*, p. 185.

14 Hugo Vickers, *op. cit.*, diary entry for 14 January 1965, p. 491.

15 *Ibid.*, diary entry for 27 September 1966, p. 508.

16 *Ibid.*, diary entry for April 1965, p. 491.

17 Ed. Richard Buckle, *op. cit.*, diary entry for 28 April 1965, p. 377.

18 Cecil Beaton, *The Restless Years*, p. 24.

19 *Ibid.*, p. 25.

20 *Ibid.*, p. 57.

21 Ed. Richard Buckle, *op. cit.*, diary entry for February 1960, p. 321.

22 *Ibid.*, p. 324,

23 Cecil Beaton, 'Designs for the Theatre – Rex Whistler', *The Masque*, no. 2, London 1947.

24 Stephen Tennant to Hugo Vickers in Hugo Vickers, *op. cit.*, introduction, p. xxiv.

25 Ed. Richard Buckle, *op. cit.*, introduction, p. xxiii.

Costume Designs for Saki's 'The Watched Pot', c. 1924 (Private Collection)

THE TYRANNY OF THE EYE

THE THEATRICAL IMAGINATION OF CECIL BEATON

Ian Jeffrey and Dr David Mellor

Cecil Beaton's life in the theatre, although triumphant in the end, never did run smooth. He was a *Wunderkind* who, after Cambridge, paradoxically took time to establish himself. One of the most poignant entries in his diary records an attempt to break into the upper echelons of show business. In 1925, he took examples of his work to C. B. Cochran, the great impresario, but 'he didn't look at half the things I showed him'.[1] Cochran, who staged prize fights, operettas, and almost anything that an audience might care to watch, may have been too busy to look very thoroughly, or his eye may not have been discerning – by his own admission, he had failed to give due recognition to Noël Coward in the early 1920s. Alternatively, Beaton's work might have been below par and the showman's indifference a fair assessment.

Cochran had new ideas about design in the theatre, and they are well expressed in *I Had Almost Forgotten . . .*, a rambling memoir of 1932. He praised Gladys Calthrop, Coward's designer through the 1920s, as 'an indefatigable worker with a fine sense, rather than great knowledge, of period. It is the sense that counts in theatrical design. Accuracy can be obtained from recourse to the library.' Cochran added that she had 'a strong feeling for late Victorian and early Edwardian settings and furniture', which associates her with Cecil Beaton, at least with his work from the mid-thirties onward.[2]

Perhaps Cochran's objection to Beaton's designs was that Beaton put 'great knowledge' in place of 'fine sense'. He researched his designs for Pirandello's *Henry IV*, staged by the Cambridge Amateur Dramatic Company in 1924, and his designs for *Volpone*, acted by the Marlowe Society in 1923, look authentic and detailed. In 1924 he also made costume designs for Saki's *The Watched Pot*, and some of the drawings are reproduced in *Cecil Beaton: Stage and Film Designs* by Charles Spencer. These drawings, headed 'terribly rough sketches for the dress maker', read like a critical essay on contemporary fashion and its terminology. This is his note alongside a dark, drooping costume with heavy cuffs: 'Afraid Shaftesbury Avenue and Wardour Street are already a mass of leopard skin but we must have a little here. It's so nice even if it is common.' Mrs Vulpy, a character from Saki's play, appears in 'a little three cornered hat of straw like the hats of the hags that sell flowers in Piccadilly Circus – trimmed smartly with cocks feathers', the same Mrs Vulpy whose 'orange feather fan (very luscious) goes with her carrot silk hair'. Perhaps Cochran recognized that the young man from Cambridge was a couturier, a historical revivalist and a social observer with a too-particular sense of both past and present.[3]

Cecil Beaton entered the world of British theatre at a moment of paradigm shift, and he came

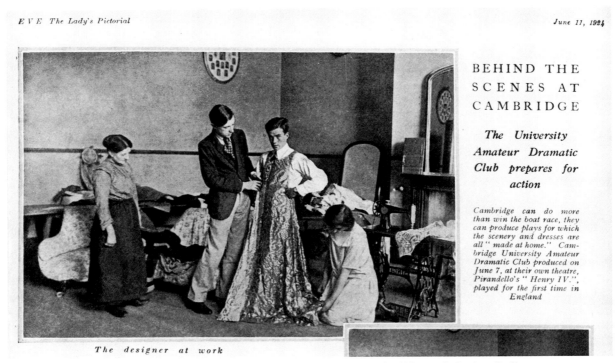

BEHIND THE
SCENES AT
CAMBRIDGE

*The University
Amateur Dramatic
Club prepares for
action*

Cambridge can do more
than win the boat race, they
can produce plays for which
the scenery and dresses are
all " made at home." Cam-
bridge University Amateur
Dramatic Club produced on
June 7, at their own theatre,
Pirandello's " Henry IV.",
played for the first time in
England

The designer at work

Beaton Fitting Costumes at Cambridge University ADC, 1924 (Cecil Beaton's *Cuttings Book*)

in as an exponent of the old mode. The ending of the First World War had no immediate effect on the London stage. In 1922, for instance, a Pinero revival at The Royalty Theatre was a major event. It began with the harsh play *Mid-Channel*, which had been condemned for its brutishness in 1909; in it 'practically every important member of the cast is a mess of quivering ganglions from beginning to end' (*Daily Telegraph*, 31 October, 1922). Pinero's influence can be detected in Coward's *The Vortex*, which was first played in 1923 and which, as his first success, brought silk shirts into fashion and inaugurated 'an extravagant amount of publicity'. *The Vortex* is marked by hysteria and changes of heart, and ends with the exposure of the theatrical Bliss family: 'I'm seeing for the first time how old you are – it's horrible – your silly fair hair – and your face all plastered and painted.'[4] In *Hay Fever*, an even greater success of 1925, artifice triumphs everywhere at the expense of trade, tragedy, commonsense and 'genuine' feeling – and ends triumphantly with the words, 'I really am going to return to the stage'. The sympathies of Beaton, the literalist and close observer, lie with the earlier Coward; his drawings for *The Watched Pot* amount to an astute perception of the characters.

For Beaton, the theatrical imagination of the 1920s was rich in unacceptable options. Coward's mature characters lived in a modern dreamworld, somewhere above Society. High Bohemia, on the other hand, was exotic and adventurous. Beaton's first sponsor, Osbert Sitwell, saw all the world as an affecting and dangerous stage. Sitwell warmed, for example, to d'Annunzio, the poet-terrorist who occupied Fiume with his para-military groups, the Arditi and the Wolves of Tuscany. He met them on a train: 'It was a strange mixture of efficient militarism, high ideals, and a somewhat theatrical *vie de Bohème*, but there flickered like a flame, through the noisy, rapid chatter, an enthusiasm that had died out of the other poor and war-worn nations of the West.'[5] D'Annunzio and his realm 'appeared to offer an escape from the normal European misery and vulgarity'.[6] Sitwell looked for glamour and *frisson*. His imagination was prompted by Franz-Josef, 'the charlatan Emperor', by the almost forgotten King Christopher of Haiti, a builder of châteaux in the jungle, and by those ancient dynasties put to the sword and replaced by 'the . . . less picturesque gum-chewing ogres of Oil and Big Business'.[7] But it was gum-chewing, and all that meant in terms of poor style, that was to become the norm.

Beaton may have been worried by the onset of bad taste on a world scale, but he was never a tragedian or dark dreamer in Sitwell's sense. Nor was he influenced much by the Ballets Russes, whose modern stage design set a precedent for the 1920s and for most of the 1930s. Adrian Stokes introduced his own book of 1935, *Russian Ballets*, as 'a pioneer work . . . long overdue . . . that will finally close a gap in aesthetic studies'. Diaghilev's ballet had been celebrated since it created its first sensation in Paris in 1909, but a satisfactory critical framework had never been found – and thus the ballet remained unpoliced. Stokes writes tentatively, making appreciative asides with respect to an art form which is more eternal than local, eg: 'In *Présages* we contemplate the heart and its movements and its emotions with our eyes.'[8] André Levinson, in an introduction to *The Designs of Léon Bakst for 'The Sleeping Princess'* praises the designer in similar terms as being free of 'all pedantry and erudition . . . the creator of an atmosphere, not a gravedigger rummaging among tombs'.[9]

Briefly, ballet had begun with the barbaric richness of *Prince Igor*, *Thamar* and *Scheherazade* and had then diversified during the 1920s and 1930s. In 1933, Cyril Beaumont identified a turning point: 'There was one final orgy of colour in the ballet *Chout*, given in 1921, and the virile hues of the Russian decorators gave place to the pale, clear tints inaugurated by Picasso, slowly to descend the colour scale until they reached the whites and greys of the costumes in *Ode* [1928]'.[10] By the early 1930s a change was taking place under the direction of Colonel de Basil, whose ballets included *Cotillon*, *La Concurrence*, *Scuola di Ballo* and *Le Beau Danube*, all produced for the first time in 1933. Stokes ascribes them to de Basil's *fouetté* period; they are witty, dandified, elegant, light. Stokes expands his views in relation to the Kochno ballet *Cotillon*, with its scenery and costumes by Christian Bérard: 'It is rare that anything as *mondain* should be as beautiful, as strenuous and as lyrical. Chabrier contrived to gain a light comprehensiveness, so modern in ideal, from the Victorian Age in which he lived. Bérard's prismatic-coloured frocks and the ladies' coiffures are of the period 1870–80. By means of a series of episcopes were are offered the quintessence of the evening occasion, fortuitous upshots, telepathic alliances, electrified common-places, and those polite primeval games which give some parties the character of a hastily convened séance.'[11] For the first time the Ballets Russes, with Bérard's 'prismatic-coloured frocks' and specific reference to recent history, begins to sound like a contributory element to the Beaton story.

Beaton waited, and taste changed in his favour. It changed towards a sardonic nationalism, epitomized by Noël Coward's *Cavalcade*, his 'Play of the Century', launched in 1931. *Cavalcade*, made up of three acts and nineteen scenes, begins in 1899 with champagne and ends in 1930 with the singing of the national anthem. It is a collage of songs and vignettes prompted by a photograph of a troopship leaving for the Boer War, seen by Coward in a back number of the *Illustrated London News*.[12] Beaton turned to similar sources; he ransacked his own bound copies of *The Sketch* to assemble a research archive for *My Fair Lady*.[13] *Cavalcade* was more than simple revivalism, and more than

K32 *Costume Design for The First Shoot from
the Revue 'Follow the Sun'*, 1936 (Roy Astley)

K34 *Costume Design for Mrs Erlynne, Act III
'Lady Windermere's Fan'*, 1945 (Roy Astley)

nostalgia. Coward's twentieth century careers downhill into a chaos which the Union Jack and *God
Save the King* will never put right. The great days were Edwardian; they were heroic and picturesque,
and family life was stable and assured. But the butler becomes a drunkard, the *Titanic* sinks, and
a surviving youngest son is killed almost on Armistice Day.

Two weeks after *Cavalcade* opened at Drury Lane, a general election resulted in a sweeping Conservative majority. Coward, 'bleakly uninterested in politics', put it down to fate which pointed
him towards the Boer War rather than to the storming of the Winter Palace in St Petersburg.[14]
Cavalcade established the myth of the Edwardian Age as gilded, vivacious, confident. The idea was
already in the air; C. B. Cochran's revue of 1929, *Wake Up and Dream*, featured an Empire Parade
in 1910. In 1936, Beaton worked on the décor and costumes for Osbert Sitwell's ballet *The First
Shoot*, included in *Follow the Sun*, another Cochran revue. The subject was Edwardian and its heroine
a Gaiety Girl peeress – the humbly-born Fanny had almost made the same grade in *Cavalcade*.

That Edwardian dream of parades, high society balls and folk pageantry emerges spectacularly
in *My Fair Lady*, first in the Lerner and Loewe stage version of 1956, and then in the film of 1963,
which is at least a generation after Noël Coward first broached the subject. It was an enduring

and discreet myth, and above all it was elaborate, involving a way of life. W. MacQueen-Pope's best-seller of 1947, in *Carriages at Eleven: The Story of the Edwardian Theatre*,[15] analyses the structure of Edwardian life, and the theatre in particular. It was still an intimate world. Advertising was done by word of mouth and performers sang and recited, unassisted by electronics, in theatres where audiences were treated as guests of the great actor- and house-managers. Decorum, in MacQueen-Pope's account, was insisted on, and the total impression is of an integrated community in which Society beauties clothed in silk belonged to the same world as kerb-side entertainers. The writer is as moved by the circumstance of theatre as by Theatre itself; he describes a set of buskers and their songs, lists programme advertising, and evokes every one of the hundreds of personalities who went to make up the Edwardian theatre. For example, 'Sir Squire Bancroft, one of the few moustached actors, was an unforgettable figure, his silver hair, his bearing, his monocle with its broad black ribbon, his grey frock coat and topper – a universal celebrity'.[16]

P22 *Princess Turandot's Headpiece,* 1961 (Metropolitan Opera, New York)

Hats for the Ascot Scene, 'My Fair Lady', 1963
(Sotheby's, London)

When Cecil Beaton thought of Edwardian London, he thought in terms of *Carriages at Eleven*, and his account of *Lovely Lily Elsie*, written in 1974, depends on MacQueen-Pope's definitive work. But Beaton was a mere child during the heyday of Edwardian musical comedy: 'When I had reached the age of eleven I was able to admire this lady, through a pair of binoculars, as she sat one late Sunday morning smoking cigarettes with laughing friends on a balcony at the Grand Hotel, Folkestone.'[17] Nevertheless, it was, in retrospect, a comfortable and coherent world where 'audiences were in the nature of one large family'.[18] At times his Edwardian world seems homely and ideal. At other times it comes to life in an uneasy, macabre fashion. A visit to Lily Elsie in old age is recounted in detail: 'By degrees I was able to scrutinize my companion as she sat enveloped in the anonymous disguise of old age. The beautiful cleft chin had now grown a full double chin, and there was puffiness under the eyes, but her complexion was faultlessly white and singularly unlined . . . I noticed through the dark glasses that the eyes had "gone": they were half their usual size and the skin had sagged in a little swag by the bridge of the nose.' This is not an uncharacteristic piece of observation by Beaton the photographer, who was cruelly sharp-eyed, almost victimized by his own powers of perception. By comparison, MacQueen-Pope, although an evocative writer, deals in generalities,[19] while Beaton falls under the tyranny of his eye.

This power of, and delight in, observation fitted Beaton for the cinema rather than for the stage, even though the stage was his confessed interest. *Anna Karenina*, for which he designed the costumes in 1948, is one of his lesser achievements. *Gigi*, on which he worked in 1958, is of a higher order, a preparation for the Cukor film of *My Fair Lady*, released in 1963. In 1956, Beaton had worked on the costumes of the stage version of *My Fair Lady*. At one level these films, with their many formal occasions in great houses, in ballrooms and at race meetings, rehearse Edwardian themes. The

Audrey Hepburn in 'My Fair Lady', 1963 (Sotheby's, London)

presence of picturesque street characters, inherited from Shaw's *Pygmalion* and intensified in *My Fair Lady*, reinforces the idea of intimacy which MacQueen-Pope puts at the heart of the Edwardian myth. The Pygmalion story itself, although carrying a classical sanction, takes its local colour from late Victorian and Edwardian examples of social ascent. Gaiety Girls and musical comedy actresses often married into the peerage, for example, the Countess of Orkney, Lady Churston, Countess Ostheim, Lady George Cholmondeley, the Countess of Suffolk, and many more.[20]

This Edwardian revival may have been important to Beaton the artist as a reminder of his lost childhood and as an idyll, yet it was a powerful fiction which allowed him to envisage other meanings. *My Fair Lady* is, at first sight, just such an Edwardian revival with costumes out of the most graceful Society portraiture of 1910. The subject of Shaw's play, on the other hand, involves such themes as truth, a coming to consciousness and rites of passage. Eliza is purified by her professor, and introduced to a (literally) refined language which allows her to be herself. Beaton honours this theme in Shaw's play, for Eliza enters mismatched and cacophonous; her 'trade' costume is bottle-green over burgundy in colour with a black hat, ornamented with pink, yellow and apricot flowers (worn on her first visit to the phoneticist's laboratory). The onset of her purification is symbolized by her being stripped and scrubbed offstage by a governess. She re-appears in grey-collared schoolgirl dresses, and is then given her first public trial at Ascot in a discordant costume of black and white. She appears as a product, packaged by modern design in a prefiguration of the 1920s. Her Ascot launch is a disaster, for the package, as the angles and discords of the costume suggest, has been improperly tied and the language of the old Eliza breaks through in the excitement of a close finish to the race. Shaw's Eliza never went to Ascot, but in the Lerner and Loewe version that visit and that dress are central. She recovers her composure, and finally comes of age in a white ball-gown which also signifies a return to Edwardian values.

For Shaw, writing in Edwardian England, a purified, national language was something to be worked for without reservation. In Beaton's costume allegory, on the other hand, Shaw's Modernist ideology is sabotaged. Purification robs a culture of its flavour and Beaton's perversely costumed cast ensure that a distinctive local flavour remains. And the mature Eliza becomes an Edwardian lady, an anachronism that speaks more for the power of Beaton's myth of Britishness than Shaw's ideas on efficiency. Professor Higgins, too, is enlisted by Beaton in the undermining of the modern ideal. In *Pygmalion*, he appears as an exemplary Edwardian, 'dressed in a professional-looking black frock-coat with a white linen collar and black silk tie', but in Rex Harrison's version he is rather more of a suburban enthusiast in a comfortable cardigan.[21] *Anna Karenina* had served as a preparation of sorts for *My Fair Lady* in that it, too, featured a distinction between an efficient, thoughtful Modernism, represented by Kitty and the curate-like Constantin, and a glamorous court life. Vronsky enters, uniformed and with epaulettes like pancakes, but makes his final appearance in a civilian suit, enfeebled and exiled in Venice. The meaning of *Anna Karenina*, as directed by Julien Duvivier and costumed by Cecil Beaton, involves a failure on the part of a reformed, tolerant, liberal society to catch at the imagination. There is nothing, they suggest, to match pearls, the opera and military braid.

And yet – the artist equivocates. A modern, sensible or suburban society lacks the glamour of that old world of dressing up, occasion and decorum. But the costumed world itself is no unmitigated good thing. In *Gigi* the girl bride is taken to a night club where bright dresses and a dominant master of ceremonies constitute a kind of hell. Beaton's designs imply an elementary colour-coding with the low dressed up in lilac or paraded as bright confections. And a dress might signify entrapment: Gigi, for instance, as a child undergoing instruction, appears striped and checked and chevroned, and the early Eliza is uniformed; just as middle-period Eliza is a package, Gigi, too, when she goes out into the wide world, dressed in white, wears bows at her shoulders, quite as though she might be untied, as a gift. If he took anything from the Ballets Russes it was this stress on costume as an independent element; in Bakst's designs, for example, fabric dominates figure – in Cecil Beaton's very much more tentative theatre drawings, by contrast, swaying figures blend with their costumes. But his filmed figures are, predominantly, constrained by costume. Again and again they come decked in high collars or ruffs, or enhanced by necklaces and necklets. Heads are thus held apart by costume-like artifice, and rather as fetish objects than as mirrors of soul or spirit. The head, often elaborately coiffed or brightly ornamented in a feathered hat, stands as an intensification of the rest, but at moments of unusual truth, beauty or revelation the heroine – Anna, Gigi or Eliza – appears bare-headed, for once free from the constraint of her costume. His major figures have their major moments when they appear to transcend society, yet the artist never declares for one world rather than the other. Perhaps he wanted to, but never believed in transcendental moments and ideals. His account of Lily Elsie moves from her early beauty, touchingly told, to her decline 'wrapped in a cocoon of elderly fat'.[22] This account of Gaby Deslys is worthy of the early Otto Dix: 'They gasped as she appeared clad from head to foot in magenta with a windmill of paradise feathers on her head, or dressed entirely in black and white furs, to step into the Rolls-Royce of "elephants' breath" that awaited her. She died of cancer of the throat at an early age.'[23] Beaton knew that perfection could never last, but had an idea that decay and failure might be shut out, that a welter of sequins, tassels and feathers or good form, carefully maintained, might dispose of time, for a while at least.

1 Quoted by Charles Spencer in *Cecil Beaton: Stage and Film Designs*, London, 1975, p. 22.

2 Charles B. Cochran, *I had almost Forgotten . . .*, London, 1932, pp. 148–9.

3 Charles Spencer, *op. cit.*, p. 20.

4 '*The Vortex* was written in 1923 and produced on 25 November at the Everyman Theatre, Hampstead', Noël Coward, *Play Parade*, introduction, p. x.

5 Osbert Sitwell, *Discussions on Travel, Art and Life*, London, 1925, p. 228.

6 *Ibid.*, p. 221.

7 Osbert Sitwell and Margaret Burton (eds.), *Sober Truth: A Collection of Nineteenth-century Episodes, Fantastic, Grotesque and Mysterious*, London, 1930, p. 19.

8 Adrian Stokes, *Russian Ballets*, London, 1935, p. 128.

9 André Levinson, *The Designs of Léon Bakst for 'The Sleeping Princess'*, London, 1923, preface.

10 Cyril Beaumont, *Serge Diaghilev*, London, 1933, p. 85.

11 Adrian Stokes, *op. cit.*, p. 185.

12 Noël Coward, *op. cit.*, p. viii.

13 Eileen Hose, in conversation with David Mellor.

14 Noël Coward, *op. cit.*, pp. ix–x.

15 W. MacQueen-Pope, *Carriages at Eleven: The Story of the Edwardian Theatre*, London, 1947. Chapter VI, *Daly's, the delectable*.

16 W. MacQueen-Pope, *op. cit.*, p. 12.

17 Cecil Beaton, 'Lovely Lily Elsie', in *The Rise and Fall of the Matinée Idol*, ed. Anthony Curtis, London, 1974, p. 14.

18 Cecil Beaton, *op. cit.*, p. 3.

19 Cecil Beaton, *op. cit.*, p. 16. In this short essay the author remembers his first experience of the theatre, a scene from *The Merry Widow*, in which Lily Elsie starred: 'I was too young to remember anything of the afternoon of dazed delight except that in the last act a lady did a high-kicking dance on the supper table at Maxim's'. The scene on the supper table lived on as an image from *The Merry Widow*; it was illustrated performance, and is vignetted on the cover of *Fortune's Favourite: The Life and Times of Franz Lehar*, by W. MacQueen-Pope and D. L. Murray, London, 1953.

20 Forbes Wilsford, *Daly's*, London, 1944, p. 133.

21 G. B. Shaw, *Pygmalion*, first produced in London and New York, 1914. Professor Higgins's costume is described in the introduction to Act II.

22 Cecil Beaton, *op. cit.*, p. 16.

23 Cecil Beaton, *From Gladys Cooper to Gertrude Lawrence*, also in *The Rise and Fall of the Matinée Idol*, ed. Anthony Curtis, pp. 55–6.

F25 *Cecil Beaton* by Paul Tanqueray, 1937 (Private Collection)

OPEN SECRETS

IDENTITY, PERSONA AND CECIL BEATON

Stuart Morgan

Both more and less than a portrait, Paul Tanqueray's study of Cecil Beaton reveals, but refuses to analyse, a tangle of fictions which sustained him. The most obvious is concealment; surrogates, in the form of photographic portraits pinned to his suit, are employed as camouflage, or even armour. Of equal importance is display – not only done but seen to be done, as Beaton makes eye-contact with the viewer while permitting himself an expression of bored superiority. If he appears disdainful of his audience, he is just as disdainful of the squadron of sub-Cecils he commands. While calling attention to his own creativity, the ability to summon a multitude of alternative selves, he deprecates it too. Retention and expenditure, production and consumption, release and repression are kept in perfect equilibrium. And the result is a prodigy: a Burning Bush of a man whose capacity for the proliferation of images keeps pace with the rate of their natural dissolution, a man who exists by virtue of a process of constant renewal, defying time by mastering the very operations of time itself. The tone of Tanqueray's portrait is ambiguous. Is it satirical or complimentary? One thing, at least, is certain. As the viewer becomes aware of the overlay of imagery by which Beaton is defined, the picture slips into another mode completely. In Shakespeare's *Henry V* an actor appears as Rumour, in a costume covered with tongues. The man in this photograph may also be an allegory of something. But what? The search for an answer involves an analysis of the creative act as Beaton saw it.

Beaton's reports of his early years reveal divergent attitudes to his own identity. 'I want only to be Cecil Beaton', he commented, on seeing his initials on a box he had to take to school.[1] Yet this sense of ineradicable difference from others was countered by 'a secret feeling of inadequacy' physical, social, sexual and financial – which preyed on him for the rest of his life, and was accompanied by an unusual eagerness for change.[2] ('I'd like to change my whole self', he wrote after seeing Fred Astaire.)[3] In the first volume of his diaries, *The Wandering Years*, the conflict between these alternatives is heightened by the need to find work, a point at which *Bildungsroman* ceases and picaresque begins. Gradually the debate on selfhood takes the form of a discussion of the appropriate way of life for an artist. Having renounced frivolity, Boy Le Bas reminds his erstwhile devotee that the self brooks no alteration. But young Cecil thinks differently and they part for ever. 'Life is deeper than thought', he wrote much later.[5] In his case choosing 'life' meant opting for change and levity, but above all for a histrionic metaphor which would eventually come to dominate his entire aesthetic.

When Beaton decided to tour North America as a professional speaker in 1953, the lecture he chose to deliver again and again was one with a venerable history on the lecture circuit. It concerned

B33 *Cecil Beaton and a Group of Bright Young People on a Wooden Bridge*, Wilsford, from left to right: Rex Whistler, Cecil Beaton, Georgia Sitwell, William Walton, Stephen Tennant, Zita Jungman, Theresa Jungman, *c.* 1928 (Sotheby's, London)

the problem of vocation. Given the dilemma of having to preserve selfhood at all costs while never ceasing to adjust the presentation of that self, Beaton drew on his deepest instincts when faced with the need to survive. Masquerades had provided the occasion for his best early photography. Already Beaton had found his medium. Later he was to use the phrase 'living picture' to describe his own theatre designs. But it was something resembling *tableau vivant* in its proper sense which preoccupied Beaton for his entire career. As described by Goethe in *Die Wahlverwandtschaften* and Jane Austen in *Mansfield Park*, the *tableau vivant* was a household entertainment, sometimes highly elaborate, in which sets, costumes, poses and lighting were employed to create a sculptural rendering of a given painting. The proscenium arch was crucial to such reconstruction, enabling two dimensions to turn into three, the effect of depth being dependent on a frame. Theatre was referred to merely in terms of setting; the participants were no more than life models. One object of the exercise was to stimulate thought about the complex relationship between life and art. In a more worldly sense, it provided social lubrication. Ironies in casting would be noted, unexpected groupings might be assessed on their potential in real terms. Performers would be thrown together unexpectedly and the audience was given permission to discuss them. Suddenly relations between people were sharpened and changed.

Beaton's own *tableaux* were constructed in free space. Framed by his camera, imaginatively illumin-ated, and developed by trial, error and experiment, the scenes appeared totally deliberate. The product could be regarded as a flattering portrait, an 'abstract' illustration in the Pictorialist vein or simply a souvenir of one piece of improvized fun. Yet each of the best of these photographs has the potential to be more than the sum of its parts. As in the boyhood works of Lartigue, the secret lay in that sense of heightened possibility experienced in play, captured by making the act of photo-graphy one element in the game. At its peak, *tableau vivant* was the true heir of the defunct court masque. As in the masque, an image of an ideal community lay at its core. The rhetoric which served to convince spectators of that social perfection succeeded at an aesthetic moment when each separate unit could be regarded in its own terms yet, by 'willing suspension of disbelief', acted also as part of a totality with perfect political, as well as artistic, justification. When distinctions between children and adults, men and women, contemporaneity and history, reality and fiction imploded, and for a second it seemed that anything was possible, Beaton's camera not only captured that carnivalesque moment; it also transmitted and perpetuated it.

B39 *Mrs Ronald Armstrong-Jones as Perdita Robinson*
in the Pageant of Hyde Park, 1928 (Sotheby's, London)

The repercussions of this moment, when art meets life on its own terms by breaking its bounds, literally gaining another dimension, are visible throughout Beaton's career. The disguise, which was no disguise at all because only by penetrating it was it possible to experience the full impact of the pose, retained all its attraction for an artist who, it was said, could remember 'a period when for eight or ten days at a stretch he did not ever confront the world in ordinary costume but having removed his fancy dress to go to bed stepped straight into a new disguise as soon as he emerged from slumber'.[5] Eventually all dress became fancy dress for Beaton, an extension of that flair for mimickry he so admired in Pavel Tchelitchew or Frederick Ashton, natural Brechtians who 'acted' without ever surrendering their individuality.[6] In psychological terms, disguise might have reflected a need to be present when the 'aesthetic moment' took place and he, like all the other participants in the *tableau*, would be transformed, not least in status. What did he have to lose? As a self-confessed snob and a social climber, he just wanted to be accepted as an equal by those in whose circles he tried to move. The objection to this theory is obvious. It is that far from simply being a bit actor, Beaton had it in his power to bring about the rearrangement he so desired. Of course, he had to do both. When he had achieved his aim, when he had become a 'society photographer' who was himself a member of Society, he continued to act out both sides of the predicament at once. In new guises, those two views of selfhood were taken to logical extremes: on the one hand Beaton was playing God (the secret motive of any photographer who employs the 'directorial mode') and on the other he was submitting to permanent metamorphosis, making himself a walking reminder of some fault in the system. A single example of the simultaneous use of both approaches will suffice. In 1933, at rue de la Boëtie in Paris, Beaton photographed Pablo Picasso. He faces us, his back to a mirror in which Beaton's head is reflected, a reminder that our audience with the great man has been granted only at the intercession of someone he respects. Hanging, apparently, on the very wall at which Picasso is gazing, Beaton's framed face resembles a portrait exchanged in an act of gratitude.

The management of a public persona had now become a complicated matter. Beaton's diaries were edited to give an account of his life as 'Cecil Beaton', no longer merely a photographer but a gentleman artist, modelled on Noël Coward, who lectured him on his attire early in his career, and Beverley Nichols, who opened his eyes to sex. For Beaton, the edited version of the diaries and his other publications which often repeated the same anecdotes, supplied a running subtext for a body of photographs which, like *tableaux vivants*, seemed to incline towards narrative. Their personal use was as a record of self-cultivation. And the qualities Beaton most wanted to cultivate were those of an actor. (As if to prove a point, to himself most of all, he eventually played on Broadway.) 'Great acting', he wrote as late as 1957, 'is always the highest artificiality.'[7]

'Artificiality', the maintenance of what Coward called a 'façade' in both personal and professional spheres, was a preoccupation of male homosexuals from the 1890s onwards. The continued distaste for the middle-class concept of 'nature' and sincerity persisted long after the pronouncements of the Aesthetic Movement had ceased. Indeed, the very persistence of a set of cultural habits, a private vocabulary, an emotional range and particular ways of expressing it, demonstrated how little the lot of this particular minority had improved in the course of a century which had been prefaced by the trial of Oscar Wilde. Within the terms of this subculture, Cecil Beaton's behaviour and artistic preferences followed a well-worn path. Like Beaton, Aubrey Beardsley preferred to be known as a man of letters rather than an artist.[8] Like Beaton, the young Wilde entertained actresses, including Lillie Langtry, while Ronald Firbank, whose favourite word was 'artificial', kept an album filled

F3 *Self-portrait in Mirror with Picasso*, 1933 (Sotheby's, London)

with picture postcards of musical comedy beauties during his school years. Biographical coincidences between Beaton and this set of contemporaries could be expanded indefinitely. Particularly in the earlier part of the century, the cultivation of a style which was too eroticized or too satirical, too opulent or too clipped indicated the flouting of norms: Wilde's overloaded descriptions in his stories and epigrams in his plays; Firbank's exotic, languid sentences and abstract precision, as in Chapter XX of *Inclinations*, which in its entirety reads 'Mabel! Mabel! Mabel! Mabel! Mabel! Mabel! Mabel! Mabel!'; or Beardsley's rococo flounces and economic line. The use of cosmetics; a tone of voice pitched either too high or too low, confusing people wherever possible; and the use of theatrical behaviour as a protection against vulnerability, all constituted a defence from, and an attack on,

[115]

those bourgeois values which homosexuals did surprisingly little to try to disrupt. A common denominator exists in Beaton's taste for travesty; his deliberate avoidance of cliché and sentimentality in the choice of the most ugly shot from a Judy Garland contact sheet; his deliberate use of the same qualities in his 1947 portrait of Her Majesty the Queen, posed in front of a Christmas card setting; the flagrant grotesque of Elsa Maxwell's total baldness in 1960; and his purely artistic deployment of religious iconography in Lady Diana Cooper's portrait of 1930. The sexual glances inferred

B16 *The Miracle: Lady Diana Cooper*, 1930 (Sotheby's, London)

09 *Judy Garland*, 1953 (Sotheby's, London)

in his photographs of servicemen during wartime and his documentary photographs of London in ruins, many resembling theatre sets, show an unusually effete and perverse approach to the wartime situation which faced him. As so many of his travel pictures and royal portraits show, Beaton was happiest when not confronting his own time and place. Armed with a limited number of themes, contexts and approaches, he often played at jumbling them up, so that a European spire looks like a Hollywood set, or a savage tribesman resembles one of the chorus line in a bad musical.[9] Perhaps Beaton's most characteristically homosexual act was the urge to modify his 'image', to try to show a 'front' to the world while, oddly, giving himself away at every turn. Perhaps he thought that the English were hypocrites who would find him acceptable if only he went through the motions of trying to conform. It is possible. But it is more possible still that he was falling into a pattern of events which had been repeated so often during his formative years that it constituted an identifiable stance. André Gide regarded Oscar Wilde's entire body of work as the product of a simultaneous desire for advertisement and secrecy. In his *Journals* Gide wrote, '1st October 1927: I believe . . . that this affected aestheticism was for him merely an ingenious cloak to hide, while half revealing, what he could not let be seen openly; to excuse, to provide a text, and even apparently motivate, but that very motivation is a pretence. . . . Always he managed in such a way that the uninformed reader could raise the mask and glimpse under it the true usage (which Wilde had good reason to hide).'[10]

Johnnie Weissmuller, Hollywood, 1932 (Sotheby's, London)

Sailor Relaxing, 1944 (Sotheby's, London)

If the strategy of concurrent revelation and concealment pervaded every aspect of Cecil Beaton's life, the reason might have been that it represented the only possible compromise between his incompatible views of his own selfhood. An 'actor' in the sense of having rejected a life of contemplation, he lived as if on a stage. Yet he changed his parts at will in an attempt to handle the materials of his existence as an artist manipulates his medium. So while he admired figures such as Cocteau for having taken control of the 'design' of their lives, by which he meant that they never allowed themselves to be seen except as they wanted, he himself may have craved a 'grand design' which would determine all his choices. He ended as a moral relativist and an artistic split personality, wavering between the avant garde and the academy, between revolution and revivalism. Never really part of Society, however much he dreamed of it, he was not antagonistic to it either. Of all fictional characters, he most resembles Thomas Mann's Felix Krull who, when asked whether he was a socialist, replied 'Certainly not, Herr Generaldirektor! I find society charming just the way it is and I am burning to win its favour.' Perhaps Beaton always expected more of both art and life than they could really offer. His distress can best be seen in his view of disorganization, the jumble of his hotel bedroom, the back lots in Hollywood, the confusion of the masked ball. His own reaction to these was touchingly indecisive, reminiscent of that total estrangement which Beerbohm sensed in Beardsley. He wished only to be close to it all, to those focal points of glamour, High Society and Hollywood, which he felt poetically fertile. There and only there play could arise, personae could be lost and found, stars could be born. If for him photography became an agent of transformation, clothes represented the harsh facts of survival, a capitulation to the world outside him. Nudity has no place in Beaton's scheme of things. His pictures of Dolores del Rio wearing Oceanic garlands or Johnny Weissmuller, relaxing under a tree, might equally well be Sander-esque studies of people at work or remakings of the myth of Adam and Eve, with little sympathy for their predicament. There is no escape from the role-playing mankind is forced to accept. In the words of Felix Krull, 'He who truly loves the world shapes himself to be pleasing to it.' Beaton would have nodded vigorously.

Who knows what Paul Tanqueray thought of Beaton that day in his studio. A pleasing young man, but one who had picked his brains. No shortage of talent. Too much for his own good, perhaps. The embarrassment of one photographer photographing another who he knew in time would pre-empt him. But what to do about it? Praise him to the skies? See him in hell? Suddenly it all became clear. He would turn him into something like a playing card or a chess-piece. Only Beaton would have properly understood the allegory. As he sat there under the hot lights, his mind a blank, he became Fashion. Or Photography. Or maybe both at once.

1 Cecil Beaton, *Diaries 1922–1939: The Wandering Years*, London, 1961, p. 30.
2 Cecil Beaton, *It Gives Me Great Pleasure*, London, 1955, p. 4.
3 Cecil Beaton, *The Wandering Years*, p. 59.
4 *Ibid.*, p. 214.
5 Peter Quennell, *Time Exposure*, London, 1941, p. 43.
6 See Cecil Beaton, *Diaries: 1939–1944 The Years Between*, 1965, p. 78.
7 Cecil Beaton, *The Face of the World*, London, 1957, p. 150.
8 Stanley Weintraub, *Beardsley: A Biography*, London, 1967, p. 159.
9 Cecil Beaton, *Far East*, London, 1945.
10 Philippe Jullian, *Oscar Wilde*, London, 1971, p. 229.

E38 *Summer Evening Dresses, hand-tinted fashion photographs*, 1937 (Condé Nast)

L20 *How To Keep Cool, Helen Bennett, c.* 1946 (Sotheby's, London)

L14 *Adèle Simpson Two-piece Hostess Gown*, 1945 (Sotheby's, London)

P42 *'La Traviata'*, 1966 (Private Collection)

κ38 *'Lady Windermere's Fan'*, 1946 (Private Collection)

s42 *Jean Shrimpton*, 1964 (Sotheby's, London)

L39 *Evening Gown*, late 1950s (Sotheby's, London)

s46 *The Great Indoors, Maudie James and the Myers Twins*, 1968 (Sotheby's, London)

834 *Mick Jagger on the Set of 'Performance'*, 1968 (Sotheby's, London)

P4I *'Look After Lulu'*, *set for Act I*, 1959 (Private Collection)

A51 *'Volpone', costume design,* 1923 (Michael Parkin Fine Art Ltd)

L2I *Fashion photograph in the style of Mary Cassatt, Carmen, 1946 (Sotheby's, London)*

L25 *Summer Shorts, fashion photograph*, 1948 (Sotheby's, London)

N39 *HRH Princess Margaret,* 1949 (Private Collection)

N40 *HM Queen Elizabeth*, 1948 (Private Collection)

M41 *Cut Flowers, Reddish, c.* 1960 (Sotheby's, London)

❧ THE CATALOGUE ❧

A

Early Years to 1927

B

Personalities of the Twenties

C

New York and Hollywood

D

Ashcombe

E

Fashion I and II: Twenties and Thirties

F

Personalities of the Thirties and Travel

G

Royalty in the Thirties

H

Wartime – the Home Front

I

Wartime – the Near East

J

Wartime – the Far East

K

Theatre and Film in the Thirties and Forties

L

Fashion III: Forties and Fifties

M

Reddish and Garbo

N

Royalty in the Forties and Fifties

O

Fifties Personalities

P

Theatre and Film in the Fifties and Sixties

Q

Gigi

R

My Fair Lady

S

The Sixties

T

Late Work of the Seventies

A42

A I

Unknown photographer

'Cecil Beaton and his Mother'

[*c.* 1906]

Silver print photograph
21.0 × 16.5 cm
Condé Nast Publications (American *Vogue*)

Outside the family home, 21 Langland Gardens,
Hampstead, where Beaton was born
and lived until 1911.

A2

Lallie Charles

Family Group :
Cecil (far left) with his mother Etty
and brother Reggie

[*c.* 1908]

Silver print copy photograph
28.0 × 20.0 cm
Private Collection
(illus. on p. 46)

Lallie Charles and her sister, Rita Martin, were two of the
best-known society and stage photographers of the early
1900s and took many of the photographs of stage stars
that were produced as postcards.

Repr.: Cecil Beaton, *Photobiography*,
facing p. 16

A3

Unknown photographer

Cecil Beaton in Bed Reading

[*c.* 1910]

Tinted snapshot print
10.2 × 10.0 cm
Sotheby's, London
(illus. on p. 8)

Repr.: Cecil Beaton, *Beaton Portraits*, p. 7;
British *Vogue*, November 1968, 'A Day in the Life of
Cecil Beaton', p. 120

A4

Bea Belton

Cecil Beaton

[*c.* 1912]

Silver print photograph, on brown card mount
14.0 × 9.6 cm
Signed on mount
Private Collection

A5

J. Weston & Sons of Folkestone

Cecil and Reginald Beaton

[*c.* 1909]

Silver print photograph, mounted on card in presentation
folder with tissue overlay
25.0 × 19.8 cm
Signed on print
Sotheby's, London

Beaton's Aunt Jessie had a house in Folkestone and this
photograph was probably taken on a holiday there.

A6, A7, A8

Foulsham and Banfield

Miss Lily Elsie

[*c.* 1910]

Original photographic postcards
All 13.5 × 8.5 cm
Private Collection

The photographer Arthur C. Banfield and businessman
Frank Foulsham operated one of the most successful firms
specializing in theatrical postcards, usually published by
the Rotary Photo Co.

A9

Foulsham and Banfield

Miss Lily Elsie

[*c.* 1905]

Modern print
24.0 × 15.2 cm
Private Collection

This enlargement from an original postcard came from
Beaton's own collection.

A 10
Unknown photographer
Lily Elsie in 'The Dollar Princess'
[1909]
Modern copy print
9.6 × 21.2 cm
Private Collection

Another copy print of this musical comedy heroine,
also from Beaton's collection (see Cat. A9).

A 11
*'Cecil Beaton's Mother
[taken] when he was Fourteen Years Old'*
[c. 1919]
Silver print photograph
24.1 × 14.0 cm
Private Collection

This print was taken by Beaton with his Kodak 3A
folding camera.

A 12
*'Sunday in Hyde Park/My Father and Mother/
An Attempt to Take a Society Picture'*
[c. 1920]
Silver print photograph
20.0 × 15.0 cm
Private Collection

The decoration on Mrs Beaton's dress has been
retouched on the negative.

A 13
Alice Collard
*Beaton Family Group: Cecil with his sisters and
mother in a garden*
[c. 1916]
Silver print photograph
13.7 × 24.2 cm
Sotheby's, London

Repr.: Cecil Beaton, *The Wandering Years*, pp. 340–1

A 14
Baba Beaton with Cecil Beaton in Mirror
[c. 1917]
Silver print photograph
24.0 × 17.5 cm
Sotheby's, London
(illus. on p. 47)

This is the first known example of Beaton's work in which
he deliberately included himself in a composition by
means of a mirrored reflection, a motif he employed
throughout his career.

A 15
Nancy and Baba Beaton
[c. 1919]
Silver print photograph
24.2 × 15.0 cm
Sotheby's, London

A 16
The Family on the Sands
[c. 1925]
Modern print
19.5 × 23.0 cm
Sotheby's, London

Repr.: *The Wandering Years*, pp. 52–3

A 17
*Self-portrait with the Beaton Family
at Hyde Park Street, Christmas 1924*
[1924]
Modern print
29.0 × 17.5 cm
Private Collection

Repr.: Cecil Beaton, *My Bolivian Aunt*, pp. 100–1

A 18
Alice Collard
*Self-portrait in Family Group, Church Parade:
Nancy, Baba, Aunt Jessie and Cecil
outside their house in Hyde Park Street*
[c. 1925]
Modern print
14.7 × 25.5 cm
Sotheby's, London

A 19
Mrs Beaton as Madame de Pompadour
[1925]
Silver print photograph
20.5 × 15.5 cm
Sotheby's, London

A 20
*Mrs Beaton reflected in a
Dressing-Table Mirror*
[c. 1925]
Silver print photograph
22.0 × 17.0 cm
Sotheby's, London
(illus. on p. 31)

A21

Mrs Beaton

[*c.* 1925]

Silver print photograph
21.0 × 16.5 cm
Sotheby's, London

A22

Alexander Bassano

*Jessie Suarez and Members of
her Husband's Family*

[*c.* 1908]

Silver print photograph, mounted on card
26.5 × 21.0 cm
Sotheby's, London

Beaton's Aunt Jessie married the Bolivian colonel Don
Pedro Suarez, who was appointed Bolivian Consul-
General to London in 1902.

Repr.: *My Bolivian Aunt*, pp. 140–1

A23

*Cecil Beaton in his Lodgings at 47 Bridge Street,
Cambridge*

[1924]

Modern print
18.0 × 29.5 cm
Sotheby's, London

Repr.: *The Wandering Years*, pp. 18–19

A24

Cecil Beaton at Cambridge

[*c.* 1924]

Silver print photograph
27.0 × 21.0 cm
Condé Nast Publications (American *Vogue*)

A25

Self-portrait

[*c.* 1926]

Silver print photograph
10.5 × 13.5 cm
Sotheby's, London
(illus. on p. 16)

A26

Unknown photographer

Cecil Beaton in Harlequin Costume, Venice

[1926]

Silver print photograph
17.0 × 12.25 cm
Sotheby's, London

Taken in front of the Excelsior Hotel on the Lido
during a visit to Venice; while on this trip Beaton met
Serge Diaghilev.

A27

Hills & Saunders, Cambridge

*Cecil Beaton as Donna Matilda,
with other members of the cast
in a scene from Pirandello's Henry IV*

[*c.* 1925]

Silver print photograph
19.5 × 27.5 cm
Sotheby's, London

As well as designing the sets and costumes, Beaton acted
in this play, produced by the Cambridge ADC.

A28

Cecil Beaton's Mother

[1920s]

Watercolour
38.1 × 27.9 cm
Private Collection

Exh.: Parkin Gallery, *Cecil Beaton Memorial Exhibition*,
1983, cat. 12

A30

A29

Cecil Beaton's Kodak 3A Folding Camera

[*c.* 1944]

Fox Talbot Museum Collection, The National Trust,
gift of Miss E. Hose

A30

Still Life with Cup and Saucer

[*c.* 1910]

Pencil and watercolour
29.9 × 22.9 cm
Private Collection

Exh.: Parkin Gallery, *Cecil Beaton and Friends*, 1985, cat. 3

A31

Book Cover Design for 'The President's Hat'

[*c.* 1926]

Watercolour
36.0 × 29.0 cm
Private Collection

The President's Hat by Robert Herring was Beaton's first
commercial commission, published by Longman, 1926.

A32

Baba in the Garden

[*c.* 1915]

Watercolour
22.9 × 10.2 cm
Private Collection

Exh.: Parkin Gallery, *Cecil Beaton Memorial Exhibition*,
1983, cat. 15

A33

Judgement of Paris

[1927]

Pen, ink and watercolour
34.5 × 37.0 cm
Private Collection
(illus. on p. 93)

Exh.: Cooling Galleries, 1927, cat. 5
Repr.: *Eve*, 7 December 1927, p. 552

A34

*Princess Angelica
'The Rose and the Ring'*

[1923]

Pen, ink and watercolour
30.0 × 25.1 cm
Signed and inscribed: 'Act I scene II showing her
drawing to Lorenzo/Angelica fecit'
Private Collection

A34

A35

Design for the Set of 'The Gyp's Princess'

[1923]

Watercolour
25.0 × 31.0 cm
Private Collection

A36

*A Page from Cecil Beaton's Cambridge Photo-Album,
with Six Postcards*

[*c.* 1923]

Sepia prints
29.0 × 40.0 cm; page size
Inscribed: 'Boy and Cecil at Cambridge'
Private Collection

A37

*Costume Design, Princess Tecla,
'The Gyp's Princess', Act II*

[1923]

Pen and ink
35.2 × 25.2 cm
Private Collection

A38

Early Theatre Design

[*c.* 1922]

Crayon and watercolour
15.3 × 17.2 cm
Private Collection

A39

Fan Design with Girl Picking Flowers

[*c.* 1912]

Pencil and watercolour
12.2 × 25.0 cm
Private Collection

Exh.: Parkin Gallery, *Cecil Beaton Memorial Exhibition*, 1983, cat. 4

A40

Still Life

[*c.* 1912]

Pencil and watercolour
25.0 × 21.7 cm
Private Collection

Exh.: Parkin Gallery, *Cecil Beaton*, 1976, cat. 2

A38

A35

A39

A41
King George V and Queen Mary

[1935]

Pen, ink and wash
24.1 × 20.3 cm
Private Collection

Exh.: Parkin Gallery, *Cecil Beaton and Friends*, 1985,
cat. 45
Repr.: British *Vogue*, 21 August 1935, p. 27;
Cecil Beaton, *Cecil Beaton's Scrapbook*, p. 7

A42
*Gaby Deslys as The Charm of Paris
in 'The New Aladdin'*

[*c.* 1930]

Pen, ink and wash with glitter additions
27.2 × 20.5 cm
Signed
Private Collection

Repr.: Cecil Beaton, *The Book of Beauty*, p. 23

A43
Nancy Beaton

[*c.* 1918]

Watercolour
26.0 × 19.0 cm
Private Collection

Exh.: Parkin Gallery, *Cecil Beaton*, 1976, cat. 6

A44
Baba Beaton

[*c.* 1918]

Watercolour
26.7 × 18.4 cm
Private Collection

Exh.: Parkin Gallery, *Cecil Beaton*, 1976, cat. 6a

A45
Lily Elsie

[*c.* 1916]

Watercolour
30.0 × 25.0 cm
Private Collection

Exh.: Parkin Gallery, *Cecil Beaton*, 1976, cat. 5

A46
*Design for the Pageant of Great Lovers,
New Theatre, London*

[1927]

Pen, ink and watercolour
25.0 × 47.0 cm
Leslie Esterman

This charity matinée was arranged by Olga Lynn; the
costume was designed by Beaton for Lady Diana Cooper.

A47
Percy Anderson
Lily Elsie

[1907]

Pen, ink and watercolour
22.0 × 16.8 cm
Inscribed: 'Lily Elsie/September 1943' and 'Original
design by Percy Anderson for Lily Elsie's Marisovian
costume for the original/production of the Merry Widow/
Given to Cecil Beaton by Mr Norman F. Summers [1943]
Leslie Esterman

A48
Unknown artist
A Figure from a Musical Comedy

[1907]

Pen, ink, watercolour and paper on board
Monogrammed and dated
29.0 × 16.4 cm
Leslie Esterman

This was once in Beaton's own collection.

A49

Unknown artist

A Figure from a Musical Comedy

[1907]

Pen, ink and watercolour on board
Monogrammed and dated
30.0 × 15.0 cm
Leslie Esterman

This was also once in Beaton's collection.

A50

Camille Clifford, 'The Gibson Girl'

[1929]

Pen, ink and wash
24.1 × 16.5 cm
Inscribed: '1906 From a photo by Bassano August 1929'
Michael Parkin Fine Art Ltd

Repr.: *The Book of Beauty*, p. 8

A51

Fine Madame Politique Would Be, 'Volpone'

[1923]

Pen, ink and watercolour
38.1 × 26.7 cm
Michael Parkin Fine Art Ltd
(illus. on p. 131)

Exh.: Parkin Gallery, *Cecil Beaton and Friends*, 1985, cat. 7

A52

Princess Tecla, 'The Gyp's Princess'
Set Design for Act I, Scene I

[1923]

Pen, ink and watercolour
34.9 × 24.1 cm
Michael Parkin Fine Art Ltd

Exh.: Parkin Gallery, *Cecil Beaton and Friends*, 1985, cat. 6

A53

Jug and Cup

[*c.* 1910]

Pencil and watercolour
25.4 × 22.9 cm
Michael Parkin Fine Art Ltd

Exh.: Parkin Gallery, *Cecil Beaton and Friends*, 1985, cat. 2

A54

A Girl with Flowers

[*c.* 1910]

Pencil and watercolour
22.9 × 8.9 cm
Michael Parkin Fine Art Ltd

Exh.: Parkin Gallery, *Cecil Beaton and Friends*, 1985, cat. 1

A55

House in Hampstead

[1914]

Watercolour
29.5 × 27.3 cm
Signed and dated
Private Collection

A56

Lady de Grey

[1954]

Pen and ink
36.6 × 25.6 cm
Private Collection

After a photograph by Baron de Meyer of the 1910s
(see ill. on p. 70)

Repr.: Cecil Beaton, *The Glass of Fashion*, p. 297

A57

Head of Queen Mary

[*c.* 1915]

Electroplate
20.0 cm high
Private Collection

A58

W. and D. Downey

Two Framed Portraits of King Edward VII
and Queen Alexandra

[1901 & 1902]

Platinum photographs
25.4 × 16.8 cm
19.9 × 15.8 cm
National Portrait Gallery, London

A59

'Gaby Deslys – 1912'

[1954]

Brush, pen and ink
38.0 × 33.0 cm
Inscribed: 'Gaby Deslys – 1912'
Leslie Esterman

Repr.: *The Glass of Fashion*, p. 39

❧ B ❧

PERSONALITIES OF THE TWENTIES

B I

*Mrs Mosscockle in the Kennels at
Clewer Park, Windsor*

[1926]

Silver print photograph
24.0 × 16.5 cm
Sotheby's, London

Repr.: Cecil Beaton, *The Wandering Years*, pp. 100–1

B I

B 2

Mrs Mosscockle

[*c.* 1926]

Silver print photograph on card
19.5 × 23.0 cm
Sotheby's, London

Repr.: Cecil Beaton, *Cecil Beaton's Scrapbook*, p. 87

B 3

Lady Oxford

[*c.* 1927]

Silver print photograph
32.5 × 22.0 cm
Sotheby's, London

In this portrait, photographed from behind, Beaton almost certainly sought to emulate a style of photography pioneered by Henry Van Der Weyde, who had taken similar portraits of Lillie Langtry and other great beauties of the Edwardian era.

Variant repr.: Cecil Beaton, *The Book of Beauty*, plate II (frontal pose); British *Vogue*, 5 February 1928, p. 40.

B 4

The Dashwood Family

[*c.* 1929]

Silver print photograph
33.5 × 24.0 cm
Sotheby's, London

A revival of the Conversation Piece genre.

Repr.: British *Vogue*, 17 August 1932, p. 32;
Cecil Beaton's Scrapbook, p. 12

B 5

Debutantes of 1928

[1928]

Silver print photograph
18.0 × 15.0 cm
Sotheby's, London

From left to right: the Hon. Georgina Curzon, Lady Anne Wellesley, Nancy Beaton and Deidre Hart-Davis.

Repro.: British *Vogue*, 8 August 1928, p. 34;
The Book of Beauty, plate X

в6

Baba and Nancy Beaton

[*c.* 1927]

Silver print photograph
19.0 × 17.5 cm
Sotheby's, London

Exh.: London Salon of Photography, 1929, cat. 13
Repr.: *Photograms of the Year*, 1929, cat. XLVI

в7

Nancy Beaton

[*c.* 1929]

Silver print photograph
30.5 × 25.5 cm
Sotheby's, London
(illus. on p. 24)

в8

Baba Beaton

[1926]

в9

в3

Silver print photograph
25.5 × 21.0 cm
Sotheby's, London

Published under Beaton's pseudonym, Carlo Crivelli.

в9

Nancy Beaton as a Shooting Star

[1929]

Silver print photograph
30.0 × 23.0 cm
Sotheby's, London

This costume, worn by Nancy Beaton to the Galaxy Ball held at the Park Lane Hotel London, on 14 November 1929, was designed for her by Beaton and Oliver Messel.

Exh.: Cooling Galleries, 1930, cat. 15;
London Salon of Photography, 1930, cat. 13
Repr.: *Tatler*, 13 November 1929, p. 318

в10

Baba Beaton

[*c.* 1928]

Silver print photograph
21.5 × 13.3 cm
Condé Nast Publications (American *Vogue*)

B 1 1

Baba Beaton

[*c.* 1927]

Silver print photograph, multiple exposure
21.0 × 24.0 cm
Condé Nast Publications (American *Vogue*)

Repr.: *The Wandering Years*, pp. 100–1

B 1 2

Portrait of Nancy and Baba Beaton

[*c.* 1928]

Photogram and positive print combined
25.2 × 21.1 cm
Condé Nast Publications (American *Vogue*)

B 1 3

Lady Lavery

[*c.* 1930]

Silver print photograph
31.0 × 26.0 cm
Sotheby's, London

Hazel Martyn, Lady Lavery, was the second wife of the
fashionable portrait painter Sir John Lavery. At Harrow,
Beaton acquired a passion for her through seeing
photographs of her by E. O. Hoppé, which appeared
regularly in *The Sketch* and *Tatler*.

Repr.: *The Book of Beauty*, plate XIII

B 1 4

*'Lady Lavery' Impersonators
at the Chicago Pageant*

[*c.* 1931]

Silver print photograph
24.4 × 19.0 cm
Condé Nast Publications (American *Vogue*)

Repr.: American *Vogue*, 15 January 1932, p. 16

B 1 5, B 1 6, B 1 7

Three Photographs of Lady Diana Cooper

[1930]

Silver print photographs
B 1 5 22.0 × 17.0 cm
B 1 6 24.5 × 19.0 cm
B 1 7 23.5 × 17.0 cm
Sotheby's, London
(B 1 6 illus. on p. 116)

B 1 5 and B 1 7 are reproduced, cropped, in British *Vogue*,
25 June 1930, p. 52; they show Lady Diana Cooper posing
as the Madonna from a painting by an unknown
Tuscan artist for a *tableau* at the Gaiety Theatre charity
event, *Living Pictures from Italian Masterpieces*. B 1 6 shows
her in *The Miracle*, her most celebrated thirties role.

B 1 2

B 1 8

Lady Alexander

[1930]

Silver print photograph
24.0 × 19.5 cm
Sotheby's, London

Lady Alexander was the widow of Sir George Alexander
(1858–1918), the famous actor-manager. Photographed
at Sussex Gardens, in front of a portrait of Beaton's
mother, she is dressed for the Jewels of the Empire Ball.

Repr.: *The Sketch*, 3 December 1930, p. 445

B 1 9

Miss Lillie Langtry

[1928]

Silver print photograph
26.0 × 20.7 cm; irregular
Sotheby's, London

Repr.: *The Book of Beauty*, plate IV

B23

B20

Lady Milbanke

[1927]

Silver print photograph
26.0 × 21.2 cm
Condé Nast Publications (American *Vogue*)

Repr.: *Tatler*, 14 December 1921;
Cecil Beaton and Peter Quennell, *Time Exposure*, p. 11

B21

*Paula Gellibrand,
The Marquise de Casa Maury*

[1929]

Silver print photograph
28.0 × 21.5 cm; irregular
Condé Nast Publications (American *Vogue*)

Variant repr.: *The Sketch*, 15 January 1930, frontispiece

B22

Edith Sitwell

[1927]

Silver print photograph, mounted on card
21.3 × 16.2 cm
Signed on mount
Condé Nast Publications (American *Vogue*)

Repr.: *Münchner Illustriete Presse*, 13 October 1929, p. 1379

B23

Edith Sitwell

[1928]

Silver print photograph
11.5 × 8.9 cm
Sotheby's, London

B24

Edith Sitwell

[1927]

Silver print photograph, mounted on card
Signed in wash on mount
36.8 × 27.3 cm
Paul Walter, New York

B25

Edith Sitwell receiving Breakfast in Bed at Renishaw

[1930]

Modern print, mounted on card
Signed in wash on mount
49.0 × 39.0 cm
Sotheby's, London
(illus. on p. 48)

Exh.: Cooling Galleries, 1930, cat. 14
Repr.: British *Vogue*, 1 October 1930, p. 72

B26

Edith Sitwell

[1930]

Modern print
48.0 × 39.0 cm
Sotheby's, London

Exh.: Cooling Galleries, 1930, cat. 1
Repr.: British *Vogue*, 1 October 1930, p. 68

B27

Reresby Sitwell and his Nanny

[1927]

Silver print photograph
19.0 × 21.0 cm
Paul Walter, New York

Variant repr.: *The Sketch*, 29 June 1927

B28

Georgia Sitwell

[1930]

Silver print photograph
20.0 × 24.0 cm
Sotheby's, London

Exh.: Cooling Galleries, 1930, cat. 23
Repr.: British *Vogue*, 1 October 1930, p. 73

B29

Osbert Sitwell

[*c.* 1929]

Silver print photograph
9.5 cm diameter; tondo format
Paul Walter, New York

B30

Conversation Piece: the Sitwell Family

[1930]

Modern print
33.0 × 20.0 cm
Sotheby's, London

Exh.: Cooling Galleries, 1930, cat. 4
From left to right: Sacheverell, Sir George, Georgia,
Reresby, Lady Ida, Edith and Osbert.

B31

The Jungman Twins

[1927]

Silver print photograph
29.7 × 22.6 cm
Paul Walter, New York

Repr.: *Tatler*, January 1927, p. 125;
The Book of Beauty, plate XI;
Time Exposure, p. 11

B32

Lady Pamela Smith

[*c.* 1928]

Silver print photograph on card with pink cellophane
29.2 × 22.6 cm
Signed in wash on mount
Paul Walter, New York

B33

*Cecil Beaton and a Group of Bright Young People
on a Wooden Bridge, Wilsford*

[*c.* 1928]

Modern print
26.5 × 44.5 cm
Sotheby's, London
(illus. on p. 112)

From left to right: Rex Whistler, Cecil Beaton, Georgia
Sitwell, William Walton, Stephen Tennant, Zita and
Theresa Jungman.

B34

Tallulah Bankhead

[1927]

Silver print photograph
21.6 × 21.0 cm
Paul Walter, New York

Variant repr.: *Eve*, 22 June 1927, p. 662

B35

Rex Whistler

[*c.* 1930]

Modern print from original Kodak 3A negative
50.0 × 70.0 cm
Sotheby's, London

Repr.: *Cecil Beaton's Scrapbook*, p. 86

B35

B36, B37

Rex Whistler

[*c.* 1930]

Modern prints
Both 70.0 × 50.0 cm
Sotheby's, London

B38

The Hon. Stephen Tennant

[1927]

Silver print photograph
27.0 × 19.0 cm
Sotheby's, London

This portrait of Stephen Tennant shows him costumed as
Prince Charming, the role he took in the Lovers Through
the Ages pageant. He is posed as a medieval tomb
sculpture, like the earlier photograph of Edith Sitwell.

B39

Mrs Ronald Armstrong-Jones as Perdita Robinson

[1928]

Modern print
23.0 × 16.0 cm
Sotheby's, London
(illus. on p. 113)

This is the role played by Mrs Armstrong-Jones in
The Pageant of Hyde Park matinée at
Wyndham's Theatre.

B40

Oliver Messel

[1929]

Silver print photograph
25.0 × 19.5 cm
Sotheby's, London

Messel is surrounded by papier maché masks which he
had made for various theatre productions at the end of
the 1920s.

B41

Self-portrait (Four Heads)

[1927]

Silver print photograph, mounted on card
38.1 × 30.5 cm
Signature in red wash
National Portrait Gallery, London

Exh.: Cooling Galleries, 1927, cat. 27
Repr.: Cooling Galleries exhibition catalogue, 1927,
frontispiece

B42

Nancy Cunard

[*c.* 1929]

Pencil and wash
33.2 × 20.32 cm
Private Collection

Exh.: Parkin Gallery, *Cecil Beaton and Friends*, 1985,
cat. 84

B43

Modern Venus

[1928]

Pen and ink
33.0 × 17.8 cm
Private Collection

Exh.: Parkin Gallery, *Cecil Beaton Memorial Exhibition*,
1983, cat. 29
Repr.: British *Vogue*, 24 November 1928, p. 49

B44

Lady Sybil Colefax

[1928]

Watercolour
80.0 × 30.5 cm
Private Collection

Exh.: Parkin Gallery, *Cecil Beaton Memorial Exhibition*,
1983, cat. 24
Repr.: British *Vogue*, 5 January 1928, p. 52,
with the caption, 'Even Lady Colefax must take
her place in the queue'

B45

Lady Diana Cooper

[1945]

Coloured chalk
35.6 × 25.4 cm
Signed, dated and inscribed: 'Darling Diana with love C.B.'
Private Collection

Exh.: Parkin Gallery, *Cecil Beaton and Friends*, 1985,
cat. 70

B46

Lady Ottoline Morrell

[1929]

Pencil
40.6 × 27.9 cm
Private Collection

Exh.: Parkin Gallery, *Cecil Beaton Memorial Exhibition*,
1983, cat. 51

B47

Self-portrait

[*c.* 1928]

Pen, ink and wash
24.1 × 26.7 cm
Private Collection

B48

Paula Gellibrand: A Page from a Photo-Album

[1928]

Eight silver print photographs in various states, mounted
on card
33.0 × 41.5 cm
Private Collection

B49

Curtis Moffat and Olivia Wyndham

Portrait of Cecil Beaton

[*c.* 1928]

Silver print photograph
28.9 × 24.0 cm
Signed on mount
National Portrait Gallery, London

B50

*The Book of Beauty:
Artwork for Title Page*

[1930]

Pen and ink
55.7 × 42.6 cm
Private Collection

B51

*The Book of Beauty:
Artwork for Vignette*

[1930]

Pen and ink
27.5 × 21.6 cm
Private Collection
Repr.: British *Vogue*, 20 February 1929

B52, B53, B54

*Three Designs for Osbert Sitwell's
'All At Sea'*

[1927]

Pen, ink and watercolour
B52 10.5 × 14.4 cm
B53 13.2 × 14.3 cm
B54 11.8 × 12.8 cm
Michael Parkin Fine Art Ltd

B55, B56, B57, B58

*Four Illustrations for
'Twilight of the Nymphs'*

[1928]

Collotypes
All 16.4 × 13.4 cm
Michael Parkin Fine Art Ltd
(B55 illus. on p. 92)

Pierre Löuys's book, *Twilight of the Nymphs*, was illustrated
with photograms by Cecil Beaton with ink additions.

B59

Ethel Levey in 'Yes'

[*c.* 1928]

Pen and ink
34.6 × 24.2 cm
Signed in ink
Inscribed: 'Singing, Swinging down the Lane'
Leslie Esterman

B60

Katherine Cornell

[*c.* 1928]

Pen and ink
50.6 × 35.4 cm
Signed in ink
Inscribed: 'Katherine Cornell a vision of beauty in a
white bustle and gardenias in the age of innocence'
Leslie Esterman

B61

Oliver Messel

[*c.* 1930]

Modern print
23.2 × 18.3 cm
Leslie Esterman

B62

Paul Poiret

[1931]

Pen and ink
33.0 × 23.0 cm
Private Collection

Exh.: Parkin Gallery, *Cecil Beaton Memorial Exhibition*,
1983, cat. 41
Repr.: Cecil Beaton, *My First 50 Years*, Victor Gollancz,
London, 1931, frontispiece

C

NEW YORK AND HOLLYWOOD

C1

Fred and Adèle Astaire

[1930]

Multiple-exposure silver print photograph
27.0 × 24.0 cm
Sotheby's, London
(illus. on p. 49)

The Astaires (brother and sister) were regular visitors to
England in the 1920s as a dance act. Beaton first saw
them perform in Birmingham in *Stop Flirting*, and was to
meet them later that year in London.

Exh.: Cooling Galleries, 1930, cat. 32
Repr.: *Tatler*, 7 May 1930, p. 255, with the caption
'From All Angles'

C2

Adèle Astaire and Cecil Beaton

[1931]

Silver print photograph
25.0 × 16.5 cm
Sotheby's, London

Taken in the apartment of Condé Nast, New York.

Repr.: *The Sketch*, 28 October 1931

C3

Anita Loos

[1929]

Modern print
24.3 × 19.2 cm
Sotheby's, London

Repr.: American *Vogue*, 25 May 1929, p. 67;
Cecil Beaton, *The Best of Beaton*, p. 30

C4

Self-portrait

[*c.* 1929]

Silver print photograph
19.7 × 19.4 cm
Sotheby's, London

Taken on Brooklyn Bridge, New York.

Repr.: Cecil Beaton, *Cecil Beaton's Scrapbook*, p. 1

C5

*'Sunday Morning' : Self-portrait
with New York Sunday Times*

[1937]

Silver print photograph
14.3 × 20.0 cm
Sotheby's, London

Repr.: Cecil Beaton, *Cecil Beaton's New York*, p. 70;
Cecil Beaton, *Portrait of New York*, p. 49

C3

C4

c6
Self-portrait in New York
[*c.* 1936]
Silver print photograph
23.9 × 24.1 cm
Sotheby's, London

Beaton is standing beneath a poster of Joe Louis, then
heavyweight boxing champion of the world.

Repr.: *Portrait of New York*, pp. 44–5

c7, c8
George Platt-Lynes

Two Portraits of Cecil Beaton
[*c.* 1935]
Silver print photographs
Both 23.5 × 19.5 cm
c7 Private Collection;
c8 Sotheby's, London

c9
Michael Caputo

Cecil Beaton and Mary Taylor at the Opening of Beaton's Scrapbook Exhibition, New York
[1937]
Silver print photograph
25.5 × 20.5 cm
Sotheby's, London

c10
'Abraham Lincoln in Nuts'
[*c.* 1936]
Silver print photograph
26.0 × 26.0 cm
Sotheby's, London

A shop window spectacle, as in Atget's photography.

Repr.: *Cecil Beaton's New York*, p. 141

c11
Macy's Parade
[Late 1930s]
Silver print photograph
26.0 × 26.0 cm
Sotheby's, London

Repr.: *Cecil Beaton's New York*, p. 123

c12
Attraction of 42nd Street
[*c.* 1947]
Silver print photograph
20.5 × 20.7 cm
Sotheby's, London

Repr.: *Portrait of New York*, p. 76

c13
James Van Der Zee

Funeral Parlor in Harlem
[*c.* 1936]
Composite silver print photograph
20.5 × 25.5 cm
Sotheby's, London

Variant repr.: *Cecil Beaton's New York*, p. 178

c14
A Photomontage Sheet of Sixteen Contact Prints of New York
[*c.* 1936 and *c.* 1946]
Silver print photograph
25.5 × 27.0 cm
Sotheby's, London

c15
Self-portrait with Anita Loos
[January 1930]
Silver print photograph
13.8 × 8.0 cm
Sotheby's, London
(illus. on p. 50)

Repr.: *Tatler*, 12 March 1930, p. 481

C16

Unknown photographer

Cecil Beaton in Hollywood

[1929–30]

Modern print
25.5 × 20.3 cm
Sotheby's, London

C17

Unknown photographer

Cecil Beaton in a Hollywood Studio

[*c.* 1932]

Silver print photograph
23.5 × 18.6 cm
Sotheby's, London

Photographed on the set of the film *Edmund Goulding*.

Repr.: Cecil Beaton, *The Wandering Years*, pp. 164–5

C18

Bert Longworth

Cecil Beaton and Douglas Fairbanks

[1931]

C23

Silver print photograph
24.5 × 19.0 cm
Private Collection

Taken on Beaton's second Hollywood visit.

C19

Karen Morley, Hollywood

[1929]

Silver print photograph mounted on card
34.2 × 26.9 cm
Signed on mount
Paul Walter, New York

C20

Alice White

[1929]

Silver print photograph
24.3 × 19.0 cm
Sotheby's, London

On the set of her film *Show Girl in Hollywood*.

Repr.: Cecil Beaton, *The Book of Beauty*, 1930, plate XVIII;
The Best of Beaton, 1968, p. 40

C21

Ernst Lubitsch

[1929]

Silver print photograph
24.2 × 15.0 cm
Sotheby's, London

The German-born film director was then at work on his
film *The Love Parade* (1930). Beaton recorded in his diary
on 23 December 1929 that his earlier film *The Marriage
Circle* (1924) was 'The first good film I ever saw'.

C22

The Marx Brothers

[1932]

Silver print photograph
24.3 × 19.2 cm
Sotheby's, London

Taken by Beaton during his third visit to Hollywood in
January 1932; the Marx Brothers were then filming *Horse
Feathers*, following the success of *Monkey Business* in 1931.

C23, C24

Two Portraits of Buster Keaton

[1929]

Silver print photographs
C23   10.2 × 8.1 cm
C24   23.8 × 18.4 cm
Sotheby's, London

C25

Jackie Coogan

[1932]

Silver print photograph
18.7 × 23.5 cm
Sotheby's, London

Repr.: *The Sketch*, 8 August 1932;
The Best of Beaton, p. 109

C26

Lillian Gish

[1929]

Silver print photograph
24.1 × 19.3 cm
Sotheby's, London

Repr.: *The Book of Beauty*, plate xv;
British *Vogue*, 25 July 1930, p. 28

c26

C27

Johnny Weissmuller

[1932]

Silver print photograph
19.1 × 24.1 cm
Sotheby's, London

The former Olympic athlete was to appear in the first of
many Tarzan films.

Repr.: Cecil Beaton and Peter Quennell, *Time Exposure*,
p. 32
Variant repr.: *The Best of Beaton*, p. 43

C28, C29

Two Portraits of Gary Cooper

[1931]

Silver print photographs
c28 30.8 × 24.4 cm
c29 29.4 × 21.5 cm
Sotheby's, London
(c28 illus. on p. 50)

Repr.: *Vanity Fair*, October 1931

C30

Cecil and Gary Cooper in the early 1930s

[*c.* 1930]

Silver print photograph
25.5 × 20.3 cm
Paul Walter, New York

This print was formerly in the collection of the artist
Sir Francis Rose.

C31

Katharine Hepburn

[*c.* 1936]

Photomontage, silver print photograph on card
25.0 × 45.5 cm; irregular
Sotheby's, London

Original artwork produced for *Cecil Beaton's Scrapbook*,
1937, p. 31

C32

Self-portrait

[1928]

Pen, ink, wash and pencil
39.0 × 35.0 cm
Terence Pepper
(illus. on p. 95)

Repr.: American *Vogue*, 5 January 1929, with the caption
'Deep but Hasty Homage to El Greco, Carl Erickson,
Room 1806 of the Ambassador Hotel, and to myself.'

C31

C33

'Cecil Beaton's New York':
Artwork for Frontispiece

[1937]

Watercolour on red board
49.0 × 39.2 cm
Private Collection

C34

Hollywood Postcards

[1929]

Watercolour on photographic prints
17.3 × 29.2 cm
Private Collection

Variant repr.: British *Vogue*, 19 March 1930, p. 52;
Cecil Beaton's Scrapbook, p. 28

C35

New York Impressions

[1937]

Pen, ink and mixed media
51.0 × 39.6 cm
Private Collection

Repr.: *Cecil Beaton's Scrapbook*, p. 65

C36

Joan Crawford

[1932]

Pen, ink and watercolour
2.5 × 19.0 cm
Michael Parkin Fine Art Ltd
(illus. on p. 97)

An early, full length study for this portrait was published
in *Vanity Fair*, December 1932.

Exh.: Parkin Gallery, *Cecil Beaton and Friends*, 1985,
cat. 52
Repr.: *Cecil Beaton's Scrapbook*, p. 38

C37

Clark Gable

[*c.* 1935]

Watercolour
31.0 × 34.0 cm
Private Collection

Exh.: Parkin Gallery, *Cecil Beaton*, 1976, cat. 24

C38

Mae West

[1929]

Pen and ink
37.0 × 49.0 cm
Private Collection

Exh.: Parkin Gallery, *Cecil Beaton*, 1976, cat. 20
Repr.: British *Vogue*, 16 February 1929

D2

D

ASHCOMBE

D1

Millar & Harris

Ashcombe: Interior

[1932]

Silver print photograph
20.0 × 15.5 cm
Private Collection

D2

Millar & Harris

Ashcombe: Circus Bedroom

[1932]

Silver print photograph
21.0 × 15.5 cm
Private Collection

D3

Millar & Harris

*Ashcombe: Murals Painted by Guests
in the Circus Bedroom*

[1932]

Silver print photograph
21.5 × 15.5 cm
Private Collection

The harlequin was painted by Beaton, the fat lady by Rex Whistler and the negro figure by Oliver Messel.

D4

Millar & Harris

Ashcombe: Circus Bedroom

[1932]

Silver print photograph
20.5 × 16.0 cm
Private Collection

D5

Millar & Harris

Ashcombe: Hallway to the Studio

[1932]

Silver print photograph
20.0 × 15.0 cm
Private Collection

Repr.: Cecil Beaton, *Ashcombe*, facing p. 17

D6

Millar & Harris

Ashcombe: Dining Room

[1932]

Silver print photograph
16.0 × 20.5 cm
Sotheby's, London

D7

Millar & Harris

Ashcombe: Circus Bedroom

[1932]

Silver print photograph
16.0 × 21.0 cm
Inscribed on reverse: 'p. 14, House and Garden Book,
19/2/36'
Sotheby's, London

D8

Millar & Harris

Ashcombe: Drawing Room

[1932]

Silver print photograph
14.5 × 21.0 cm
Sotheby's, London

D9

Millar & Harris

Ashcombe: Sitting Room

[1932]

Silver print photograph
16.0 × 21.0 cm
Sotheby's, London

Repr.: *Ashcombe*, facing p. 16

D11

D10

Millar & Harris

Ashcombe : Circus Bedroom

[1932]

Silver print photograph
20.5 × 15.5 cm
Sotheby's, London
(illus. on p. 48)

D11

Millar & Harris

Ashcombe : Drawing Room

[1932]

Silver print photograph
16.0 × 20.5 cm
Sotheby's, London

D12

Self-portrait with sisters Nancy and Baba

[Early 1930s]

Silver print photograph
19.4 × 27.2 cm
Private Collection

D13

Family Group under the Ilex

[*c.* 1935]

Silver print photograph
18.0 × 22.3 cm
Private Collection
(illus. on p. 80)

Repr.: *Ashcombe*, facing p. 5

D14

Mrs Beaton in Fancy Dress at Ashcombe

[Late 1930s]

Silver print photograph
27.0 × 25.8 cm
Sotheby's, London

D15

Ruth Ford at Ashcombe

[Late 1930s]

Silver print photograph
26.8 × 24.9 cm
Sotheby's, London

Repr.: Cecil Beaton and Peter Quennell, *Time Exposure*,
p. 73, top

D16

Ashcombe: The Studio; with decorations for a Fête Champêtre

[1937]

Silver print photograph
26.9 × 25.6 cm
Sotheby's, London

D17

Ivan Moffat at Ashcombe

[1930s]

Silver print photograph
25.9 × 24.7 cm
Sotheby's, London

D18

Tilly Losch at Ashcombe

[1930s]

Silver print photograph
20.0 × 25.0 cm
Sotheby's, London

D19

Tilly Losch at Ashcombe

[Late 1930s]

Silver print photograph
25.0 × 19.7 cm
Sotheby's, London

D20

Tilly Losch as Ariel

[Late 1930s]

Silver print photograph
24.1 × 19.4 cm
Sotheby's, London

Repr.: *Time Exposure*, p.48

D21

Self-portrait with Peter Watson

[1930s]

Silver print photograph
19.6 × 19.5 cm
Private Collection

D22

Filming 'The Sailor's Return'

[1935]

Silver print photograph
19.7 × 24.5 cm
Private Collection

Preparations for an amateur film version of David Garnett's novel.

D23

Self-portrait as a Scarecrow

[1937]

Silver print photograph
19.3 × 23.0 cm
Sotheby's, London

Repr.: *The Sketch*, 3 February 1937

D24

John Smiley at Ashcombe

[c. 1940]

Silver print photograph
26.3 × 24.5 cm
Sotheby's, London

Variant repr.: *Time Exposure*, p.69

D18

D25

D30

D25

John Smiley at Ashcombe

[*c.* 1940]

Silver print photograph
26.2 × 25.1 cm
Sotheby's, London

Repr.: *Time Exposure*, p.131

D26

John Smiley at Ashcombe

[*c.* 1940]

Silver print photograph
27.7 × 26.7 cm
Sotheby's, London

D27

Photographic Backdrops: Twelve Contact Prints and Two Enlargements

[Late 1930s–early 1940s]

Silver print photographs of various sizes
Sotheby's, London

D28

Still Life with a Bust of Marie Antoinette

[1943]

Silver print photograph
25.1 × 19.3 cm
Sotheby's, London

D29

Still Life with Skull

[Late 1930s]

Silver print photograph
25.0 × 19.0 cm
Sotheby's, London

Repr.: *Time Exposure*, p.57, bottom left

D30

'Farewell to Ashcombe': self-portrait

[1946]

Silver print photograph
22.0 × 18.9 cm
Sotheby's, London

Repr.: *Ashcombe*, facing p. 123

D31
Sir Francis Rose
Cecil Beaton at Ashcombe
[1939]
Oil on canvas
38.1 × 63.5 cm
Private Collection
Exh.: Parkin Gallery, *Cecil Beaton and Friends*, 1985,
cat. 147

D32
Unknown artist
Eighteenth-century Landscape View of Ashcombe
[*c.* 1720]
Oil on canvas
226 × 284 cm
Salisbury and South Wiltshire Museum
Repr.: *Ashcombe*, facing p. 24

D33
'Plastikos'
Mask of Cecil Beaton
[*c.* 1930]
Gilded and painted plaster
34.8 × 15.5 cm; irregular
Private Collection

D34
Sir Francis Rose
The Glittering Room
[1937]
Watercolour
49.4 × 64.0 cm
Signed and dated in ink
Inscribed: 'The Glittering Room/Ashcombe House'
Leslie Esterman

D35
Ashcombe House
[1935]
Watercolour
52.0 × 63.7 cm
Private Collection
This painting was formerly in the collection of Sir Brian
Batsford.

D36
Frank Dobson
Bust of Cecil Beaton
[1930]
Bronze
49.5 cm high
Signed on bronze
Private Collection

D37
Gordon Anthony
Cecil Beaton in Fancy Dress Costume
[1937]
Silver print photograph
25.0 × 20.0 cm
Sotheby's, London
(illus. on p. 2)

E5

E

FASHION I AND II:
TWENTIES AND THIRTIES

E1
Clothes and the Car – At Claridges
[1927]
Silver print photograph
22.6 × 16.2 cm
Sotheby's, London

A lemon-beige quilted Chantal coat from Maison Ross, with the new Invicta car. Chauffeur's uniform from Harrods.

Repr.: British *Vogue*, 5 October 1927, p. 60

E2
Clothes and the Car – At the Theatre
[1927]
Silver print photograph
21.0 × 16.5 cm
Sotheby's, London

Irfé evening coat and Daimler painted in two shades of grey. 'The lady in the apple green velvet opera coat was the first of my fashion photographs to be published. The No. 3A Kodak was used on a tripod – the $\frac{1}{4}$ second bulb exposure being long enough to give the desired effect of speed as the bus passed along Piccadilly' (Cecil Beaton, *The Best of Beaton*, 1968, p. 58).

Unpublished photograph for British *Vogue*,
5 October 1927

Repr.: *The Best of Beaton*, p. 58 (misdated 1928)

E3
Untitled Fashion Photograph
[*c*. 1926–8]
Silver print photograph
21.7 × 12.0 cm
Sotheby's, London

E4
The Bridal Veil – the Chic Bride
[1928/9]
Silver print photograph
19.3 × 14.5 cm
Sotheby's, London

E4
Cream-pink satin dress with tulle veil in turban effect from Jay-Thorpe.

Variant repr.: American *Vogue*, 2 March 1929, p. 78

E5, E6
Marion Moorehouse in Condé Nast's New York apartment
[1929]
Silver print photograph
E5 11.6 × 8.3 cm
E6 12.0 × 8.1 cm
Sotheby's, London

Taken in Condé Nast's opulently decorated apartment, which provided the setting for many of Steichen's fashion photographs.

Repr.: *The Best of Beaton*, p. 60

E 7

Charles James Hat

[1930]

Silver print photograph
23.9 × 19.2 cm
Sotheby's, London

Variant repr.: *The Best of Beaton*, p. 60

E 8

Eno's Tea Gown

[1933]

Silver print photograph
24.7 × 19.5 cm
Sotheby's, London

Repr.: British *Vogue*, 6 September 1933, p. 49

E 9

In the Manner of Edwardians

[1935]

Modern copy print
10 × 12.5 cm
Sotheby's, London

The years 1935–7 witnessed the peak of Beaton's most successful early fashion photography. His taste for rococo and baroque trappings can be traced to his visits to Austria the previous summer. See Cecil Beaton, *Photobiography*, p. 70.

Repr.: American *Vogue*, 1 May 1935, p. 51; *Photobiography*, facing p. 65

E 10

Midsummer Pageant: 'Lady Daphne Finch-Hatton in Glenny's slim column of parma romaine set afloat by clouds of tulle'

[1935]

Silver print photograph
24.7 × 20.2 cm
Sotheby's, London

Repr.: British *Vogue*, 12 June 1935, p. 56

E 11

Mary Taylor wearing Majorette's Hat

[1935]

Silver print photograph
25.3 × 20.3 cm
Sotheby's, London

The symbol of the American eagle emblazoning Taylor's hat was ubiquitous in American popular culture in the period 1933–5, and represents the Roosevelt administration logo for the National Recovery Agency.

Repr.: British *Vogue*, 1 May 1935, p. 112; American *Vogue*, February 1935, p. 36

E 12, E 13

Two Fashion Studies with Mary Taylor as Model

[1935]

Silver print photographs
E 12   25.3 × 20.3 cm
E 13   24.0 × 19.2 cm
Sotheby's, London

The background painting by Pavel Tchelitchew (1898–1957) was commissioned for Prince Matchabelli's salon. E 12 shows Mary Taylor modelling a Bergdorf Goodman fashion design. E 13 is a variant pose, fashion unidentified.

E 12 repr.: American *Vogue*, 1 July 1935, p. 42, in colour; E 13 repr.: Cecil Beaton, *Cecil Beaton's Scrapbook*, p. 71

E 12

E14

Mary Taylor in a Dress of Cloque Rayon by Molyneux

[1935]

Silver print photograph
25.3 × 20.3 cm
Sotheby's, London
(illus. on p. 68)

Repr.: American *Vogue*, 1 July 1935, p. 43, in colour

E15

Fashion Study against Draped Net

[November 1935]

Silver print photograph
23.8 × 17.9 cm
Sotheby's, London

The motif of netting and filigree in this fashion study, and E16 and E17 following, can be traced to the influence of Cocteau on Beaton as well as Beaton's fascination with the Victorian and Edwardian use of the doily as a compositional device.
Compare with the full-length figure published in American *Vogue*, November 1935, p. 42.

E16

Unidentified Fashion modelled by Lud

[November 1935]

Silver print photograph
24.0 × 18.0 cm
Sotheby's, London

E17

Unidentified Fashion modelled by Lud

[November 1935]

Silver print photograph
24.0 × 18.0 cm
Sotheby's, London

Repr.: *Cecil Beaton's Scrapbook*, p. 58

E18

*'Shadow her : she is the new image . . .'
A Lelong Gown of White Crêpe modelled by Lud*

[1935]

Silver print photograph
16.5 × 22.0 cm
Sotheby's, London

Repr.: American *Vogue*, 1 December 1935, p. 71
Variant repr : British *Vogue*, 25 December 1935, p. 33

E18

E19

*Lights ! Camera !
Focus on Mainbocher's straight and narrow shaft of white crêpe, with gold-beaded leaves*

[1935]

Silver print photograph
23.5 × 17.9 cm
Sotheby's, London

Repr.: American *Vogue*, 1 December 1935, p. 34

E20

*'Nouvelles de l'Été', or 'New Items'
Schiaparelli fashions*

[1935]

Silver print photograph
24.0 × 17.9 cm
Sotheby's, London

In *Photobiography* Beaton explains the circumstances of these highly influential pictures in the history of fashion photography: 'Long before the war had accustomed us to scenes of destruction I decided it might give added piquancy to the artificial smartness of fashion models if instead of being photographed in drawing-rooms . . . they were portrayed amid scenes of ruin and destruction' (p. 73).

Repr.: American *Vogue*, 1 January 1936, pp. 66–7;
French *Vogue*, March 1936, p. 29
Variant repr.: British *Vogue*, 19 February 1936, pp. 72–3

E21

'For the Lace Ball'

[1936]

Silver print photograph
23.9 × 16.9 cm
Sotheby's, London

Madame Labeuf modelling a dinner suit of thick white
cotton lace by Maggy Rouff.

Variant repr.: American *Vogue*, 1 February 1936, p. 48;
British *Vogue*, 5 February 1936

E22

Dress modelled by
Louise de Vilmorin

[1936]

Silver print photograph
23.9 × 17.8 cm
Sotheby's, London

E23, E24

Schiaparelli Hats
made of Cellophane

[1936]

Silver print photographs
E23 17.8 × 25.5 cm
E24 19.4 × 19.5 cm
Sotheby's, London

Variant repr.: American *Vogue*, 15 May 1936, p. 57

E25

Large Trimmed Hat (unidentified fashion)

[1936]

Silver print photograph
24.0 × 19.0 cm
Sotheby's, London

E26

Lucile Paray Pink Chiffon Dress from Maison Ross

[1936]

Silver print photograph
21.6 × 17.9 cm
Sotheby's, London

Repr.: American *Vogue*, May 1936, p. 60;
British *Vogue*, 24 June 1936, p. 52

E27

Mock Puppet Theatre
(Angelica Welldon and Nina Matleva)

[1936]

Silver print photograph
20.4 × 25.3 cm
Sotheby's, London

Repr.: American *Vogue*, 15 June 1936, p. 63

E28

Hat by Hattie Carnegie

[1936]

Silver print photograph
25.8 × 20.5 cm
Sotheby's, London

Repr.: American *Vogue*, 15 July 1936, p. 22

E27

E29

Blue Butterfly-encrusted Hat by Bergdorf Goodman

[1936]

Silver print photograph
25.8 × 20.5 cm
Sotheby's, London

Variant repr.: American *Vogue*, July 1936, p. 23

E30

Straight Capes

[1936]

Silver print photograph, with retouching instructions
25.8 × 21.0 cm
Sotheby's, London

Left: grey astrakhan cape with military collar from
Bergdorf Goodman.
Right: shorter cape of Alaska sealskin.

Repr.: American *Vogue*, 1 August 1936, p. 38, retouched
print

E31, E32

Aage Thaarup Hats

[1936]

Silver print photographs
E30 25.4 × 20.1 cm
E31 25.2 × 20.1 cm
Sotheby's, London

Sequin-strewn dunce's hat (E31) and grey felt hat with
blackbirds on top (E32).

Repr.: British *Vogue*, 19 August 1936, p. 46 (both)

E33

Charles Creed Black Worsted Suit with Talbot Hat

[1936]

Silver print photograph
24.0 × 18.0 cm
Sotheby's, London

Repr.: American *Vogue*, September 1936, p. 71

E34

Molyneux Dress

[1936]

Silver print photograph
22.0 × 16.0 cm
Mrs Fiona Cowan

Repr.: French *Vogue*, September 1936, p. 13
British *Vogue*, 14 October 1936, p. 93

E35, E36, E37

'Ilka Chase in "The Florist's Box"
A Tragedy in three acts
Gown by Henri Bendel
Jewels by Tiffany & Company
Settings by Cecil Beaton'

[1937]

Silver print photographs
E35 18.9 × 21.6 cm
E36 18.7 × 21.2 cm
E37 19.0 × 21.8 cm
Sotheby's, London

The first pose shows the receipt of flowers with
expectation, the second the reading of the accompanying
note, the third the collapse of the model after reading the
note. Ilka Chase was the daughter of Edna Woolman
Chase, *Vogue*'s editor-in-chief, and later became an actress
and playwright.

Repr.: American *Vogue*, 15 March 1937;
Cecil Beaton and Peter Quennell, *Time Exposure*, p. 54

E38, E39

'Fresh as Paint'
Two Hand-coloured Photographs of
Summer Evening Dresses

[1937]

Hand-tinted silver print photographs
Both 25.5 × 24.0 cm
Condé Nast Publications (American *Vogue*)
(E38 illus. on p. 121)

Repr.: American *Vogue*, 1 May 1937, p. 78, in colour,
with the caption 'Cecil Beaton, moved by the sheer,
unalloyed romanticism of these fragile evening dresses,
has reverted to the sentimental technique of the hand-
tinted post-card. He hasn't forgotten a single dove, a
single stylized drapery, a single quasi-Grecian urn; and
when it came to colouring them he employed all the
traditional apple-greens, icing-pinks, and faint blues,
winding up with the triumphant red flush on the ladies
cheeks.'

E40

Picture Window Fashion

[*c.* 1937]

Silver print photograph
20.3 × 25.3 cm
Sotheby's, London

The multi-framing device of the wall, window and
curtains is typical of Beaton's creative imagination as
applied to fashion photography.

~ F ~

PERSONALITIES OF THE THIRTIES
AND TRAVEL

F 1

Self-portrait, London

[*c.* 1935]

Silver print photograph, mounted on card
24.8 × 19.0 cm
Sotheby's, London

F 2

Self-portrait in Fancy Dress

[*c.* 1935]

Silver print photograph
25.4 × 17.0 cm
Sotheby's, London

F 3

Self-portrait in Mirror with Picasso

[1933]

Silver print photograph, mounted on card
21.0 × 26.0 cm
Sotheby's, London
(illus. on p. 115)

Taken in Picasso's Paris flat in the rue de la Boëtie.

Variant repr.: British *Vogue*, 8 January 1936

F 4

Picasso

[1933]

Silver print photograph
27.0 × 25.5 cm
Sotheby's, London

Repr.: Gertrude Stein, *Picasso*, 1938, facing p. 48

F 5

Gertrude Stein and Alice B. Toklas

[Late 1930s]

Silver print photograph
18.5 × 22.0 cm
Condé Nast Publications (American *Vogue*)

Repr.: Cecil Beaton and Peter Quennell, *Time Exposure*,
p. 32, bottom right

F 6

Gertrude Stein

[Late 1930s]

Silver print photograph, with airbrush additions
23.5 × 21.0 cm
Sotheby's, London

Repr.: Cecil Beaton, *Cecil Beaton's Scrapbook*, p. 130

F 7

W. H. Auden

[1935]

Silver print photograph
27.4 × 22.6 cm
Condé Nast Publications (American *Vogue*)

Repr.: American *Vogue*, 11 November 1935

F 8

Jean Cocteau

[*c.* 1935]

Silver print photograph
22.0 × 16.2 cm
Condé Nast Publications (American *Vogue*)

Repr.: *Cecil Beaton's Scrapbook*, p. 84, last in a series of four

F 9

Salvador Dali

[1936]

Silver print photograph
23.9 × 18.3 cm
Sotheby's, London

Variant repr.: *Cecil Beaton's Scrapbook*, p. 85;
Cecil Beaton, *The Best of Beaton*, p. 89

F 10

Christian Bérard

[*c.* 1935]

Silver print photograph
20.0 × 24.0 cm
Inscribed: 'to C.B. affectuellement Ch. Berard'
Hugo Vickers

Repr.: *Cecil Beaton's Scrapbook*, p. 85

F6

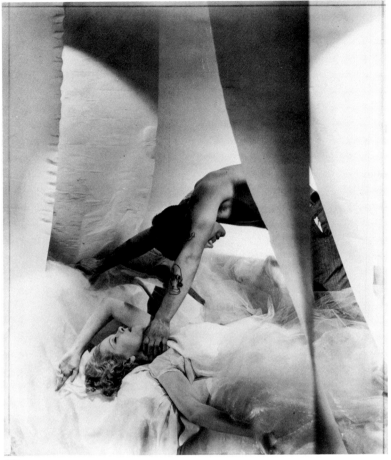

F17

F I I

Max Beerbohm

[1936]

Silver print photograph, mounted on card
19.1 × 23.6 cm
Sotheby's, London

Repr.: American *Vogue*, 8 July 1936, p. 40

F I 2

'Coco' Chanel

[1937]

Silver print photograph
24.5 × 19.4 cm
Sotheby's, London

F I 3, F I 4, F I 5

Three Photographs of Elizabeth Bergner

[1934]

Silver print photographs
All 27.5 × 21.0 cm
Condé Nast Publications (American *Vogue*)

F I 5 repr.: American *Vogue*, 7 March 1934, p. 93;
Vanity Fair, May 1934, p. 52

F I 6

Nathalie Paley

[*c.* 1935]

Silver print photograph
22.0 × 17.5 cm
Sotheby's, London

F17, F18

Nathalie Paley and Victor Kraft

[*c.* 1935]

Silver print photographs
F17 24.0 × 19.5 cm
F18 24.0 × 19.0 cm
Sotheby's, London

A ballet film improvization, directed by Pavel
Tchelitchew.

Rep.: British *Vogue*, 11 November 1935;
The Best of Beaton, p. 63

F19, F20, F21

Three Photographs of Marlene Dietrich, New York

[1937]

Silver print photographs
F19 24.5 × 19.3 cm
F20 18.7 × 24.6 cm
F21 13.5 × 10.3 cm
Sotheby's, London
(F20 illus. on p. 29)

Repr.: *Cecil Beaton's Scrapbook*, p. 41 top; p. 43 (2nd from
top) and p. 43 (bottom)

F22

Marlene Dietrich, Salzburg

[1930]

Silver print photograph
21.3 × 19.3 cm
Sotheby's, London

Repr.: *Cecil Beaton's Scrapbook*, p. 42

F24

F23

Mrs William Rhinelander Stewart

[*c.* 1935]

Silver print photograph
22.0 × 18.5 cm
Condé Nast Publications (American *Vogue*)

Repr.: *Cecil Beaton's Scrapbook*, p. 90

F24

F. J. Gutmann (Francis Goodman)

Cecil Beaton

[1933]

Silver print photograph, mounted on card
Signed on mount
24.0 × 19.0 cm
Sotheby's, London

Repr.: *Modern Photography 1934–5*, 1934, plate 38

F25

Paul Tanqueray

Cecil Beaton

[1937]

Modern print from an original negative
50.8 × 40.6 cm
Private Collection
(illus. on p. 110)

F26

Unknown photographer

Cecil Beaton

[Late 1930s]

Silver print photograph, mounted on card
15.5 × 20.6 cm
Sotheby's, London

F27

Elsa Maxwell, Social Dictator

[1934]

Silver print photograph
24.6 × 19.3 cm
Sotheby's, London

Repr.: *Vanity Fair*, May 1934, p. 24;
Cecil Beaton's Scrapbook, p. 57

F28

Mrs Patrick Campbell

[1938]

Silver print photograph
29.3 × 24.5 cm
Sotheby's, London

F27

F29
Lady Oxford
[1937]
Silver print photograph
25.0 × 19.7 cm
Sotheby's, London

Repr.: American *Vogue*, June 1937, p. 54

F30
Frederick Ashton
[1939]
Silver print photograph
25.7 × 25.9 cm
Sotheby's, London

Ashton in travesty for Beaton's publication *My Royal Past*
(1939).

F31

Mme Edouard Bourdet

[Late 1930s]

Solarized photograph
26.8 × 24.0 cm
Paul Walter, New York

Wife of the Director of the Comédie Française, Mme Bourdet was a frequent model for Beaton in the late 1930s.

F32

Tunisian Boy

[*c.* 1933]

Silver print photograph, with photomontage on card
22.0 × 20.0 cm
Sotheby's, London

Repr.: *Cecil Beaton's Scrapbook*, p. 17

F33

'Moroccan Fly-Paper'

[*c.* 1933]

Silver print photograph
21.6 × 19.4 cm
Sotheby's, London

Repr.: *Time Exposure*, p. 96

F32

F31

F34

Ouled Nails

[1933]

Silver print photograph
24.3 × 24.3 cm
Sotheby's, London

The circumstances in which this photograph and the group F34–8 were taken are related in Cecil Beaton's *The Wandering Years*, Part XI; they lay the foundations for Beaton's Orientalist photography a decade later in North Africa and Asia.

F35

Ouled Nails

[1933]

Silver print photograph
26.6 × 25.3 cm
Sotheby's, London

Repr.: *Time Exposure*, p. 93, bottom

F36
Ouled Nails
[1933]
Silver print photograph
26.8 × 25.8 cm
Sotheby's, London

Variant print of F35.

F37
Ouled Nails
[1933]
Silver print photograph
25.5 × 24.3 cm
Sotheby's, London

Variant repr.: *Time Exposure*, p. 92, top (close-up)

F38
Ouled Nails
[1933]
Silver print photograph
24.3 × 24.0 cm
Sotheby's, London

Variant repr.: *Time Exposure*, p. 92, bottom

F39
North African Casbah
[1930s]
Silver print photograph
25.6 × 24.5 cm
Sotheby's, London

Repr.: *Time Exposure*, p. 82

F40
North African Casbah
[1930s]
Silver print photograph
25.7 × 24.6 cm
Sotheby's, London

Repr.: *Time Exposure*, p. 91, bottom right

F41
Pavel Tchelitchew
Portrait of Cecil Beaton
[c. 1937]
Brown wash
28.6 × 18.4 cm
Private Collection

Exh.: Parkin Gallery, *Cecil Beaton and Friends*, 1985, cat. 162

F42
Denton Welch
Lord Berners
[c. 1940]
Oil on canvas
83.8 × 61.0 cm
Private Collection

Exh.: Parkin Gallery, *Cecil Beaton and Friends*, 1985, cat. 176

F43
Cecil Beaton's Rolleiflex
[1933]
Fox Talbot Museum, Lacock, Wiltshire

Beaton began to use a Rolleiflex camera during his visit to North Africa in 1933, on the advice of George Hoyningen-Huene, Paris *Vogue*'s chief photographer.

F44
Christian Bérard
Portrait of Cecil Beaton
[1937]
Ink and wash
47.0 × 27.5 cm
Private Collection

Repr.: *Cecil Beaton's Scrapbook*, frontispiece

F45
Dorothy Hyson
[Late 1930s]
Pencil and wash
54.0 × 37.5 cm
Inscribed: 'Dorothy Hyson'
Private Collection

F46
Christian Bérard
Portrait of Cecil Beaton
[1937]
Watercolour
37.0 × 42.0 cm
Hugo Vickers

Repr.: *Cecil Beaton's Scrapbook*, tailpiece

F47
Mrs Simpson
[November 1936]
Watercolour
35.0 × 68.0 cm
Hugo Vickers

F44

F48
Christian Bérard
Portrait of Cecil Beaton
[1938]
Oil on canvas
73 × 100 cm
National Portrait Gallery, London

For an account of the painting of this portrait, which formed part of Beaton's own collection, see *The Wandering Years*, pp. 360–71 and illus. facing p. 261.

Repr.: *Time Exposure*, p. 26, bottom right (showing Bérard and Beaton)

F49
Stephen Tennant
The Gay Life
[*c.* 1935]
Pen and ink with watercolour
47.0 × 34.3 cm
Michael Parkin Fine Art Ltd

Exh.: Parkin Gallery, *Cecil Beaton and Friends*, 1985, cat. 167

F50
Pavel Tchelitchew
Portrait of Cecil Beaton
[1937]
Brush and ink
29.4 × 18.8 cm
Signed and dated
Inscribed: 'to my dearest Cecil/with love/ Pavlik/ 11 July/ 1937'
Leslie Esterman

G 1

The Duchess of Windsor

[1937]

Silver print photograph
23.2 × 17.0 cm
Sotheby's, London

Repr.: American *Vogue*, 1 June 1937, p. 55

G 2

Wedding Photographs of the Duke and Duchess of Windsor, Château de Candé

[1937]

Silver print photograph
19.8 × 19.4 cm
Private Collection

A description of the taking of this photograph is given in Cecil Beaton, *The Wandering Years*, p. 308–13.

Variant repr.: Cecil Beaton and Peter Quennell, *Time Exposure*, p. 41

G 3

HRH The Duke of Windsor

[1937]

Silver print photograph
21.1 × 16.6 cm
Private Collection

Repr.: *Time Exposure*, p. 40, top right;
Cecil Beaton, *Photobiography*, facing p. 80
Variant repr.: American *Vogue*, 1 July 1937

G 4

HRH The Duchess of Kent with Princess Olga

[c. 1938]

Silver print photograph
20.4 × 19.3 cm
Private Collection

G 5

HRH The Duke of Kent

[1936]

Silver print photograph
25.0 × 20.0 cm
Private Collection

Possibly a variant print from the session reproduced in American *Vogue*, 15 January 1937.

G 6

HRH The Duchess of Kent

[1938]

Silver print photograph
24.9 × 18.0 cm
Private Collection

Repr.: *Photobiography*, pp. 152–3

G 7

HRH The Duchess of Kent

[1938]

Silver print photograph
20.3 × 19.2 cm
Private Collection

'I photographed the Duchess in National Greek costume, in shepherdess hats', *Photobiography*, p. 130.

G 8

HM Queen Elizabeth

[1939]

Silver print photograph
25.3 × 24.0 cm
Signed twice by HRH Queen Elizabeth,
the Queen Mother, on print and card
Paul Walter, New York

'The climax to date of my photographic career',
The Wandering Years, p. 372. For an account of Beaton's first portrait session with HRH Queen Elizabeth,
the Queen Mother, see *The Wandering Years*, pp. 372–7.

G 9

HM Queen Elizabeth

[1939]

Silver print photograph
24.5 × 17.2 cm
Private Collection

G10

HM Queen Elizabeth

[1939]

Silver print photograph
24.7 × 19.7 cm
Private Collection

Repr.: *Time Exposure*, p. 115, bottom left

G11

HM Queen Elizabeth

[1939]

Silver print photograph
24.5 × 19.8 cm
Private Collection

G12

HM Queen Elizabeth

[1939]

Silver print photograph
25.5 × 20.0 cm
Private Collection

A cropped version of this portrait, together with a portrait of HM King George VI, was given as a Christmas greetings postcard in 1939 to every member of the British Forces.

Variant repr.: *Time Exposure*, p. 116

G13

HM Queen Elizabeth

[1939]

Silver print photograph
24.8 × 19.7 cm
Private Collection

G14

HM Queen Elizabeth

[1939]

Silver print photograph
24.5 × 20.0 cm
Private Collection

G15, G16, G17

*Three Photographs of HM Queen Elizabeth
in the Garden at Buckingham Palace*

[1939]

Silver print photographs
G15   10.0 × 10.0 cm
G16   10.2 × 10.3 cm
G17   10.3 × 10.0 cm
Private Collection

G15 repr.: Cecil Beaton, *Royal Portraits*, unpaginated

G18

HM Queen Elizabeth

[1939]

Silver print photograph
25.9 × 24.9 cm
Private Collection
(illus. on p. 53)

G19

HM Queen Elizabeth

[1939]

Silver print photograph
24.0 × 23.9 cm
Private Collection

Repr.: *Photobiography*, pp. 136–7

G20

HM Queen Elizabeth

[1939]

Silver print photograph
26.9 × 24.7 cm
Private Collection

Variant repr.: *Royal Portraits*, unpaginated

G21

Princess Marina of Kent

[*c.* 1935]

Watercolour
21.6 × 16.5 cm
Private Collection

Exh.: Parkin Gallery, *Cecil Beaton Memorial Exhibition*, 1983, cat. 96

G22

HM Queen Elizabeth

[1937]

Watercolour
50.2 × 44.0 cm
Roy Astley

Repr.: British *Vogue*, 12 May 1937, p. 24

G23

Wallis Simpson, Duchess of Windsor

[1936]

Watercolour
35.6 × 20.3 cm
Private Collection

For a full account of the portrait sitting see Beaton's article 'Mrs Simpson', American *Vogue*, February 1937

Exh.: Parkin Gallery, *Cecil Beaton Memorial Exhibition*, 1983, cat. 87

WARTIME –
THE HOME FRONT

H1

Blitzed Buildings in the City of London

[1940/41]

Silver print photograph
24.4 × 24.6 cm
Sotheby's, London

Variant repr. (cropped): Cecil Beaton, *History Under Fire*, p. 2, with the caption 'Chaos by St. Paul's: looking from Ave Maria Lane across the site of Paternoster Row'

H2

The Blitz: Lambs Conduit Street, London

[1940]

Silver print photograph
21.2 × 20.3 cm
Sotheby's, London

Repr.: *History Under Fire*, p. 97, with the caption 'Bloomsbury Scene'

H3

Blitzed City Church

[1940]

Silver print photograph
20.6 × 19.6 cm
Sotheby's, London

H4

The Plinth of Milton's Monument

[1940]

Silver print photograph
26.4 × 25.2 cm
Sotheby's, London

Repr.: *History Under Fire*, p. 25 with the caption 'Milton's statue blown from its pedestal outside St. Giles Cripplegate. In the church the poet worshipped and was buried'

H5

Blitz, City of London

[1940/1]

Silver print photograph
19.4 × 19.1 cm
Sotheby's, London

H6

Remains of a Messerschmitt

[1940]

Silver print photograph
26.0 × 21.0 cm
Paul Walter, New York

H7

Hairdresser's Establishment

[1940]

Silver print photograph
20.5 × 19.7 cm
Sotheby's, London

Repr.: *The Sketch*, 13 November 1940, p. 209 with the caption 'The blast of the Blitzkrieg has bombed London into surrealism! Cecil Beaton has only to take his camera out after the "All Clear" has sounded to find well posed subjects on every hand'

H8

Eileen Dunne

[1940]

Silver print photograph
24.6 × 24.3 cm
Sotheby's, London
(illus. on p. 54)

Life's cover caption read, 'Air Raid Victim: The wide-eyed young lady on the cover is Eileen Dunne, aged 3¾. A German bomber, whose crew had never met her, dropped a bomb on a North England village. A splinter from it hit Eileen: she is sitting in hospital'.

Repr.: *Illustrated London News*, 21 September 1940, cover; *Life*, 23 September 1940, cover

H9

Mr Dove, Father of the Gardener at Ashcombe, in Air Raid Warden's Helmet

[October 1941]

Silver print photograph
28.3 × 26.0 cm
Sotheby's, London

Variant repr.: Cecil Beaton, *Ashcombe*, facing p. 89

H9

H10

H10

*Churchill's Bed,
No. 10 Downing Street, London*

[1940]

Silver print photograph
25.7 × 25.0 cm
Sotheby's, London

Censored at the Ministry of Information, this print is inscribed on the *verso*, 'Not to be published'. Other photographs taken during this session were published with the article 'The Lady of No. 10', *Picture Post*, 23 November 1940, pp. 23–5, which 'upset Mrs Churchill' according to Beaton in his *Cuttings Book*, vol. XXVIII.

H11 & H12

*Two Photographs of Winston Churchill,
Prime Minister*

[1940]

Silver print photographs
Both 25.4 × 16.6 cm
Condé Nast Publications (American *Vogue*)
(H11 illus. on p. 53)

H11 repr.: *Daily Express*, 23 December 1940, with the caption 'with the Churchill chin at its most undaunted angle'
H12 repr.: *The Sketch*, 18 December 1940, p. 371, with the caption 'The Man at the Helm. He looks the typical British bulldog'

H13

'An English Fighter Pilot, DFC and Bar'

[1941]

Silver print photograph
24.5 × 18.0 cm
Sotheby's, London
(illus. on p. 34)

H14

Fighter Pilot

[1941]

Silver print photograph
21.0 × 19.8 cm
Sotheby's, London

H15

'Cecil Beaton takes off his hat to a fighter pilot . . .'

[1940/41]

Silver print photograph
21.5 × 20.0 cm
Sotheby's, London

H16

H16

*Rear Turret of RAF Bomber,
with Cecil Beaton's Reflection*

[1941]

Silver print photograph
21.0 × 20.0 cm
Sotheby's, London

H17

Scott's Delivery Van

[Early 1940s]

Silver print photograph
20.8 × 19.1 cm
Sotheby's, London

H18

Augustus John

[c. 1940]

Silver print photograph
20.4 × 16.8 cm
Sotheby's, London
(illus. on p. 27)

Repr.: Cecil Beaton and Peter Quennell, *Time Exposure*,
facing p. 17

H19

Noël Coward in 'In Which We Serve'

[1942]

Silver print photograph
18.4 × 18.7 cm
Sotheby's, London

A still of Noël Coward impersonating Lord Louis
Mountbatten in the filmed wartime hagiography.

H20

James Agate

[c. 1943]

Silver print photograph
25.6 × 20.5 cm; irregular
Sotheby's, London

Diarist and theatre correspondent of *The Sunday Times*.

Repr.: British *Vogue*, August 1944

H21

Sir Kingsley Wood

[1940]

Silver print photograph
24.2 × 11.6 cm
Sotheby's, London

Sir Kingsley Wood was appointed Chancellor of the
Exchequer in Churchill's government of 1940.

Variant repr.: *The Sketch*, 9 October 1940 (cropped)

H22

Lord Halifax

[1940]

Silver print photograph
23.6 × 15.8 cm
Sotheby's, London

Viscount Halifax had been Secretary of State for Foreign
Affairs since 1938.

Repr.: *The Sketch*, 30 October 1940, p. 141

H23

Lady Diana Cooper in the British Embassy, Paris

[c. 1946]

Silver print photograph
19.4 × 18.5 cm
Sotheby's, London

H25

H24

Edith Olivier, Mayor of Wilton

[*c.* 1940]

Silver print photograph
24.0 × 24.4 cm
Sotheby's, London

Variant repr.: *Ashcombe*, facing p. 88

H25, H26

Two Photographs of Henry Green

[*c.* 1944]

Modern prints
H25 25.0 × 20.0 cm
H26 25.8 × 20.3 cm
Sotheby's, London

The novelist Henry Green forbade any representation of his face, hence Beaton's treatment which recalls his previous portrait of Lady Oxford, 1928.

H27

Quintin Hogg, MP

[1945]

Silver print photograph
25.5 × 20.0 cm
Sotheby's, London

H28

Richard Walter Sickert

[1941]

Silver print photograph
21.5 × 20.5 cm
Condé Nast Publications (American *Vogue*)

H29

*Richard Walter Sickert and his wife,
Thérèse Lessore*

[1941]

Silver print photograph
24.5 × 24.7 cm
Sotheby's, London

Variant repr.: 'Walter Sickert – Painter', *Picture Post*,
9 August 1941, pp. 20–1

H30

H30

President Camorna of Portugal

[1942]

Silver print photograph
29.9 × 24.3 cm
Sotheby's, London

Repr.: Cecil Beaton, *Near East*, facing p. 142

WARTIME – THE NEAR EAST

12

11

Self-portrait in the Western Desert

[1942]

Silver print photograph
21.3 × 20.4 cm
Sotheby's, London

12

Sandstorm

[1942]

Silver print photograph
20.4 × 19.6 cm
Negative no. (Imperial War Museum) CBM 1358
Private Collection

Repr.: Cecil Beaton, *Near East*, facing p. 56

13

*Cecil Beaton in his Tent,
'The Ritz', Western Desert*

[1942]

Silver print photograph
21.5 × 20.5 cm
Sotheby's, London

14

British Dispatch Rider in Syria

[1942]

Silver print photograph
19.1 × 19.5 cm
Negative no. (Imperial War Museum) CBM 2098
Sotheby's, London

15

Mount of Olives

[1942]

Silver print photograph
19.4 × 19.7 cm
Negative no. (Imperial War Museum) CBM 2483
Sotheby's, London

Repr.: *Near East*, facing p. 110

16

'"Souvenir" of the Dome of the Rock'

[1942]

Silver print photograph
20.5 × 20.1 cm
Negative no. (Imperial War Museum) CBM 1731
Sotheby's, London
(illus. on p. 35)

Repr.: *Near East*, facing p. 115

17

Self-portrait in the Wax Museum, Cairo

[1942]

Silver print photograph
19.1 × 19.4 cm
Sotheby's, London

18

18

*'Tobruk Fire Station After a Visit
from German Bombers'*

[1942]

Silver print photograph
19.1 × 19.4 cm
Negative no. (Imperial War Museum) CBM 1860
Sotheby's, London

19

Tobruk Interior

[1942]

Silver print photograph
21.3 × 20.2 cm
Negative no. (Imperial War Museum) CBM 2490
Sotheby's, London

Repr.: *Near East*, facing p. 63

110

'Enemy Skeletons'

[1942]

Silver print photograph
20.0 × 20.9 cm
Negative no. (Imperial War Museum) CBM 2485
Sotheby's, London

Repr.: *Near East*, facing p. 38, bottom

111

'An Arab Desert Shrine'

[1942]

Silver print photograph
25.3 × 24.4 cm
Negative no. (Imperial War Museum) CBM 2148
Sotheby's, London

112

'Film Stars in Cairo'

[1942]

Silver print photograph
25.7 × 21.3 cm
Negative no. (Imperial War Museum) CBM 1583
Sotheby's, London

Repr.: *Near East*, facing p. 27, bottom right

113

Prince Mohammed Ali of Egypt

[1942]

Silver print photograph
26.7 × 17.2 cm
Negative no. (Imperial War Museum) CBM 1598
Sotheby's, London

'The Prince has superb manners that only Edwardians
seem to possess today', wrote Beaton in *Near East*, 1943,
p. 35.

114, 115, 116

Three Photographs of Prince Faisal of Iraq

[1942]

Silver print photographs
114 20.8 × 20.0 cm
115 21.0 × 14.4 cm
116 13.5 × 14.0 cm
Negative nos. (Imperial War Museum) CBM 2389, 2392,
2393
Sotheby's, London

Repr.: 'Life Calls on Boy King of Iraq', *Life*, 1942, in
Cecil Beaton, *Cuttings Book*, vol. XXXI; *Near East*, facing
p. 106

117

Glubb Pasha

[1942]

Silver print photograph
19.4 × 18.7 cm
Sotheby's, London

Repr.: *Illustrated*, 31 July, 1943;
see *Near East*, pp. 116–7.

118

'Men of the Iraq Levies'

[1942]

Silver print photograph
25.6 × 24.4 cm
Sotheby's, London

Repr.: *Near East*, facing p. 102 ('Kurd Recruit')

119

Arab Legionnaire

[1942]

Silver print photograph
25.8 × 24.5 cm
Negative no. (Imperial War Museum) CBM 2449
Sotheby's, London

Repr.: *Near East*, facing p. 119

120, 121

Two Photographs of Nigerians, Lagos

[1942]

Silver print photographs
120 17.2 × 16.0 cm
121 17.3 × 14.2 cm
120 Negative no. (Imperial War Museum) CBM 2881
Condé Nast Publications (American *Vogue*)

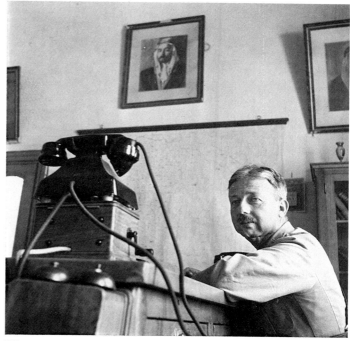

117

119

122, 123

Two Photographs of a West African Dancer

[1942]

Modern prints
Both 30.5 × 30.5 cm
Negative nos. (Imperial War Museum) CBM 2874, 2875
Imperial War Museum, London

122 repr.: British *Vogue*, December 1942, p. 58 top, with
the caption 'Devil Dancer in Ceremonial Dress'

124

Cactus Autographed by Troops

[1942]

Modern print
30.5 × 3.05 cm
Negative no. (Imperial War Museum) CBM 1511
Imperial War Museum, London

125

African Boy with British Officers

[1942]

Modern print
30.5 × 30.5 cm
Negative no. (Imperial War Museum) CBM 1065
Imperial War Museum, London

[191]

J11

J

WARTIME –
THE FAR EAST

J1
William Henderson, New Delhi

[1944]

Silver print photograph
18.9 × 14.5 cm
Sotheby's, London

Repr.: Cecil Beaton, *Far East*, facing p.8

J2
British Officer and Indian Servant

[1944]

Silver print photograph
19.7 × 19.9 cm
Sotheby's, London

J3, J4
*Two Photographs, Still Lives in
the Room of Lt. Tony Liddel*

[1944]

Modern prints
Both 30.5 × 30.5 cm
Negative nos. (Imperial War Museum) IB 65, 66
Imperial War Museum, London

J5
*'The Laundry Out Today on the
Grounds of Government House', New Delhi*

[1944]

Silver print photograph
12.5 × 20.2 cm
Negative no. (Imperial War Museum) IB 428
Sotheby's, London

J6
Sleeping Indians

[1944]

Silver print photograph
19.1 × 19.2 cm
Sotheby's, London

J7
*Self-portrait: 'Reflection in an
ornamental glass mirror in the
Temple of Jain, Calcutta'*

[1944]

Silver print photograph
51.4 × 49.0 cm
Sotheby's, London

Repr.: *The Sketch*, 13 June 1945, p. 329
Cecil Beaton and Peter Quennell, *Time Exposure*, 2nd
edition, frontispiece

J8
*Self-portrait:
The Palace of Amber, Jaipur*

[1944]

Silver print photograph
25.4 × 24.4 cm
Negative no. (Imperial War Museum) IB 631
Sotheby's, London

J9
*Filigree Screen in the
Palace of Amber, Jaipur*

[1944]

Silver print photograph
51.4 × 49.0 cm
Negative no. (Imperial War Museum) IB 624
Sotheby's, London

J10
*'A Boy in Front of an Ornamental Mirror':
Jain Temple, Calcutta*

[1944]

Silver print photograph
25.5 × 24.5 cm
Sotheby's, London

Repr.: Cecil Beaton, *Indian Album*, p. 72

J11
Palace of Amber, Jaipur
[1944]
Silver print photograph
25.4 × 24.5 cm
Negative no. (Imperial War Museum) IB 664
Private Collection

J12
*Admiral Lord Louis Mountbatten
in his Delhi H.Q.*
[1944]
Silver print photograph
25.4 × 24.4 cm
Negative no. (Imperial War Museum) IB 120
Sotheby's, London

J13
*Self-portrait with Admiral Lord Louis Mountbatten,
Faridkot House, Delhi*
[1944]
Silver print photograph
16.9 × 15.2 cm
Sotheby's, London
(illus. on p. 15)

J14
Lady Wavell, Viceroy's House, Delhi
[1944]
Silver print photograph
25.5 × 20.5 cm
Sotheby's, London

J15
The Old Fort, Golconda, India
[1944]
Silver print photograph
20.5 × 19.6 cm
Sotheby's, London
Repr.: *Indian Album*, p. 54

J16
The Ajanta Caves, Hyderabad
[1944]
Silver print photograph
50.9 × 48.3 cm
Negative no. (Imperial War Museum) IB 743
Paul Walter, New York

J17
Indian Flautist
[1944]
Silver print photograph
50.9 × 48.3 cm
Negative no. (Imperial War Museum) IB 1413
Paul Walter, New York
Repr.: *Far East*, facing p. 4

J18
Coolie in River Boat, China
[1944]
Modern print
20.0 × 25.5 cm
Paul Walter, New York

J19
Two Pigs by Riverside, China
[1944]
Modern print
19.0 × 19.0 cm
Paul Walter, New York

J20
Chinese Commandos
[1944]
Silver print photograph
24.7 × 24.4 cm
Sotheby's, London
Repr.: *Indian Album*, p. 56

J21
Man in Sunlight, Chengtu, China
[1944]
Silver print photograph
19.2 × 19.1 cm
Private Collection
Repr.: *Far East*, facing p. 105

J22
Chinese Actor
[1944]
Silver print photograph
25.0 × 24.0 cm
Sotheby's, London

J23
General Carton de Wiart
[1944]

[194]

Silver print photograph
25.4 × 24.4 cm
Negative no. (Imperial War Museum) IB 3450
Sotheby's, London
(illus. on p. 55)

J24

*Self-portrait in Mirror
with General Grimsdale*

[1944]

Silver print photograph
24.5 × 24.4 cm
Negative no. (Imperial War Museum) IB 191
Sotheby's, London

J25

Chinese Flag Maker, Chengtu

[1944]

Silver print photograph
25.2 × 24.1 cm
Negative no. (Imperial War Museum) IB 2425c
Sotheby's, London

Repr.: Cecil Beaton, *Chinese Album*, p. 59

J26

Police at ARP Headquarters, Chengtu

[1944]

Silver print photograph
23.3 × 24.2 cm
Negative no. (Imperial War Museum) IB 2437c
Private Collection

Repr.: *Far East*, 1945, facing p. 92

J27

Chinese Surprise Troops in Training, Pihu

[1944]

Silver print photograph
25.0 × 23.2 cm
Sotheby's, London

Repr.: *Far East*, facing p. 74, top

J28

*Blossom Growing by the Riverside,
Ningtu, China*

[1944]

Silver print photograph
50.0 × 47.0 cm
Negative no. (Imperial War Museum) IB 3075
Sotheby's, London

Repr.: *Far East*, facing p. 43

J26

J29

Chinese Salt Wells, Tselichung

[1944]

Silver print photograph
25.5 × 24.5 cm
Negative no. (Imperial War Museum) IB 2779c
Sotheby's, London

Repr.: *Far East*, facing p. 56, top right

J30

After the Battle, Arakan

[1944]

Silver print photograph
50.0 × 50.0 cm
Negative no. (Imperial War Museum) IB 263
Sotheby's, London

Repr.: *Far East*, facing p. 29

J31

Red Cross Hospital, Changsha

[1944]

Silver print photograph
25.8 × 24.5 cm
Sotheby's, London

Repr.: *Chinese Album*, p. 39

K1

K I

Bill Brandt

Portrait of Cecil Beaton

[*c.* 1945]

Silver print photograph
23.2 × 19.9 cm
Sotheby's, London

Repr.: *Harper's Bazaar*, October 1953, p. 185

K 2

*Self-portrait: At Work on Designs for
'Lady Windermere's Fan'*

[1946]

Silver print photograph
21.8 × 16.5 cm
Sotheby's, London

For an account of the development of the revival
production of this play, see Cecil Beaton, *The Happy Years*,
pp. 41–5.

K 3

A Still from 'The Young Mr Pitt'

[1941]

Silver print photograph
21.8 × 20.3 cm
Sotheby's, London

This film was made in 1941 and directed by Carol Reed.
Robert Morley, who played Charles James Fox, is seen
here against the background of Whitehall.

K 4

Mrs Gillian Sutro

[1945]

Silver print photograph
19.5 × 18.6 cm
Sotheby's, London

A still from an uncompleted experimental film.

Repr.: *Queen*, 25 July 1945

K 5

Ralph Crane

*Cecil Beaton Painting a Hat for the
American Production of 'Lady Windermere's Fan'*

[1946]

Silver print photograph
24.0 × 18.8 cm
Sotheby's, London

Repr.: *Life*, 13 September 1946

K 5

K6, K7, K8, K9
*Four Photographs from the
American Production of 'Lady Windermere's Fan'*
[1946]
Silver print photographs
K6 25.0 × 19.5 cm
K7 20.5 × 19.7 cm
K8 20.4 × 19.9 cm
K9 20.6 × 19.5 cm
Sotheby's, London

K6 repr.: *Time*, 28 October 1946
K8 repr.: *Cue*, 26 October 1946

KIO
John Reed of Hollywood
*Cecil Beaton and Rex Evans as Cecil Graham
and Lord Augustus Lorton in
'Lady Windermere's Fan' (American Production)*
[1946]
Silver print photograph
24.9 × 19.5 cm
Sotheby's, London

K16

For Beaton's experiences in the cast of the American
production of *Lady Windermere's Fan*, see *The Happy Years*,
pp. 104–5.
Repr.: *Life*, 13 September 1946

KII
*Michael Wilding, Diana Wynyard and Alexander
Korda on the Set of 'An Ideal Husband'*
[1947]
Silver print photograph
25.8 × 25.8 cm
Sotheby's, London

For Beaton's account of the filming of 'An Ideal
Husband' see *The Happy Years*, pp. 120–7

KI2
*Still from 'An Ideal Husband' with
Constance Collier*
[1945]
Silver print photograph
25.7 × 24.5 cm
Sotheby's, London

KI3
*Self-portrait at the British Embassy, Paris,
with Laurence Olivier and Vivien Leigh*
[c. 1945]
Silver print photograph
15.5 × 14.8 cm
Sotheby's, London

Repr.: *The Happy Years*, p. 150
Variant repr.: Cecil Beaton and Kenneth Tynan, *Persona
Grata*, 1953, facing p. 75 (portrait of Olivier)

KI4
*Still from 'Caesar and Cleopatra'
with Vivien Leigh*
[1945]
Silver print photograph
19.0 × 18.5 cm
Sotheby's, London

KI5
*Still from 'Anna Karenina'
with Vivien Leigh*
[c. 1948]
Silver print photograph
25.8 × 22.8 cm
Sotheby's, London

к16

Vivien Leigh as Anna Karenina

[1948]

Silver print photograph
21.4 × 24.4 cm
Sotheby's, London

к17

*A Sheet of Contact Prints of Stills
from 'Great Expectations'*

[1946]

Silver print photograph
25.9 × 20.4 cm
Sotheby's, London

к18

Still from 'Great Expectations'

[1946]

Silver print photograph
18.9 × 17.9 cm
Private Collection
(illus. on p. 31)

Martita Hunt, playing Miss Havisham, is seen together
with Valerie Hobson as Estella.

к19

*Dorothy Hyson in the Title Role,
'Lady Windermere's Fan', London*

[1945]

Silver print photograph
24.3 × 18.9 cm
Condé Nast Publications (American *Vogue*)

Costume of apricot satin brocade designed by Beaton.

Repr.: American *Vogue*, 15 February 1946, p. 35

к20

*Cecil Beaton and Cornelia Otis Skinner
in 'Lady Windermere's Fan'*

[1946]

Modern colour print from transparency
25.0 × 20.0 cm
Private Collection

к21

Silk Scarf for 'Lady Windermere's Fan'

[1945]

89.0 × 89.0 cm

Signed by Cecil Beaton, John Gielgud and members of
the cast including Isabel Jeans, Athene Seyler, Dorothy
Hyson, Geoffrey Toone and Griffith Jones
Hugo Vickers

Formerly the property of Athene Seyler.

к22

Set Design for 'Dandy Dick'

[1945]

Pen, ink and watercolour
30.5 × 43.0 cm
Private Collection

к23

Rex Whistler

Wake up and Dream

[1929]

Pencil, pen, ink and watercolour
36.0 × 25.4 cm
Michael Parkin Fine Art Ltd

Exh.: Parkin Gallery, *Cecil Beaton and Friends*, 1985,
cat. 182

к24

Manon Lescaut

[*c.* 1938]

Pen, ink, crayon and watercolour
43.5 × 32.0 cm
Signed and inscribed: 'medallion for rose, turquoise
framed in pearls – / coarse white lace skirt over satin – /
over drapery of stiff grey on shrimp pink satin'
Leslie Esterman

Drawing of a costume for an abortive film project which
was to have starred Merle Oberon.

к25

Set Design for 'Our Betters'

[1946]

Watercolour
53.0 × 74.0 cm
Private Collection
(illus. on p. 99)

к26

Costume Design for an 'Ideal Husband'

[1948]

Pen and ink
27.8 × 21.5 cm
Roy Astley

Glynis Johns, for whom Beaton designed this costume,
played the part of Mabel Chilton.

K27
Preliminary Sketch for 'Lady Windermere's Fan'

[1945]

Pen and ink
27.8 × 21.1 cm
Roy Astley

K28
Design for a Programme Cover for 'Apparitions'

[1936]

Ink on card
40.6 × 28.4 cm
Inscribed: 'Apparitions/Cecil Beaton'
Roy Astley

K29
Mrs Candour's Costume in 'The School for Scandal'

[1949]

Pen, ink and watercolour
36.5 × 25.2 cm
Roy Astley

For an account of Beaton's involvement in the play see
The Strenuous Years, pp. 18–19.

Repr.: *School for Scandal*, Folio Society edn, 1949, p. 115

K30
Costume Design

[*c.* 1935]

Pen, ink and wash
51.0 × 31.5 cm
Private Collection

Exh.: Parkin Gallery, *Cecil Beaton and Friends*, 1985,
cat. 14
Repr.: Cecil Beaton, *Cecil Beaton's Scrapbook*, p. 111

K31
Edith Evans in 'Heartbreak House'

[1943]

Pen, ink and watercolour
35.6 × 24.4 cm
Roy Astley

'The evening gown: of Oyster Satin and Chiffon:
a corsage of purple roses, wreathed by a dangle of
amythysts.' See Cecil Beaton, *The Years Between*, pp. 221–3;
an illustration of Edith Evans's costume for the role of
Hesione Hushabye faces p. 224.

K32
*Costume Design for
The First Shoot from the Revue 'Follow the Sun'*

[1936]

Pen, ink and watercolour
46.4 × 34.2 cm
Roy Astley
(illus. on p. 104)

K33
*Set Design for Front Cloth and Gauze
with Medallion of Queen Victoria*

[Early 1930s]

Pen, ink and watercolour
25.5 × 41.5 cm
Roy Astley

K34
*Costume Design for Mrs Erlynne,
'Lady Windermere's Fan'*

[1945]

Pencil, pen, ink and wash
40.0 × 26.6 cm
Roy Astley
(illus. on p. 104)

Repr.: *The Masque*, No. 3, 1947, cover

K35
Dorothy Dickson in 'Our Betters'

[*c.* 1945]

Pen, ink, wash and coloured chalks
40.0 × 28.0 cm
Roy Astley

A revival production directed by Ivor Novello.

K36 & K37
*A Pair of Costume Designs for
'An Ideal Husband'*

[1948]

Pencil and watercolour, with fabric additions
Both 42.5 × 32.7 cm
Roy Astley

K38
'Lady Windermere's Fan'

[1946]

Modern colour print from 10 × 8 in transparency
Private Collection
(illus. on p. 125)

к39
Sir Cedric Hardwick in 'Candida'
[1946]
35 × 24 cm
Conté crayon
Private Collection

к40
Marlon Brando and Katherine Cornell in 'Candida'
[1946]
28 × 44 cm
Conté crayon
Private Collection

к41
Mildred Nantwich in 'Candida'
[1946]
44 × 28 cm
Conté crayon
Private Collection

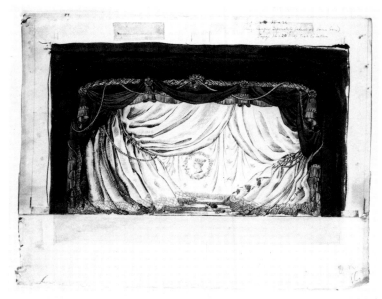

к33

к30

к35

L I

*Mrs Reginald Fellows Wearing a Paquin Shamrock
Hat and Fire-fighting Gloves*

[1941]

Silver print photograph
24.4 × 19.4 cm
Sotheby's, London

Repr.: British *Vogue*, June 1941, p. 37;
Cecil Beaton, *The Best of Beaton*, p. 136

L9

L2, L3, L4, L5, L6, L7, L8

*Fashion is Indestructible
(Digby Morton suit)*

[1941]

L2–7 Silver print photographs
L2   12.7 × 12.8 cm
L3   12.9 × 12.8 cm
L4   12.8 × 12.8 cm
L5   12.9 × 12.8 cm
L6   12.9 × 12.8 cm
L7   12.7 × 12.7 cm
L8 Modern print from 2¼ × 2¼ in negative
12.9 × 12.8 cm
Sotheby's, London

A series of seven studies including one taken in the bomb-
damaged Temple that was published in *Vogue*. Part of
Vogue's wartime function was to keep up morale by
continuing to appear despite direct bomb hits and
chronic paper shortages. The optimistic caption reads:
'Her poise unshaken, she reads about the other fire of
London in which the earlier Temple was destroyed'.

Repr.: British *Vogue*, September 1941, p. 32

L9

Bridal Gown by Bianca Mosca at Jacqmar

[1943]

Silver print photograph
24.2 × 19.3 cm
Sotheby's, London

The use of a gauze screen through which to photograph
a subject was pioneered by Baron de Meyer.

Variant repr.: British *Vogue*, February 1948, p. 48

L I O

*Hattie Carnegie Strapless Evening Gown
of Black Silk Velvet*

[1944]

Silver print photograph
25.6 × 20.5 cm
Sotheby's, London

Repr.: American *Vogue*, 15 October 1944, p. 78

LII

Bergdorf Goodman Persian Broadtail Cape

[1944]

Silver print photograph
25.5 × 20.5 cm
Sotheby's, London

Repr.: American *Vogue*, 15 October 1944, p. 80 (cropped)

LI2

*Czettel Dinner Dress of Satin and Crêpe
wide-woven Stripes from Jay Thorpe
(Andrea Johnson)*

[1944]

Silver print photograph
25.2 × 20.7 cm
Sotheby's, London

Repr.: American *Vogue*, 15 October 1944, p. 82;
Cecil Beaton, *Photobiography*, facing p. 128

LI3

*Brown Wool Overcoat by
Fira Benenson at Bonwit Teller*

[1944]

Silver print photograph
25.5 × 20.5 cm
Sotheby's, London

Variant repr.: American *Vogue*, 15 October 1944, p. 83

LI4

*Adèle Simpson Two-piece Hostess Gown
with Bare Midriff*

[1945]

Modern colour print from 10 × 8 in transparency
Sotheby's, London
(illus. on p. 123)

Repr.: American *Vogue*, 1 January 1945 (cover)

LI5

*Paris Collections:
Bruyère Pink Woollen House-gown
Embroidered with Mother-of-pearl Tracery*

[1945]

Silver print photograph
30.3 × 27.4 cm
Sotheby's, London

Repr.: American *Vogue*, 15 December 1945, p. 58;
British *Vogue*, November 1945, p. 46

LI6

*Paris Collections:
Pierre Balmain Chinese Brown Woollen
Coat with Trousers*

[1945]

Silver print photograph
22.0 × 16.5 cm
Sotheby's, London
(illus. on p. 74)

In the caption that appeared in American *Vogue* in 1945,
Beaton concluded that he had taken 'some pictures that
are outside the usual fashion sphere . . . in particular, one
. . . of a girl standing in an artist's back yard in a flannel
Chinese blouse, in which I have tried for some of the
lighting of a Corot portrait. I think it is one of the best
I have ever taken.'

Repr.: American *Vogue*, 15 December 1945, p. 59;
British *Vogue*, November 1945, p. 53;
Photobiography, facing p. 128

LI7

*Dorian Leigh Modelling a Suit
amidst Unpacked Clothing*

[c. 1946]

Silver print photograph
24.2 × 19.1 cm
Sotheby's, London

Unpublished photograph for American *Vogue*.
For Beaton's description of Dorian Leigh as a model, see
Photobiography, p. 177.

LI8, LI9

Day Suit and Evening Dress

[c. 1946]

Silver print photographs
LI8 25.5 × 20.8 cm
LI9 25.7 × 20.0 cm
Sotheby's, London

The written note that the model is holding in Cat. LI9
was probably inspired by similar motifs frequently
included in the late 1930s fashion photographs of Peter
Rose Pulham.

Unpublished photographs for American *Vogue*.

L20

How to Keep Cool (Helen Bennett)

[c. 1946]

Modern colour print from 10 × 8 in transparency
Sotheby's, London
(illus. on p. 122)

For further details see *Photobiography*, p. 71.

L21

Photograph in the Style of Mary Cassatt (Carmen)
Summer Dress by Sophie of Saks, Fifth Avenue

[1946]

Modern colour print from 10 × 8 in transparency
Sotheby's, London
(illus. on p. 132)

Variant repr.: American *Vogue*, July 1946, pp. 66–7;
British *Vogue*, August 1946, p. 40;
The Art and Techniques of Color Photography, 1951, pp. 54–5

L22

Charles James Shapes a Suit Jacket of Black Faille

[1948]

Silver print photograph
24.3 × 19.4 cm
Sotheby's, London

Variant repr.: American *Vogue*, 1 March 1948, p. 214

L23

Charles James Evening Dresses

[1948]

Modern colour print from reject 10 × 8 in transparency
Private Collection

Photographed in French and Company's eighteenth-century French panelled room, this is undoubtedly Beaton's greatest Conversation Piece fashion study.

Variant repr.: American *Vogue*, June 1948, pp. 112–3
The Art and Techniques of Color Photography, 1951, pp. 52–3

L24

Charles James Evening Dresses

[1948]

Modern print from 10 × 8 in negative
Sotheby's, London
(illus. on p. 76)
See Cat. L23

L25

Young Fashion: Summer Shorts

[1948]

Modern colour print from 10 × 8 in transparency
Sotheby's, London
(illus. on p. 133)

Variant repr.: American *Vogue*, June 1948

L26

Summer Fashion, Los Angeles

[1948]

Silver print photograph
19.0 × 19.4 cm
Sotheby's, London

Photographed in the Los Angeles flower market.

Variant repr.: British *Vogue*, July 1948, p. 52, in colour;
American *Vogue*, June 1948, p. 136, in colour

L27

London Collections:
Coats by Digby Morton, Hardy Amies, Mattli,
Peter Russell and Norman Hartnell

[1948]

Silver print photograph
24.3 × 19.4 cm
Sotheby's, London

The models include Barbara Goalen (far right), Wenda Rogerson (Mrs Norman Parkinson; centre back), Della Oake and Pat Kenyon.

Repr.: British *Vogue*, September 1948, p. 61 (cropped)

L28

L28

Clarissa Churchill in Coat by Angèle Delanghe

[1950]

Silver print photograph
24.4 × 19.5 cm
Sotheby's, London

The first of a portfolio of four pictures captioned 'Elegance – four women who possess this fastidious formality'. Clarissa Churchill, the niece of the Prime Minister Winston Churchill, was Features Editor of British *Vogue* at this time.

Repr.: British *Vogue*, January 1950, p. 43

L29

*Dorian Leigh Modelling an Evening Dress
in Beaton's Drawing Room*

[*c.* 1950]

Silver print photograph
24.7 × 19.1 cm
Sotheby's, London

L31

L30

Henri Bendel Short Taffeta Ball Gown

[1951]

Modern colour print from 10 × 8 in transparency
Sotheby's, London

Repr.: American *Vogue*, 1 March 1951, p. 160 in colour;
The Art and Techniques of Color Photography, 1951, plate 63

L31

*Irene's Spring Ball Gown of
Soufflé de Soie and Ostrich Feathers,
Modelled before a Canvas by Jackson Pollock
at the Betty Parsons Gallery,
New York*

[1951]

Silver print photograph
23.9 × 24.1 cm
Sotheby's, London

Photographs of Beaton in the thirties show him experimenting with ink-spattered sheets of cartridge paper for decorative effects, and later, with the acceptance of abstract expressionism, he acquired furnishings and carpets in a similar design.

Repr.: American *Vogue*, 1 March 1951, p. 56, in colour

L32

Balmain Taffeta Ball Gown

[1951]

Silver print photograph
25.6 × 20.4 cm
Sotheby's, London

Repr.: American *Vogue*, 1 November 1951, p. 83, in colour;
British *Vogue*, December 1951, p. 89, in colour

L33

*Fiona Campbell-Walter Modelling
a Mink Jacket by Calman Links*

[1954]

Contact print from five $3\frac{1}{2} \times 3\frac{1}{2}$ in negatives
Sotheby's, London

Vogue's star model of the 1950s was 5 ft 8 in tall with a 23 in waist, described by Beaton as being as 'finely bred as a champion greyhound'. She retired from modelling on her marriage to Baron Thyssen.

Variant repr.: British *Vogue*, August 1954, p. 30

L34, L35
*Vernier Hat of Pink Roses
Modelled by Mrs Peter Thorneycroft*
[1954]
Contact print from two $3\frac{1}{2} \times 3\frac{1}{2}$ in negatives
10.5 × 19.1 cm
Sotheby's, London

Variant repr.: British *Vogue*, June 1954, p. 57

L36
Charles James Fashions
[1955]
Contact sheet of ten studies from $2\frac{1}{4} \times 2\frac{1}{4}$ in negatives
25.5 × 20.3 cm
Sotheby's, London

These fashion studies include the butterfly ball gown, now
in the Brooklyn Museum.

L37
Charles James and his Wife
[1955]
Modern print from $2\frac{1}{4} \times 2\frac{1}{4}$ in negative
Sotheby's, London

L38
Mrs Charles James in Madison Avenue Salon
[1955]
Modern print from $2\frac{1}{4} \times 2\frac{1}{4}$ in negative
Sotheby's, London

L39
*Evening Fashion: possibly taken for Modess
advertising campaign*
[Late 1950s]
Modern colour print from 10 × 8 in transparency
Sotheby's, London
(illus. on p. 127)

L37

M 1

Self-portrait at Reddish House

[*c.* 1950]

Silver print photograph
24.9 × 19.8 cm
Sotheby's, London

Repr.: Cecil Beaton, *The Happy Years*, p. 166 with the
caption 'In Possession'

M 2

Compton Collier

Cecil Beaton and his Mother

[1951]

Silver print photograph, mounted on card
15.6 × 20.5 cm
Signed
Sotheby's, London

M 3, M 4

Richard Avedon

*Two Photographs of Cecil Beaton
and his Aunt Cada, Reddish House*

[*c.* 1955]

Silver print photographs, mounted on card
M3 21.1 × 20.5 cm
M4 20.9 × 20.3 cm
Sotheby's, London

Variant repr.: Cecil Beaton, *The Strenuous Years*, p. 73

M 5

*A Sheet of Sixteen Contact Prints
of Cecil Beaton on Television*

[*c.* 1955]

Silver print photograph
23.5 × 21.0 cm
Sotheby's, London

Taken direct from the television screen during an
interview about Reddish House.

M 6

Christmas Card : Reddish House with Snowfall

[1962]

Silver print photograph
13.0 × 12.9 cm
Inscribed in Beaton's hand : 'Happy Christmas 1962'
Sotheby's, London

M 7

*'In the Drawing Room of
Cecil Beaton's House in Wiltshire'*

[*c.* 1960]

Silver print photograph
19.2 × 19.0 cm
Private Collection

M 8

'Drawing Room of Cecil Beaton's Country House'

[*c.* 1960]

Silver print photograph
21.0 × 16.0 cm
Private Collection

M 9

Ronald Traeger

Cecil Beaton

[1965]

Silver print photograph
24.2 × 19.4 cm
Private Collection

Taken for British *Men in Vogue*, 1965.

Repr.: Australian *Vogue*, June/July 1968, p. 85

M 10

Lady Aberconway's Cat, Bodnant

[*c.* 1955]

Silver print photograph
20.9 × 20.0 cm
Sotheby's, London

Repr.: Cecil Beaton, *The Face of the World*, p. 119, with
the caption 'a favourite photograph'

M11, M12, M13, M14, M15, M16, M17

A Group of Seven Photographs of Wild Flowers

[*c.* 1960]

Silver print photographs
M11 25.5 × 20.0 cm
M12 25.0 × 20.0 cm
M13 25.0 × 20.0 cm
M14 25.0 × 20.0 cm
M15 25.1 × 20.3 cm
M16 25.1 × 19.5 cm
M17 25.2 × 20.0 cm
Sotheby's, London

From Beaton's series 'England in Spring, Wild Flowers'.
M13 was reproduced in 'Green Thoughts', his extended
essay on gardens in *The Face of the World*.

M28

M18

Daisies in Reddish House Garden

[*c.* 1960]

Modern print
15.2 × 14.6 cm
Sotheby's, London

M19

*Self-portrait with Beaton's Secretary,
Eileen Hose*

[*c.* 1958]

Silver print photograph
24.6 × 24.6 cm
Sotheby's, London

M20

*Self-portrait with Beaton's Gardener,
John Smallpeice*

[*c.* 1965]

Modern print
29.2 × 21.4 cm
Sotheby's, London
(illus. on p. 82)

M21

Greta Garbo

[1946]

Silver print photograph
40.0 × 49.0 cm
Sotheby's, London

This and the following photographs, M22 to M33, were
taken in New York in Beaton's suite at the Plaza Hotel,
and fourteen from this series were published in American
Vogue, July 1946.

M22, M23, M24

*A Group of Three Contact Sheets of
Greta Garbo, Plaza Hotel, New York*

[1946]

Silver print photographs
M22 24.6 × 19.7 cm
M23 25.5 × 19.8 cm
M24 25.6 × 20.4 cm
Sotheby's, London

M25

Greta Garbo, Plaza Hotel, New York

[1946]

Silver print photograph
35.0 × 28.8 cm
Private Collection

M26, M27, M28, M29
A Group of Four Portraits of
Greta Garbo in Pierrot Costume
[1946]
Silver print photographs
M26 29.3 × 25.5 cm
M27 27.6 × 22.3 cm
M28 30.5 × 25.2 cm
M29 27.0 × 26.4 cm
Sotheby's, London

M30, M31, M32
A Group of Three Portraits of
Greta Garbo, New York
[1946]
Silver print photographs
M30 27.6 × 25.1 cm
M31 28.3 × 24.7 cm
M32 26.6 × 16.8 cm
Sotheby's, London

M12

M33

Portrait of Greta Garbo, New York

[1946]

Silver print photograph, with pencil additions
24.6 × 26.3 cm
Sotheby's, London

M34

Garbo as Queen Christina

[1937]

Watercolour
34.0 × 62.0 cm
Hugo Vickers

Repr.: Cecil Beaton, *Cecil Beaton's Scrapbook*, p. 54

M35

Drawing of a Rose

[1950]

Pencil
27.9 × 24.0 cm
Signed and inscribed: 'Crimson/Rose/Friday/October
6th 1950'
Leslie Esterman

M36

Martin Battersby

Interior, Reddish

[c. 1950]

Oil on tin
30.6 × 23.0 cm
Private Collection

M37

Reddish House

[c. 1960]

Modern colour print from $2\frac{1}{4} \times 2\frac{1}{4}$ in transparency
20.3 × 20.3 cm
Sotheby's, London

M38

Douglas Glass

*Cecil Beaton in the Conservatory,
Reddish House*

[1958]

Modern colour print from a 10 × 8 in transparency
Sotheby's, London

M36

M39

John Smallpeice

A Map of Reddish House Garden

[1985]

Crayon, felt-tip and ink
56.0 × 78.5 cm
John Smallpeice
(illus. on p. 83)

M40

*A Group of Prize Cards for
Broadchalke Horticultural Society Show*

[1962–73]

Various sizes
John Smallpeice

Beaton's roses won first prize in the local horticultural
show on many occasions during the 1950s, '60s, and '70s.

M41

Cut Flowers, Reddish

[c. 1960]

Modern colour print from $2\frac{1}{4} \times 2\frac{1}{4}$ in transparency
20.3 × 20.3 cm
Sotheby's, London
(illus. on p. 136)

N1

HM Queen Elizabeth

[March 1942]

Silver print photograph
20.6 × 20.6 cm
Private Collection

Photographed at a charity sale of antique lace, London.

Repr.: British *Vogue*, April 1942, p. 24

N2

HM Queen Elizabeth

[1948]

Silver print photograph
24.5 × 19.5 cm
Private Collection

The backdrop was painted by Beaton's assistant Martin Battersby, while the black velvet ball gown was designed by Norman Hartnell.

Repr.: British *Vogue*, 1 November, 1949, in colour

N3

*HM King George VI with HRH Princess Elizabeth,
HRH Princess Margaret and HM Queen Elizabeth*

[1942]

Silver print photograph
25.3 × 19.8 cm
Private Collection

N4, N5

*A Pair of Photographs of the Royal Family,
Buckingham Palace*

[1942]

Silver print photographs
N4 19.0 × 18.8 cm
N5 18.9 × 14.4 cm
Private Collection

N6

*HRH Princess Elizabeth and
HRH Princess Margaret*

[1942]

Silver print photograph
18.2 × 14.3 cm
Private Collection

In his diary Beaton noted
'Together the Princesses reminded me of the beginning of my photographic career when I used to photograph Nancy and Baba as schoolchildren'.

Repr.: *The Lady*, 31 December 1942, cover

N7

HRH Princess Elizabeth

[1945]

Silver print photograph
29.4 × 24.0 cm
Private Collection

The wintery skating scene used as a backdrop was based on a picture by Rex Whistler.

N8

*HRH Princess Elizabeth in her Uniform
of Honorary Colonel of the Grenadier Guards*

[1942]

Silver print photograph
26.0 × 25.0 cm
Private Collection
(illus. on p. 54)

It was as Colonel of the Grenadier Guards, a title conferred upon Princess Elizabeth on her sixteenth birthday, that the Princess undertook one of her first public appointments.

Repr.: *Illustrated London News*, 26 December 1942, cover; *Girls' Own*, April 1943, cover (hand-tinted colour)

N9, N10, N11, N12

*A Group of Four Portraits of
HRH Princess Elizabeth*

[1945]

Silver print photographs
N9   24.2 × 19.0 cm
N10 24.4 × 17.9 cm
N11 24.2 × 19.0 cm
N12 24.2 × 19.0 cm
Private Collection

For these portraits HRH Princess Elizabeth wore a full evening dress of net embroidered with sequins, before one of Beaton's rococo photo-backdrops.

Repr.: *The Sketch*, 20 February 1946, cover;
Leader, 26 April 1947, cover;
Everybody's Weekly, 26 April 1947, p. 4

N13
HRH Princess Elizabeth and HRH Prince Charles

[December 1948]

Silver print photograph
25.0 × 19.9 cm
Private Collection

Because of concern for George VI's health, the first official photographs of Prince Charles, born on 14 November, were not taken until he was a month old, on 14 December 1948, the king's birthday.

N7

N14
HRH Prince Charles and HRH Princess Anne

[1950]

Silver print photograph
23.5 × 25.5 cm
Private Collection

First official photographs of Princess Anne taken a month after her birth at Clarence House on 15 August 1950.

N15
A Sheet of Twelve Contact Prints of HRH Princess Anne

[1950]

Silver print photograph
25.0 × 20.0 cm
Private Collection

N16, N17, N18, N19
A Group of Four Portraits of HRH Princess Margaret

[1949–1951]

Silver print photographs
N16 24.3 × 19.5 cm
N17 24.8 × 19.7 cm
N18 19.4 × 18.8 cm
N19 23.5 × 19.1 cm
Private Collection

N16 and N17 were taken as official portraits for Princess Margaret's nineteenth birthday.
N18 and N19 were taken as official portraits for her twenty-first birthday, 21 August 1951.

N19 repr.: British *Vogue*, September 1951, in colour

N20
Dr Fisher, Archbishop of Canterbury

[1953]

Silver print photograph
19.0 × 19.2 cm
Sotheby's, London

Repr.: British *Vogue*, June 1953, p. 107

N21
The Marquess of Cholmondeley, the Lord Great Chamberlain

[1953]

Silver print photograph
Inscribed: 'To Cecil from Rock . . . Lord Great Chamberlain 1953'
25.7 × 20.5 cm
Sotheby's, London

Repr.: British *Vogue*, May 1953

N22, N23
Patrick Matthews

Cecil Beaton Photographing the Royal Family,
Buckingham Palace, on Coronation Day

[1953]

Silver print photographs
N22 19.0 × 19.0 cm
N23 20.3 × 18.9 cm
Private Collection

N22 repr.: Cecil Beaton, *The Strenuous Years*, p. 200–1

N24

Princess Marie Louise of Denmark

[1953]

Silver print photograph
23.9 × 24.0 cm
Private Collection

Repr.: Cecil Beaton, *The Best of Beaton*, p. 178

N25

HRH Princess Anne, Coronation Day

[1953]

Silver print photograph
24.2 × 24.2 cm
Private Collection

N26

HRH Prince Charles and HM Queen Elizabeth,
the Queen Mother, Coronation Day

[1953]

Silver print photograph
22.2 × 19.2 cm
Private Collection

N27

HM Queen Elizabeth, the Queen Mother,
with HRH Prince Charles and HRH Princess Anne,
Coronation Day

[1953]

Silver print photograph
20.3 × 17.7 cm
Private Collection
(illus. on p. 57)

N28

HM Queen Elizabeth II, Coronation Day

[1953]

Silver print photograph
25.0 × 20.0 cm
Private Collection
(illus. on p. 57)

N29

HM Queen Elizabeth II, Coronation Day

[1953]

Silver print photograph
24.0 × 24.0 cm
Private Collection

N30

HM Queen Elizabeth II
Sovereign of the Most Noble Order
of the Garter

[1956]

Silver print photograph
24.2 × 18.5 cm
Private Collection

N9

Beaton's photograph shows Her Majesty wearing the habit and ensigns of the Order.

Repr.: *The Illustrated London News*, 23 June 1956, cover; British *Vogue*, July 1956, p. 53

N31

A Sheet of Nine Contact Prints of HRH Princess Alexandra

[1968]

Silver print photograph
19.0 × 20.0 cm
Private Collection

Repr.: *Daily Sketch*, 20 June 1968, pp. 12–13, with the caption 'How Beaton Puts the Magic into those Royal Pictures'

N32

HRH Princess Alexandra

[1959]

Silver print photograph
24.5 × 18.4 cm
Private Collection

N33

HRH Princess Marina of Kent

Portrait of Cecil Beaton

[1943]

Silver print photograph
50.0 × 37.0 cm
Signed and dated with monogram 'MK'
Private Collection

N34

Officers of the Lifeguards

[*c.* 1953]

Brush and ink
33.7 × 30.0 cm
Michael Parkin Fine Art Ltd

Exh.: Parkin Gallery, *Cecil Beaton and Friends*, 1985, cat. 82

N35

HM Queen Elizabeth II and her Photographer

[1955]

Modern colour print from 10 × 8 in transparency
25.4 × 20.3 cm
Private Collection

N36

The Coronation Procession

[1953]

Black wash
38.2 × 26.3 cm
Michael Parkin Fine Art Ltd

Exh.: Parkin Gallery, *Cecil Beaton and Friends*, cat. 82

N37

The Coronation: The Throne

[1953]

Black wash
21.3 × 13.5 cm
Michael Parkin Fine Art Ltd

N38

HRH Princess Margaret

[1949]

Modern colour print from 10 × 8 in transparency
16.0 × 11.5 cm
Private Collection

N39

HRH Princess Margaret

[1949]

Modern colour print from 10 × 8 in transparency
Private Collection
(illus. on p. 134)

N40

HM Queen Elizabeth

[1948]

Modern colour print from 10 × 8 in transparency
Private Collection
(illus. on p. 135)

01, 02, 03, 04

A Group of Four Self-portrait and Studio Photographs

[1951]

Silver print photographs
01 25.4 × 24.0 cm
02 25.3 × 20.3 cm
03 24.5 × 19.5 cm
04 24.5 × 19.5 cm
01, 02 Private Collection
03, 04 Sotheby's, London
(01 illus. on p. 63)

03 variant repr.: Cecil Beaton, *Photobiography*, book jacket
cover (tinted); used extensively for publicity purposes.

05

*Self-portrait in Fancy Dress
at the Beistegui Ball, Venice*

[1951]

Silver print photograph
20.7 × 15.5 cm
Sotheby's, London

The first major European fancy dress ball of the post-
Second World War era, the Beistegui Ball was fully
reported in *Picture Post*, 15 September 1951, pp. 13–15.
Beaton was photographed in his *curé*'s outfit.

06

Lady Diana Cooper at the Beistegui Ball, Venice

[1951]

Silver print photograph
26.5 × 24.3 cm
Sotheby's, London

Repr.: Cecil Beaton, *The Face of the World*, p. 164

07

*The Hon. Mrs Reginald Fellowes,
at the Beistegui Ball, Venice*

[1951]

Silver print photograph
28.0 × 21.0 cm
Sotheby's, London
(illus. on p. 56)

In the Palazzo Labia's Tiepolo room, Mrs Fellowes
represents 1750s America in a yellow costume by Dior.
James Caffery holds the parasol.

Repr.: American *Vogue*, 15 October 1951, pp. 94–5

08

*A Sheet of Twelve Contact Prints
of Judy Garland*

[January 1953]

Silver print photograph
25.5 × 19.5 cm
Sotheby's, London

09

Judy Garland

[1953]

Silver print photograph
10.4 × 19.5 cm
Sotheby's, London
(illus. on p. 117)

Taken shortly before the release of *A Star is Born*, 1954.

Repr.: British *Vogue*, September 1953, p. 126
Cecil Beaton and Kenneth Tynan, *Persona Grata*, pp. 44–5

010

Jacqueline and Caroline Bouvier

[1951]

Silver print photograph
25.3 × 20.3 cm
Private Collection

Repr.: American *Vogue*, 1 March 1951, p. 176

011

Yul Brynner

[1946]

Silver print photograph
24.9 × 20.0 cm
Sotheby's, London

014

012

Sugar Ray Robinson

[March 1953]

Silver print photograph
19.2 × 19.6 cm
Sotheby's, London

Beaton produced the cinematic lighting effect with a
paper cut-out.

Repr.: *The Best of Beaton*, p. 202

013

Francis Bacon

[*c.* 1955]

Silver print photograph
20.7 × 19.8 cm
Sotheby's, London

Bacon started work on a portrait of Beaton in November
1957, which continued until 1960. Beaton was shocked at
the final result and Bacon subsequently destroyed it
before Beaton could collect it.

Variant repr.: *The Face of the World*, p. 221

014

Colin Wilson

[1956]

Silver print photograph
19.7 × 19.5 cm
Sotheby's, London

Colin Wilson achieved almost overnight success with his
book *The Outsider*, 1956, which did much to popularize
Existentialism in Britain.

Variant repr.: *The Face of the World*, p. 224

015

*A Sheet of Twelve Contact Prints
of John Osborne*

[1957]

Silver print photograph
25.0 × 20.0 cm
Sotheby's, London

John Osborne's play *Look Back in Anger*, 1956, was
premièred in the same week as Colin Wilson's *The
Outsider*. Both attracted widespread press coverage and
the two men were pigeon-holed as members of a new
generation of 'angry young men'.

016

John Osborne

[1957]

011

Silver print photograph
24.7 × 24.7 cm
Sotheby's, London

Repr.: *The Face of the World*, p. 201

017, 018, 019, 020, 021

A Set of Contact Prints of Marilyn Monroe

[1956]

Silver print photographs
017 25.3 × 20.5 cm
018 25.6 × 20.7 cm
019 25.6 × 20.6 cm
020 25.6 × 20.3 cm
021 28.4 × 11.1 cm
Sotheby's, London

An account of the taking of this series of photographs is
given in Beaton's *The Face of the World*, pp. 183–8.

Repr.: *Harper's Bazaar*, September 1956

022

Marilyn Monroe

[1956]

Silver print photograph
27.1 × 25.5 cm
Sotheby's, London
(illus. on p. 58)

023

*Truman Capote, David Herbert, and
Paul and Jane Bowles in Tangiers*

[1949]

Silver print photograph
25.7 × 24.6 cm
Sotheby's, London

Repr.: British *Vogue*, February 1950, pp. 70–1

024

Ivy Compton-Burnett

[1949]

Silver print photograph
23.7 × 19.1 cm
Sotheby's, London

Repr.: British *Vogue*, September 1949, p. 87

025

Isak Dinesen, Baroness Blixen

[August 1962]

Silver print photograph
19.4 × 19.5 cm
Sotheby's, London

Beaton's macabre description of his visit to 'a beautiful
phantom' is given in *The Restless Years*, pp. 159–61.

Repr.: Cecil Beaton, *The Restless Years*, p. 157

026

Lady Mendl

[*c.* 1955]

Modern print
19.6 × 19.4 cm
Sotheby's, London

Repr.: *The Restless Years*, facing p. 24

027

Joan Crawford

[1956]

Silver print photograph
24.5 × 23.5 cm

Sotheby's, London

Repr.: *The Face of the World*, p. 190, top right

028

Augustus John

[*c.* 1955]

Silver print photograph
24.1 × 24.0 cm
Sotheby's, London

Probably taken during Beaton's visit to Augustus John in
1960, described by him in *The Restless Years*, part VI.

029

*A Sheet of Six Contact Prints
of Sir Winston Churchill*

[*c.* 1957]

Silver print photograph
18.4 × 28.8 cm
Sotheby's, London

For a description of this sitting see 'Statesman at Home',
The Face of the World, p. 129.

027

028

030
Mae Murray
[1962]
Silver print photograph
25.1 × 20.1 cm
Sotheby's, London

Taken for Beaton's book *Quail in Aspic*.

Variant repr.: *Quail in Aspic*, facing p. 80, top, with the caption 'My Dear Mother in Paris'

031
Elsa Maxwell
[1962]
Silver print photograph
25.0 × 19.7 cm
Sotheby's, London

Taken for Beaton's book *Quail in Aspic*, but not used.

032
Louise Dahl-Wolfe
Cecil Beaton and his Mother
[*c.* 1955]
Silver print photograph
27.2 × 26.2 cm
Sotheby's, London

033
Douglas Glass
Cecil Beaton, Slade School of Art,
University of London
[*c.* 1958]
Silver print photograph
20.1 × 25.6 cm
Sotheby's, London

Beaton had earlier enrolled at the Slade in the autumn of 1953, see *Illustrated*, 5 December 1953, pp. 19–21.

Repr.: 'When a Celebrity Goes Back to School', *The Sunday Times*, 9 November 1958

034
Joan Crawford
[1956]
Modern colour print from $2\frac{1}{4} \times 2\frac{1}{4}$ in transparency
25.4 × 25.4 cm
Sotheby's, London

035
Self-portrait as Curé for Beistegui Ball
[1951]
Pencil and watercolour
Signed and dated
16.7 × 21.5 cm
Leslie Esterman

036, 037
Marilyn Monroe
[1956]
Two modern colour prints from $2\frac{1}{4} \times 2\frac{1}{4}$ in transparencies
Both 25.4 × 25.4 cm
Private Collection

038
Derek Hill
[*c.* 1950]
Oil on canvas
40.0 × 52.0 cm
Private Collection

Exh.: Parkin Gallery, *Cecil Beaton and Friends*, 1985, cat. 90a

P I

Paul Tanqueray

Cecil Beaton Working on the Set for 'Quadrille'

[1952]

Silver print photograph
16.7 × 20.0 cm
Sotheby's, London

Beaton's designs for *Quadrille* in September 1952 complemented Noël Coward's romantic comedy, set in the then much revived 1880s period. See Cecil Beaton's *Cuttings Book*, vol. XXXXI.

Variant repr.: *Theatre Arts*, November 1954, p. 21

P2, P3, P4

A Group of Three Silhouette Photographs for 'The Gainsborough Girls'

[1951]

Silver print photographs
All 24.5 × 24.5 cm
Sotheby's, London

P2

Beaton's fraught diary entries during the production of his play, *The Gainsborough Girls*, are published as 'problems of playwright' in Cecil Beaton, *The Strenuous Years*, pp. 79–88.

P5

'The Gainsborough Girls'

[1951]

Silver print photograph
23.7 × 20.9 cm
Sotheby's, London

P6

'The Gainsborough Girls'

[1951]

Silver print photograph
20.5 × 14.4 cm
Sotheby's, London

The pose and costume of Gainsborough's daughter, Mary, in Beaton's play are based on Gainsborough's painting, *The Blue Boy*.

P7

Scene from 'The Gainsborough Girls'

[1951]

Silver print photograph
25.5 × 20.5 cm
Sotheby's, London

Muriel Pavlow and Josephine Stuart in the roles of Gainsborough's daughters, arriving at their new house.

Repr.: British *Vogue*, August 1951 (see Cecil Beaton's *Cuttings Book*, vol. XXXI)

P8

'The School for Scandal'

[1962]

Modern print
19.8 × 19.1 cm
Sotheby's, London

A scene from the Comédie Française production which Beaton designed.

P7

[225]

P9

*A Sheet of Twelve Contact Prints
from 'Look After Lulu'*

[1959]

Modern print
25.5 × 20.5 cm
Sotheby's, London

A series in imitation of the Art Nouveau dancer, Löie
Fuller.

Variant repr.: Charles Spencer, *Cecil Beaton: Stage and
Film Designs*, 1975, p. 56

P10

'Look After Lulu'

[1959]

Silver print photograph
25.0 × 19.3 cm
Private Collection

P11

'Look After Lulu'

[1959]

Silver print photograph
11.0 × 25.5 cm
Sotheby's, London

P12

'Look After Lulu'

[1959]

Silver print photograph
25.5 × 20.5 cm
Sotheby's, London

P13

John Bulmer

Cecil Beaton Designs for the Comédie Française

[1962]

Silver print photograph
25.6 × 17.4 cm
Sotheby's, London

Repr.: *The Sunday Times*, 6 May 1962

P14

*A Sheet of Twelve Contact Prints
from 'La Traviata'*

[1966]

Silver print photograph
25.4 × 20.5 cm
Sotheby's, London

P15

*'On a Clear Day You Can See Forever':
Barbra Streisand at the Brighton Pavilion*

[1969]

Silver print photograph
20.1 × 26.0 cm
Sotheby's, London

P15

P16

Unknown photographer

*Cecil Beaton During the Filming of
'On a Clear Day You Can See Forever'*

[1969]

Silver print photograph
21.0 × 25.0 cm
Sotheby's, London

P17

*Two Knights: Costume designs for Sir Frederick
Ashton's Ballet, 'Picnic at Tintagel'*

[1952]

Watercolour
35.6 × 24.1 cm
Michael Parkin Fine Art Ltd

Exh.: Parkin Gallery, *Cecil Beaton and Friends*, 1985,
cat. 22

P18, P19

*Two Scenes from
'The Importance of Being Earnest'*

[1960]

Watercolours
P18 58.5 × 44.0 cm
P19 61.0 × 47.0 cm
Leslie Esterman

Repr.: Oscar Wilde, *The Importance of Being Earnest*, Folio
Society (limited edn.), 1960, P18 facing p. 56; P19 facing
'First Act'

P20

Set for 'The Gainsborough Girls'

[c. 1953]

Watercolour
22.7 × 35.5 cm
Signed in pencil
Leslie Esterman

P21

*Harem Costume Design for
'The Truth About Women'*

[c. 1965]

Pen, ink and watercolour
34.0 × 23.0 cm
Inscribed: 'Harem scene / Pervenche Blue Voile
Embossed with/
Claret coloured velvet crescents/ Pale Green and white.
Stripe muslin paints/, Grape velvet over braid ceinture/
stripe pink voile turban'
Roy Astley

P10

P22

*Birgit Nillson's Costume, Fan and Headpiece
for the title role as Princess Turandot, 'Turandot'*

[1961]

With additional performance photographs
The Metropolitan Opera, New York
(illus. on p. 105)

P23

Two Costumes for the Chorus, 'La Traviata'

[1966]

The Metropolitan Opera, New York

P24

*Anna Moffo's Costume for the Title Role
as Violetta, 'La Traviata'*

[1966]

The Metropolitan Opera, New York

P25
Flower Fabric Design
[1958]
Gouache
56.0 × 47.5 cm
Paul Walter, New York

P25 and P26 were forays by Beaton into fabric design for
the British Sekers Company in the late 1950s.

P26
Sekers Flower Designs
[1958]
Gouache
58.8 × 46.0 cm
Signed
Leslie Esterman

See Cecil Beaton's *Cuttings Book*, vol. XLV.

P27
*Costume Design for
Katharine Hepburn in 'Coco', Act II Scene 2*
[1969]
Pencil and watercolour
36.8 × 27.4 cm
Signed in ink
Roy Astley

P28
*Design Detail from Set,
'The School for Scandal', Comédie Française
Production*
[1962]
Pen, ink, wash and chalk
20.2 × 22.3 cm
Roy Astley

P29
Margot Fonteyn in 'Marguerite and Armand'
[1963]
Brush and ink
46.6 × 32.6 cm
Signed
Roy Astley

P30
Preparatory Drawings for 'The Gainsborough Girls'
[1951]
Crayon
43.8 × 29.0 cm
Signed in ink
Roy Astley

P31
An Imaginary Theatre Set
[*c.* 1950]
Gouache
33.0 × 41.5 cm
Private Collection

P32, P33, P34, P35
Four Designs, 'La Traviata'
[1966]
All watercolour on photographic paper
P32   Act III no. 26   35.3 × 27.7 cm
P33   Act III no. 17   35.4 × 27.0 cm
P34   Act III no. 11   29.0 × 24.0 cm
P35   Act III no. 1   35.4 × 27.0 cm
Private Collection

P36
Costume Design, 'Quadrille'
[1952]
Pen, ink and watercolour, with fabric additions
36.0 × 27.0 cm
Roy Astley

P37
Margot Fonteyn in 'Marguerite and Armand'
[1963]
Watercolour
38.3 × 26.7 cm
Roy Astley

P38
Rudolf Nureyev in 'Marguerite and Armand'
[1963]
Watercolour
27.5 × 33.5 cm
Signed by Rudolf Nureyev
Roy Astley

P35

P34

P39
King Mark : Costume Design for Sir Frederick Ashton's ballet 'Picnic at Tintagel'

[1952]

Watercolour
24.1 × 15.9 cm
Michael Parkin Fine Art Ltd

Exh.: Parkin Gallery, *Cecil Beaton and Friends*, 1985, cat. 21

P40
Lillie Langtry

[1954]

Watercolour
27.5 × 40.0 cm
Signed
Leslie Esterman

Repr.: Cecil Beaton, *The Glass of Fashion*, p. 149 as 'The Jersey Lily'

P41
Set Design for 'Look After Lulu', Act 1

[1959]

Modern colour print from 10 × 8 in transparency
Private Collection
(illus. on p. 130)

P42
Costumes for 'La Traviata'

[1966]

Modern colour print from $2\frac{1}{4} \times 2\frac{1}{4}$ in transparency
25.4 × 25.4 cm
Private Collection
(illus. on p. 124)

Repr.: American *Vogue*, September 1966

[229]

GIGI

Q1

Howard Parker

*Cecil Beaton in Paris
during the Production of 'Gigi'*

[1957]

Silver print photograph
30.9 × 21.4 cm
Sotheby's, London

Beaton describes his labours on Vincente Minelli's film
'Gigi' in Paris, 1957, in *The Restless Years*,
Part IV, pp. 69–75. See also Beaton's article 'Gigi, the
Camera and I', *The Sunday Times*, 8 February 1959, p. 11.

Q2

Set for 'Gigi'

[1957]

Silver print photograph
19.4 × 9.2 cm
Sotheby's, London

Aunt Alicia's apartment.

Q3

*Still from 'Gigi' :
Leslie Caron and Hermione Gingold*

[1957]

Silver print photograph
25.5 × 19.7 cm
Sotheby's, London

This scene shows one of Gigi's lessons in domestic
etiquette.

Q4

Leslie Caron during the Production of 'Gigi'

[1957]

Silver print photograph
25.5 × 20.6 cm
Sotheby's, London

Q5

Leslie Caron during the Production of 'Gigi'

[1957]

Silver print photograph
19.6 × 17.0 cm
Sotheby's, London

Q6

Leslie Caron in the Studio Back Lot, 'Gigi'

[1957]

Silver print photograph
25.5 × 21.4 cm
Sotheby's, London

Q7

Still from 'Gigi' : The Beach at Trouville

[1957]

Silver print photograph
25.5 × 20.5 cm
Sotheby's, London

Q8

*Still from 'Gigi' :
Eva Gabor at Le Palais de Glace*

[1957]

Silver print photograph
30.0 × 28.0 cm
Sotheby's, London

Q9

*Still from 'Gigi' : Demi-mondaine and
the Battle of Flowers*

[1957]

Silver print photograph
25.2 × 21.5 cm
Private Collection

The Battle of Flowers in Nice was restaged by Beaton in
the Bois de Boulogne in August 1957;
see *The Restless Years*, pp. 71–2.

Repr.: French *Vogue*, Fevrier 1958, p. 100

[231]

Q10

Still from 'Gigi': the Battle of Flowers

[1957]

Silver print photograph
25.6 × 24.8 cm
Sotheby's, London

Q11

Still from 'Gigi':
Lady in the Bois de Boulogne

[1957]

Silver print photograph
28.4 × 27.8 cm
Sotheby's, London

Repr.: French *Vogue*, Fevrier 1958, p. 101, bottom right

Q12

Still from 'Gigi':
Demi-mondaine in the Bois de Boulogne

[1957]

Silver print photograph
28.8 × 28.0 cm
Sotheby's, London

Q13

Leslie Caron during the Production of 'Gigi'

[1957]

Silver print photograph
29.5 × 28.0 cm
Sotheby's, London
(illus. on p. 58)

Q12

Q17

Q14, Q15
*A Pair of Photographs of Leslie Caron
in the Role of Gigi*

[1957]

Silver print photographs
Q14 18.8 × 15.8 cm
Q15 21.0 × 14.3 cm
Sotheby's, London

Caron is posed with a column in a deliberate pastiche of
the *fin-de-siècle* studio photograph.

Q16, Q17
*A Pair of Stills from 'Gigi':
'In the pretty postcard style, 1900'*

[1958]

Silver print photographs
Q16 25.4 × 24.8 cm
Q17 25.4 × 24.9 cm
Private Collection

Repr.: 'Pretty Postcards', *Popular Photography*, 1958,
p. 28, top;
Cecil Beaton, *Cuttings Book*, vol. XLV

Q18
Girl with a Tennis Racquet, 'Gigi'

[1958]

Watercolour
27.9 × 21.6 cm
Private Collection

Exh.: Parkin Gallery, *Cecil Beaton*, 1976, cat. 96

[233]

R 1

Self-portrait with Ascot Ladies, 'My Fair Lady'
(New York Stage Version)

[1956]

Silver print photograph
21.0 × 25.6 cm
Sotheby's, London

Variant repr.: British *Vogue*, May 1956, pp. 54–5;
Cecil Beaton, *The Face of the World*, p. 136, top right

R 2

Julie Andrews in 'My Fair Lady'
(New York Stage Version)

[1956]

Silver print photograph
19.0 × 19.4 cm
Sotheby's, London

Variant repr.: *Theatre Arts*, March 1956, cover

R 3

Publicity Shot, Covent Garden, 'My Fair Lady'
(London Stage Version)

[1956]

Silver print photograph
22.6 × 24.2 cm
Sotheby's, London

Variant repr.: *Harper's Bazaar*, March 1956, p. 184

R 4

Unknown photographer

Cecil Beaton Designing 'My Fair Lady'
(Film Version)

[1963]

Silver print photograph
19.0 × 24.1 cm
Sotheby's, London

R 5, R 6

Two Sheets of Twenty-Four Contact Prints
'My Fair Lady' (Film Version)

[1963]

R8

Silver print photographs
25.6 × 20.4 cm
Sotheby's, London

R 7

Gowns for the Embassy Ball, 'My Fair Lady'
(Film Version)

[1963]

Silver print photograph
35.6 × 27.6 cm
Private Collection

R 8, R 9

A Pair of Photographs of Ascot Dresses
'My Fair Lady' (Film Version)

[1963]

Silver print photographs
R8 26.0 × 26.0 cm
R9 26.1 × 26.1 cm
Private Collection

R8 repr.: Cecil Beaton, *The Best of Beaton*, p. 192

R10

Hats for 'My Fair Lady'
(Film Version)

[1963]

Silver print photograph
24.2 × 18.9 cm
Private Collection

Variant repr.: Cecil Beaton, *Cecil Beaton's 'Fair Lady'*,
facing p. 65, top right

R11

Ascot Hat for 'My Fair Lady'
(Film Version)

[1963]

Silver print photograph
28.5 × 27.5 cm
Private Collection

R12

Audrey Hepburn in 'My Fair Lady'
(Film Version)

[1963]

Silver print photograph
34.5 × 29.0 cm
Private Collection

R13

Audrey Hepburn in Extra Girl's Ascot Dress, 'My
Fair Lady' (Film Version)

[1963]

Silver print photograph
34.3 × 25.5 cm
Private Collection

R14

Audrey Hepburn in 'My Fair Lady'
(Film Version)

[1963]

Silver print photograph
25.6 × 20.6 cm
Sotheby's, London

R15

Audrey Hepburn in 'My Fair Lady'
(Film Version)

[1963]

Silver print photograph
28.0 × 13.0 cm
Sotheby's, London

R16

Audrey Hepburn in 'My Fair Lady'
(Film Version)

[1963]

Silver print photograph, mounted on card
24.1 × 23.9 cm
Sotheby's, London

Repr.: *The Best of Beaton*, p. 197

R17

Audrey Hepburn in 'My Fair Lady'
(Film Version)

[1963]

Silver print photograph
25.5 × 20.4 cm
Sotheby's, London

R13

R17

R18

Bob Willoughby

Cecil Beaton Photographing Audrey Hepburn in 'My Fair Lady' (Film Version)

[1963]

Modern print
22.8 × 33.9 cm
Bob Willoughby

R19

Unknown photographer

Cecil Beaton with Audrey Hepburn, 'My Fair Lady' (Film Version)

[1963]

Silver print photograph
25.5 × 19.5 cm
Sotheby's, London
(illus. on p. 59)

R20

Unknown photographer

Cecil Beaton on the Set of 'My Fair Lady' (Film Version)

[1963]

Silver print photograph
25.4 × 20.6 cm
Sotheby's, London

R21

Audrey Hepburn's Ascot Costume, 'My Fair Lady' (Film Version)

[1963]

Barbican Art Gallery
Reproduction by Glyndebourne Opera Workshop, 1986.

R22

Four Ascot Gavotte Costumes, 'My Fair Lady' (Film Version)

[1963]

Barbican Art Gallery
Reproduction by Glyndebourne Opera Workshop, 1986.

R23

Costume for Dancer in Ascot Gavotte, 'My Fair Lady' (Film Version)

[1963]

Watercolour
68.0 × 50.0 cm
Hugo Vickers

R24

Summer Dress for Heather Firbank

[1963]

Modern colour print from 10 × 8 in transparency
Private Collection

Immediately before beginning his work on *My Fair Lady* in Hollywood, Beaton photographed his favourite costumes from the new Costume Court at the Victoria and Albert Museum, London.

Repr.: 'Beaton's Choice', *The Sunday Times*, 17 June 1963, p. 22

R25

Eliza's Ball Dress

[1958]

Watercolour
31.8 × 19.0 cm
Michael Parkin Fine Art Ltd

Exh.: Parkin Gallery, *Cecil Beaton Memorial Exhibition*, 1983, cat. 170

R26

Costume Sketch for 'My Fair Lady' (Film Version)

[1963]

Watercolour
45.5 × 26.8 cm
Signed
Leslie Esterman

R27

Edwardian Garden Party

[1954]

Brush and ink
33.2 × 51.0 cm
Signed
Leslie Esterman

Repr.: Cecil Beaton, *The Glass of Fashion*, p. 10

R28

Costume Design for Embassy Ball Scene, 'My Fair Lady' (Film Version)

[1963]

Watercolour over xerox
36.0 × 21.5 cm
Inscribed: 'Fitter/Lucia'
Roy Astley

R29
Costume Design for 'My Fair Lady'
(probably New York Stage Version)
[1956]
Brush and ink
35.0 × 27.5 cm
Signed in ink
Roy Astley

R30
Costume Design: Cockney Dancer, Covent Garden,
'My Fair Lady' (Film Version)
[1963]
Watercolour
34.7 × 12.5 cm
Private Collection

R31
Audrey Hepburn in the Ascot Gown,
'My Fair Lady' (Film Version)
[1963]
Modern colour print from a 10 × 8 in transparency
Sotheby's, London
Variant repr.: *The Weekend Telegraph*, 25 September 1964,
p. 36

R32
A Lady of Fashion
[c. 1953]
Brush and wash
36.0 × 13.5 cm
Private Collection
Repr.: *The Glass of Fashion*, p. 113

R32

R30

$\backsim$ S $\backsim$

THE SIXTIES

S1

Unknown photographer

*Cecil Beaton Leaving 8 Pelham Place
to receive his CBE at Buckingham Palace*

[1957]

Silver print photograph
25.0 × 19.8 cm
Sotheby's, London

Repr.: *Daily Express*, 27 March 1957

S2

Albert Finney

[1 June 1961]

Silver print photograph
20.2 × 19.4 cm
Sotheby's, London

Variant repr.: Cecil Beaton, *The Best of Beaton*, p. 237

S3

Diana Vreeland

[January 1973]

Silver print photograph
27.6 × 26.9 cm
Private Collection

S4

Rudolph Nureyev

[1963]

Silver print photograph
24.0 × 19.2 cm
Sotheby's, London

S5

Kin Hoitsma

[*c.* 1964]

Silver print photograph
34.2 × 28.0 cm
Sotheby's, London

S6

David Warner

[January 1965]

Silver print photograph
29.6 × 20.3 cm
Sotheby's, London
(illus. on p. 60)

Beaton used this photograph as a starting point for a painting which was exhibited at the Lefevre Gallery, London, in January 1966. See *The Weekend Telegraph*, 14 January 1966, illus. p. 29.

Repr.: *The Best of Beaton*, p. 240

S7

The Walker Brothers

[January 1966]

Silver print photograph
30.5 × 25.5 cm
Sotheby's, London

Formed in 1964, the Walker Brothers enjoyed their greatest success in 1965 with the world-wide hit record *Make it Easy on Yourself*.

S4

s8

*London Youth: Julian, Jane and Victoria
Ormsby-Gore*

[1965]

Silver print photograph
22.4 × 22.2 cm
Sotheby's, London

Repr.: *The Best of Beaton*, 1968, p. 240;
See Cecil Beaton, *The Parting Years*, pp. 53–4

s9

*Brian Jones, Keith Richard and Mick Jagger
of The Rolling Stones, Marrakesh*

[March 1967]

Silver print photograph
22.0 × 24.0 cm
Private Collection

See *The Parting Years*, pp. 43–6.

s10

Lord Goodman

[20 September 1968]

Silver print photograph
22.6 × 17.8 cm
Sotheby's, London
(illus. on p. 27)

Lord Goodman was one of several new sitters Beaton
photographed for possible inclusion in
The Best of Beaton.

s11

HM Queen Elizabeth II; contact sheet

[1968]

Silver print photograph
18.8 × 25.8 cm
Private Collection

Photographs taken for inclusion in the 1968
National Portrait Gallery exhibition.
Beaton photographed the Queen on 16 October;
she wore a navy blue serge Admiral's cloak.

s12

Prince Charles at Buckingham Palace

[1968]

Silver print photograph
24.0 × 23.8 cm
Private Collection

s13

Patrick Lichfield

*Cecil Beaton at his Retrospective Exhibition
at the National Portrait Gallery, London*

[1968]

Silver print photograph
30.7 × 26.0 cm
Sotheby's, London

s14

*Self-portrait with Mick Jagger
on the Set of 'Performance'*

[November 1968]

Silver print photograph
24.0 × 24.0 cm
Sotheby's, London

s11

s15

Mick Jagger on the Set of 'Performance' ;
contact sheet

[1968]

Silver print photograph
25.6 × 20.5 cm
Sotheby's, London
(illus. on p. 60)

s16

James Fox on the Set of 'Performance'

[1968]

Silver print photograph
24.3 × 24.4 cm
Sotheby's, London

s17

Barry Humphries

[1968]

Silver print photograph
23.0 × 33.5 cm
Sotheby's, London

s18

Gervase

[1968]

Silver print photograph
25.5 × 20.7 cm
Sotheby's, London

Gervase, a minor pop singer of the 1960s, first appeared
in Beaton's fashion photograph series 'The Great
Indoors', and was subsequently photographed at
Reddish.

s19

Christopher Gibbs and Marianne Faithfull

[June 1968]

Silver print photograph
24.0 × 24.3 cm
Sotheby's, London

See *The Parting Years*, pp. 50–4.

s20

The Myers Twins (Dennis and John Myers)

[1968]

Silver print photograph
28.8 × 23.5 cm
Sotheby's, London

Variant repr.: 'The Great Indoors',
British *Vogue*, December 1968

s21

The Myers Twins : Double Portrait in a Mirror

[1968]

Silver print photograph
29.3 × 20.0 cm
Sotheby's, London

s22

Patrick Procktor

[Late 1968]

Colour photograph
19.7 × 20.4 cm
Sotheby's, London

s23

Gervase as Narcissus in the
Conservtory at Reddish

[1968]

Silver print photograph
16.7 × 24.2 cm
Sotheby's, London
(illus. on p. 13)

s24

Unknown photographer

Cecil Beaton photographing
Katharine Hepburn for 'Coco'

[1969]

Silver print photograph
20.8 × 22.5 cm
Sotheby's, London

s25

Lord Harewood

[15 October 1968]

Silver print photograph
17.7 × 25.3 cm
Sotheby's, London

s26

Unknown photographer

Cecil Beaton outside Buckingham Palace

[Late 1960s]

Silver print photograph
20.1 × 25.5 cm
Sotheby's, London

827
David Warner
[*c.* 1967]
Modern colour print from $2\frac{1}{4} \times 2\frac{1}{4}$ in transparency
25.4 × 25.4 cm
Private Collection
Variant repr.: *The Best of Beaton*, p. 245

828
Derek Hill
Portrait of Cecil Beaton
[1960s]
Oil on canvas
43.8 × 48.9 cm
Signed with initials
Mr David Clark
Exh.: Parkin Gallery, *Cecil Beaton and Friends*, 1985,
cat. 116

829
Patrick Procktor
Reddish House
[*c.* 1968]
Watercolour
11.4 × 16.5 cm
Signed
Private Collection
Exh.: Parkin Gallery, *Cecil Beaton and Friends*, 1985,
cat. 138

830
Joe Louis
[1965]
Oil on canvas
54.6 × 34.3 cm
Private Collection
Exh.: Parkin Gallery, *Cecil Beaton and Friends*, 1985,
cat. 90

831
John Vassall
[1966]
Oil on canvas
55.0 × 34.0 cm
Private Collection

832
Violet Trefusis in Later Life
[*c.* 1960]

Pencil and wash
49.3 × 34.3 cm
Private Collection
(illus. on p. 94)
Exh.: Parkin Gallery, *Cecil Beaton Memorial Exhibition*,
1983, cat. 28

833
*Self-portrait with Mick Jagger
and Anita Pallenberg*
[1968]
Modern colour print from a $2\frac{1}{4} \times 2\frac{1}{4}$ in transparency
20.3 × 20.3 cm
Sotheby's, London

834
Mick Jagger on the Set of 'Performance'
[1968]
Modern colour print from a $2\frac{1}{4} \times 2\frac{1}{4}$ in transparency
25.4 × 25.4 cm
Sotheby's, London
(illus. on p. 129)

835–38
*'An Impromptu Revue Produced and Photographed
by Cecil Beaton': Fashion by Belville et Cie,
Ronald Paterson and Mary Quant*
[1962]

The following four images were taken for a montage
tableau and include Adam Faith, Shirley Anne Field, the
Hon. Chairmain Montagu-Douglas-Scott, and from
Beyond the Fringe Jonathan Miller, Alan Bennett, Peter
Cook and Dudley Moore as well as a back view of Beaton.
Repr.: American *Vogue*, 15 March 1962, pp. 78–9

835
Adam Faith and Shirley Anne Field
Contact sheet from $2\frac{1}{4} \times 2\frac{1}{4}$ in negatives
25.3 × 20.4 cm
Sotheby's, London

836
Shirley Anne Field and the Cast of 'Beyond the Fringe'
Contact sheet from $2\frac{1}{4} \times 2\frac{1}{4}$ in negatives
25.3 × 20.4 cm
Sotheby's, London

837
*Jonathan Miller with Shirley Anne Field in
White Organdie Dress with Black Polka Dots
by Belville et Cie*
Silver print photograph
30.4 × 25.5 cm
Sotheby's, London

s38
Shirley Anne Field with the cast of 'Beyond the Fringe'
Silver print photograph
30.4 × 25.5 cm
Sotheby's, London

s39–42
Jean Shrimpton
[1964]
These photographs were all taken for use in the June 1964 issue of British *Vogue*, and for the cover. Although four pages in the magazine featured Beaton's Shrimpton photographs, the cover was taken by David Bailey.

s39
Contact sheet of seven poses from 2¼ × 2¼ in negatives
25.4 × 20.4 cm; irregular
Sotheby's, London
Unpublished photograph for British *Vogue*, June 1964

s40
Contact sheet of twelve poses from 2¼ × 2¼ in negatives
25.4 × 20.4 cm
Sotheby's, London

Variant repr.: British *Vogue*, June 1964, p. 43

Beaton's image of Shrimpton, seen here wearing pure white make-up and a white wig, is a deliberate recreation in the style of Chéret, the French poster artist of the 1890s.

s41
Modern print
25.4 × 20.4 cm
Sotheby's, London

Variant repr.: British *Vogue*, June 1964, p. 45

s42
Modern print from 2¼ × 2¼ in colour transparency
Sotheby's, London
(s42 illus. on p. 126)

s43
*Picnic Fashion Group Including the Models
Jean Shrimpton and Ceila Hammond*
[1965]
Silver print photograph
30.3 × 35.7 cm
Sotheby's, London

Here Beaton recreates the idyllic picnic scenes of Ashcombe in the context of the 1960s.

Repr.: British *Vogue*, July 1965, p. 50–1

s44–5
Beaton and the Baroness
[1966]

Baroness Fiona Thyssen, formerly Fiona Campbell-Walter, returned to fashion modelling in 1966. These photographs were taken in the sumptuous flat of Roger Vivier in the Quai d'Orsay, Paris.

Repr.: *The Weekend Telegraph*, 2 September 1966

s44
With Two Borzoi
Modern colour print from 2¼ × 2¼ in transparency
Sotheby's, London

s45
Fashion by Marc Bohan of Dior
Modern colour print from a 2¼ × 2¼ in transparency
Sotheby's, London

s46–7
*The Great Indoors: Afghanistan in SW10
at Christopher Gibbs's Flat*
[1968]

s46
*The Great Indoors:
Maudie James and the Myers Twins*
Modern colour print from a 2¼ × 2¼ in transparency
Sotheby's, London
(illus. on p. 128)

Repr.: British *Vogue*, December 1968, pp. 90–1

s47
'A Houri Dances in David Hockney's flat'
Silver print photograph
30.4 × 38.2 cm
Condé Nast Publications (British *Vogue*)

Peter Schlesinger is seated on the left; the model is Maudie James.

Repr.: British *Vogue*, December 1968, p. 92

s48
Mick Jagger Taken from a Television Screen
[6 April 1967]
Modern print
23.9 × 24.5 cm
Private Collection

'Archaic are the paralytic transports of Mick Jagger', wrote Beaton of Jagger's television performances ('Telereactions', British *Vogue*, January 1967, pp. 15–16). Beaton also made drawings of Jagger, Harold Wilson, David Warner and other figures of the 'Swinging Sixties' from the television screen.
Other negatives from this series, taken the day before Beaton first photographed Jagger, show Jimi Hendrix.

LATE WORK OF THE SEVENTIES

T I

HM Queen Elizabeth, The Queen Mother

[1970]

Silver print photograph
23.9 × 24.1 cm
Private Collection

T 2

Andy Warhol and Candy Darling

[1969]

Silver print photograph
24.6 × 24.5 cm
Sotheby's, London

T 3

Self-portrait in a Mirror with Viva, New York

[January 1970]

Silver print photograph
20.8 × 25.8 cm
Sotheby's, London

T 4

Gilbert and George

[1974]

Silver print photograph
24.1 × 16.1 cm
Sotheby's, London

T 5

*Elizabeth Taylor as Ida Rubinstein
for the Rothschild 'Proust Ball'*

[1971]

Silver print photograph
22.6 × 20.0 cm
Sotheby's, London

For Cecil Beaton's report on the Rothschild costume ball,
see 'Remembrance of Things Proust', British *Vogue*,
February 1972.

T5

T 6

Liliane de Rothschild

*Cecil Beaton as the Photographer Nadar,
for the Rothschild 'Proust Ball'*

[1971]

Silver print photograph
24.0 × 20.0 cm
Private Collection
(illus. on p. 20)

Repr.: British *Vogue*, February 1972, p. 79

T7

*Marisa Berenson as the Marchesa Casati
for the Rothschild 'Proust Ball'*

[1971]

Silver print photograph
31.0 × 24.6 cm
Sotheby's, London

Repr.: British *Vogue*, February 1972, p. 78

T8

Salvador Dali

[January 1973]

Silver print photograph
25.2 × 19.8 cm
Sotheby's, London

T9, T10

*A Pair of Photographs of
the Hon. Stephen Tennant*

[1971]

Silver print photographs
Both 24.2 × 24.2 cm
Sotheby's, London

Taken on a visit to Wilsford with David Hockney.

T11

Chinoiserie (Tina Chow)

[1973]

Silver print photograph
40.9 × 50.6 cm
Condé Nast Publications (British *Vogue*)

Repr.: British *Vogue*, 15 April 1973, pp. 76–7

T12

*Dayle Haddon modelling
Givenchy Dress*

[1979]

Modern copy print
Sotheby's, London

Repr.: French *Vogue*, March 1979, p. 256

T13

Outfit by Torrente

[1979]

Modern copy print
Sotheby's, London

Repr.: French *Vogue*, March 1979, p. 283

T2

BIBLIOGRAPHY OF CECIL BEATON'S WORKS

CECIL BEATON'S BOOKS

The Book of Beauty (Duckworth, London, 1930)
Cecil Beaton's Scrapbook (Batsford, London, 1937)
Cecil Beaton's New York (Batsford, London, 1938);
    revised, second edition, *Portrait of New York*
    (Batsford, London, 1948)
My Royal Past (Batsford, London, 1939;
    republished by Weidenfeld & Nicolson, London, 1960)
History Under Fire with James Pope-Hennessy
    (Batsford, London, 1941)
Time Exposure with Peter Quennell
    (Batsford, London, 1941; revised edition, 1946)
Air of Glory (HMSO, London, 1941)
Winged Squadrons (Hutchinson, London, 1942)
Near East (Batsford, London, 1943)
British Photographers (Collins, London, 1944)
Far East (Batsford, London, 1945)
Cecil Beaton's Indian Album (Batsford, London, 1945–6)
Cecil Beaton's Chinese Album (Batsford, London, 1945–6)
India (Thacker & Co., Bombay, 1945)
Ashcombe (Batsford, London, 1949)
Photobiography (Odhams, London, 1951; also published
    in America by Doubleday, New York, 1951)
Ballet (Wingate, London, 1951)
Persona Grata, with Kenneth Tynan
    (Wingate, London, 1953)
The Glass of Fashion (Weidenfeld & Nicolson, London,
    1954; also published in America by Doubleday,
    New York, 1954; in France as *Cinquante Ans d'Elégances
    et d'Art de Vivre*,
    Amiot-Dumont, Paris, 1954;
    and in Japan by Kern Associates, Tokyo, 1954)
It Gives me Great Pleasure (Weidenfeld & Nicolson, London,
    1955; also published in America as *I Take Great Pleasure*,
    John Day, New York, 1956)
The Face of the World (Weidenfield & Nicolson,
    London, 1957)
Japanese (Weidenfeld & Nicolson, London, 1959)
Cecil Beaton's Diaries: 1922–1939 The Wandering Years
    (Weidenfeld & Nicolson, London, 1961; also published
    in America by Little Brown, Boston, 1961)
Quail in Aspic (Weidenfeld & Nicolson, London, 1962;
    also published in America by Bobbs Merrill, New York,
    1963)
Images (Weidenfeld & Nicolson, London, 1963; also
    published in America by Bobbs Merrill, New York, 1963)
Royal Portraits (Weidenfeld & Nicolson, London, 1963;
    also published in America by Bobbs Merrill, New York,
    1963)
Cecil Beaton's 'Fair Lady' (Weidenfeld & Nicolson,
    London, 1964)
Cecil Beaton's Diaries 1939–1944 The Years Between
    (Weidenfeld & Nicolson, London, 1965)
Beaton Portraits (HMSO, London, 1968)
The Best of Beaton (Weidenfeld & Nicolson, London, 1968)
Fashion: An Anthology by Cecil Beaton (HMSO, London, 1971)
My Bolivian Aunt (Weidenfeld & Nicolson, London, 1971)
Cecil Beaton's Diaries: 1944–1948 The Happy Years
    (Weidenfeld & Nicolson, London, 1972; also published

in America as *Memoirs of the Forties* McGraw-Hill,
    New York, 1972; and in France as *Les Annes Heureuses*,
    Coedition Albin Michel-Opera Mundi, Paris, 1972)
Cecil Beaton's Diaries: 1948–1955 The Strenuous Years
    (Weidenfeld & Nicolson, London, 1973)
The Magic Image, with Gail Buckland
    (Weidenfeld & Nicolson, London, 1975)
Cecil Beaton's Diaries: 1955–1963 The Restless Years
    (Weidenfeld & Nicolson, London, 1976)
Cecil Beaton's Diaries: 1963–1974 The Parting Years
    (Weidenfeld & Nicolson, London, 1978)
Self Portrait with Friends, Richard Buckle (ed.)
    (Weidenfeld & Nicolson, London 1979; also published
    in America by Times Books, New York, 1979)

ILLUSTRATIONS

Wings on her Shoulders, Katherine Bentley Beauman
    (Hutchinson, London, 1943)
Face to Face with China, Harold Rattenbury
    (Harrap, London, 1945)
The School for Scandal, Richard Brinsley Sheridan
    (The Folio Society, London, 1949)
Before the Sunset Fades, The Marchioness of Bath
    (Longleat Estate Company, 1951)
The Importance of Being Earnest, Oscar Wilde
    (The Folio Society, London, 1960)
First Garden, C. Z. Guest
    (Putnam, New York, 1976)

BOOK COVERS

The President's Hat, Robert Herring
    (Longmans, London, 1926)
All at Sea, Osbert and Sacheverell Sitwell
    (Duckworth, London, 1927)
Mrs. Lesley and Myself, Hugh Smith
    (Duckworth, London, 1927)
The Spirit of Paris, Paul Cohen Portheim
    (Batsford, London, 1937)
West Indian Summer, James Pope-Hennessy
    (Batsford, London, 1943)
A Star Danced, Gertrude Lawrence
    (Doubleday, New York, 1945)
Wars I Have Seen, Gertrude Stein
    (Batsford, London, 1945)
The Blessing, Nancy Mitford
    (Hamish Hamilton, London, 1951)
The Roman Spring of Mrs. Stone, Tennessee Williams
    (John Lehmann, London, 1950)
The Loved and the Envied, Enid Bagnold (Heinemann,
    London, 1951; Doubleday, New York, 1951)
Quadrille, Noël Coward
    (Heinemann, London, 1952)
Madame de Pompadour, Nancy Mitford
    (Hamish Hamilton, London, 1957)
Voltaire in Love, Nancy Mitford (Hamish Hamilton,
    London, 1957)
Don't Tell Alfred, Nancy Mitford
    (Hamish Hamilton, London, 1960)

❧ GENERAL BIBLIOGRAPHY ❧

SIR HAROLD ACTON, *Memoirs of an Aesthete*, London, 1948

ARTS COUNCIL OF GREAT BRITAIN,
Pictorial Photography in Britain 1900–1920, London, 1978

ARTS COUNCIL OF GREAT BRITAIN,
Modern British Photography 1919–1939, London, 1980

ARTS COUNCIL OF GREAT BRITAIN, *Late Sickert*, London, 1981

BETTINA BALLARD, *In My Fashion*, London, 1960

BARON, *Baron by Baron*, London, 1957

JEAN BAUDRILLARD, 'Fetishism and Ideology:
The Semiological Reduction'
'*For a Critique of the Political Economy of the Sign*,
USA, 1981

*Photographic Images and other Material
from the Beaton Studio*,
Sotheby Parke Bernet & Co., London, 21 November 1977

*Photographic Images and other Material
from the Beaton Studio*
Sotheby Parke Bernet & Co, London, 26 October 1979

Reddish House, Broadchalke, Wiltshire,
Christie, Manson & Woods, London, 9–10 June 1980

Cecil Beaton Memorial Exhibition, 1904–1980,
Parkin Gallery, London, 1983

CECIL BEATON, 'From Gladys Cooper to Gertrude Lawrence'
and 'Lovely Lily Elsie', ed. Anthony Curtis
The Rise and Fall of the Matinée Idol, London, 1974

CECIL BEATON, 'The Story of an Exception',
Photography as a Career, ed. A. Kraszna-Kraus, London, 1944

CYRIL BEAUMONT, *Serge Diaghilev*, London, 1935

HECTOR BOLITHO, *A Batsford Century*, London, 1943

ed. E. MARTIN BROWNE, LUIGI PIRANDELLO,
Right You Are/All for the Best/Henry IV, London, 1962

GAIL BUCKLAND, 'Introduction', Cecil Beaton,
War Photographs 1939–45, London, 1981

ed. RICHARD BUCKLE, *Self-Portrait with Friends*,
London, 1979

C. R. CAMMEL, *Memoirs of Annigoni*, London, 1956

DAVID CANNADINE,
'The Context, Performance and Meaning of Ritual:
the British Monarchy and the "Invention of Tradition"',
ed. E. Hobsbawm and T. Ranger,
The Invention of Tradition, London, 1984

EDNA WOOLMAN CHASE and ILKA CHASE,
Alway in Vogue, London, 1954

C. B. COCHRAN, *A Showman Looks On*, London, 1945

JOHN COLVILLE, 'The Fringes of Power',
Dining Street Diaries 1939–1955, London, 1985

CYRIL CONNOLLY, *Enemies of Promise*, London, 1938

DIANA COOPER, *The Light of Common Day*, London, 1959

NOEL COWARD, *Collected Sketches and Lyrics*, London, 1932

NOEL COWARD, *Play Parade*, Vol. 11, London, 1939

SALVADOR DALI, *Metamorphosis of Narcissus*, New York, 1937

LUCIEN DÄLLENBACH, *Le Récit Speculaire*, Paris, 1977

JAMES DANZIGER, Beaton, London, 1980

NIGEL DENNIS,
'Evelyn Waugh, The Pillar of Anchorage House',
Partisan Review, July/August 1943

JACQUES DERRIDA, *La Vérité en Peinture*, Paris, 1978

JACQUES DERRIDA, 'The Parergon', *October* (9), Summer 1979

ed. DAVID DILKS, *The Diaries of Sir Alexander Cadogan*,
London, 1971

WILLIAM A. EWING, *Eye for Elegance*, New York, 1980
WILLIAM A. EWING, *Hoyningen-Huene*,
London (to be published), 1986

RONALD FIRBANK, *Five Novels*, London, 1949

ed. A. FRANKOVITZ, *Seduced and Abandoned*, Sydney, 1984

PAUL FUSSELL, *The Great War and Modern Memory*,
London, 1973

PAUL FUSSELL, *Abroad*, London, 1980

MADGE GARLAND, *The Changing Face of Beauty*, London, 1957

DAVID GARNETT, *The Familiar Faces*, London, 1962

DOUGLAS GOLDING, *The Nineteen-Twenties*, London, 1945

C. GRAVES, *The Cochran Story*, London, n.d.

MICHAEL GREEN, *Children of the Sun*, London, 1977

PAUL HILL, and THOMAS JOSHUA COOPER,
Dialogue with Photography, New York, 1970

MICHAEL HOLROYD,
*Lytton Strachey and the Bloomsbury Group:
His Work and Their Influence*, London, 1971

EMILE OTTO HOPPÉ, *Book of Fair Women*, London, 1922

ed. MERVYN HORDER, *Ronald Firbank, Memoirs and Critiques*, London, 1977

GEORGINA HOWELL, *In Vogue*, London, 1975

LINDA HUTCHEON,
Narcissistic Narrative : The Metafictional Paradox,
London, 1984

FREDERIC JAMESON, 'Imaginary and Symbolic in Lacan:
Marxism, Psychoanalytic Criticism and the
Problem of the Subject', ed. Shoshana Felman,
Literature and Psychoanalysis, Baltimore, 1982

BARBARA JOHNSON, 'The Frame of Reference',
ed. Robert Young, *Untying the Text*, London, 1981

PHILLIP JULLIAN, *Oscar Wilde*, trad. V Wyndham,
London, 1971

JAMES LEES-MILNE,
Ancestral Voices ; Prophesying Peace ; Caves of Ice,
London, 1975, 1977 and 1977

ANDRÉ LEVINSON,
The Designs of Leon Bakst for 'The Sleeping Princess',
London, 1923

COMPTON MACKENZIE, *Sinister Street*, London, 1914

W. MACQUEEN-POPE,
Carriages at Eleven : The Story of the Edwardian Theatre,
London, 1974

W. MACQUEEN-POPE and D. L. MURRAY,
Fortunes Favourite : The Life and Times of Franz Lehar,
London, 1957

WALTER DE LA MARE, *Memoirs of a Midget*, London, 1921

DAVID MELLOR, 'Picturing the End of Empire',
Creative Camera, January 1982

CHRISTIAN METZ, *Psychoanalysis and the Cinema*,
London, 1982

EDGAR MORIN, *Le Cinéma oú L'Homme Imaginaire*, Paris, 1956

BEVERLY NICHOLS, *Twenty Five*, London, 1925

BEVERLY NICHOLS, *The Sweet and Twenties*, London, 1961

GRAHAM PAYN and SHERIDAN MORLEY,
The Noel Coward Diaries,
London, 1982

JOHN PEARSON,
Facades : Edith, Osbert and Sacheverell Sitwell,
London, 1978

PEARSON PHILLIPS, 'The New Look', ed. Michael Sissons,
The Age of Austerity 1945–51, London, 1963

EDEN PHILLPOTTS, *My Garden*, London, 1906

PETER QUENNELL,
'Introduction' *Cecil Beaton and Friends*,
Michael Parkin Fine Art, London, 1985

S. REYNOLDS-HOLE, *A Book about Roses*, London, 1859

S. REYNOLDS-HOLE, *About Gardens*, London, 1899

ed. ROBERT RHODES JAMES, *Chips, the Diaries of Sir ?Channon*,
London, 1967

SIR FRANCIS ROSE, *Saying Life*, London, 1961

ROYAL ACADEMY OF ARTS, *Sir Winston Churchill*, London, 1959

JEAN SAGNE, 'Introduction', L'Espace Cardin, *Cecil Beaton*,
Paris, 1984

EDWARD SAID, *Orientalism*, London, 1980

GEORGE BERNARD SHAW, *Pygmalion*, (location) 1914

OLIVER SAYLOR, *Max Reinhardt and his Theatre*,
New York, 1924

MILES F. SHORE, 'Biography in the 1980s:
A Psychoanalytic Perspective', ed. T K Rabb and R I Rothberg,
The New History, New Jersey, USA, 1982

OSBERT SITWELL, Discussions on Travel, Art and Life,
London, 1925

OSBERT SITWELL, 'Appreciation', Cecil Beaton catalogue,
Cooling Galleries, 1927

OSBERT SITWELL and MARGARET BUTTON,
*Sober Truth, A Collection of Nineteenth Century Episodes,
Fantastic, Grotesque and Mysterious*,
London, 1930

SACHEVERELL SITWELL, *Southern Baroque Art*, London, 1924

SACHEVERELL SITWELL, *German Baroque Sculpture*,
London, 1938

CHARLES SPENCER, *Cecil Beaton : Stage and Film Designs*,
London, 1975

WALTER STARKIE, *Luigi Pirandello*, USA, 1965

FRANCIS STEEGMÜLLER, *Cocteau*, Boston, 1970

ADRIAN STOKES, *Russian Ballets*, London, 1935

LYTTON STRACHEY, *Biographical Essays*, London, 1960

SIR ROY STRONG,
'Preface', *Cecil Beaton* exhibition catalogue,
Michael Parkin Gallery, London, 1976

J. L. STYAM, *Max Reinhardt*, London, 1982

HUGO VICKERS, *Cecil Beaton*, London, 1985

THORSTEIN VEBLEN, *Theory of the Leisure Class*,
London, 1925

VICTORIA AND ALBERT MUSEUM, *Oliver Messell*, London, 1983

EVELYN WAUGH, *Decline and Fall*, London, 1928

EVELYN WAUGH, *Vile Bodies*, London, 1930

STANLEY WEINTRAUB, *Aubrey Beardsley*, London, 1969

Rebecca West, 'The Future of the Press', *Time and Tide*, 2 March 1928, pp. 194–6

Laurence Whistler, *Rex Whistler*, London, 1985

F. Wilsford, *Dalys*, London, 1944

Michael Wishart, *High Diver*, London, 1977

Elsie de Wolfe, *After All*, New York, 1935

Virginia Woolf, *Orlando*, London, 1928

Percy Wyndham Lewis, *Time and Western Man*, London, 1927

Percy Wyndham Lewis, *The Apes of God*, London, 1930

ed. Kenneth Young, *The Diaries of Sir Robert Bruce Lockhart 1915–1938; 1939–1965*, London, 1973 and 1980

H. W. Yoxall, 'Fashion Photography', *Penrose Annual*, 1949 pp. 66–70

H. W. Yoxhall, *A Fashion of Life*, London, 1966

 ACKNOWLEDGEMENTS

Barbican Art Gallery would like to thank all the following for their assistance towards the selection and organisation of the exhibition:

Abbot, Terry, New York
Abdy, Lady Jane
Alison, Jane, Barbican Art Gallery
Anstee, Paul
Astley, Roy
Bailey, David
Bald, Claire, Barbican Art Gallery
Bentheim, David
Berman, Monty, of Bermans & Nathans Ltd
Butler, Susan, Co-editor of Creative Camera
Carmichael, Jane, Keeper of Photography, Imperial War Museum
Clayton, Dr Alexandra
Cullen, Lydia, Sotheby's, London
Cohen, David
Diamontopolou, Kate
Dickson, Barbara, New York
Dreusedow, Jean, Keeper of Costume, Metropolitan Museum of Art, New York
Edkins, Diana, Condé Nast, New York
Esterman, Leslie
Ewing, William A., New York
Frohlinger, Gail, Metropolitan Opera, New York
Garner, Philippe, Sotheby's, London
Goodman, Frances, Sotheby's, London
Goldhill, Judy
Henderson, Dr Mary, New York
Hely-Hutchinson, The Hon. Nicholas
Hemming, Denny, Weidenfeld & Nicolson
Hooker, Denise
Hose, Eileen
Hunnisett, Jean
Jarman, Derek
Jones, W. B. and V.
Klein, Ives-Brookes, New York
Koch, Fred, New York
Kozloff, Max, New York

Kroll, Alex, Condé Nast, London
Lassam, Bob, Fox Talbot Museum, Lacock, Wiltshire
Lloyd, Elizabeth
Marschner, Joanna
Matyjaszkiewicz, Krystyna, Barbican Art Gallery
Muir, Robin, *Vogue* Library, London
Munch, Alan, Ives-Brooks, New York
Parkin, Diana
Pepper, Terence, National Portrait Gallery, London
Pilkington, Eileen
Rainer, William, Condé Nast, New York
Redway, Nicola
Regan, Michael
Richardson, Agnes and Dorothy
Rosenberg, Linda, New York
Ross, Jane, *Vogue* Library, London
Saunders, Paul, Curator, Salisbury and South Wiltshire Museum
Sawyer, Geoffrey, Alicante, Spain
Scott, Julian
Silver, Dorian
Smallpeice, Mr and Mrs John M., Salisbury, Wiltshire
Sparke, Penny, Royal College of Art, London
Spencer, Charles
Smiley, Lady and Sir Hugh
Stracy, David, Barbican Art Gallery
Strong, Sir Roy
Tanqueray, Paul
Tuttle, Robert, Metropolitan Opera, New York
Vickers, Hugo
Vreeland, Diana, New York
Walker, Robert, New York
Walter, Paul
Williams, Alice
Wilson, Clare
Woollcombe, Tamsyn
Wooster, Francis

PHOTOGRAPHIC ACKNOWLEDGEMENTS

All photographs are from the Beaton Archive, Sotheby's, London,
apart from the following:

Courtesy *Vogue*, copyright © the Condé Nast Publications Inc. 1927,
1929, 1930, 1933, 1934, 1935, 1936, 1937, 1938,
1940, 1941, 1942, 1944, 1945, 1946, 1948, 1949, 1950,
1951, 1953, 1954, 1955, 1956, 1958, 1962, 1964, 1965,
1966, 1968 and 1972.

Francis Goodman © 1933

Paul Tanqueray © 1937

John Bullmer © 1962

The Sailor's Return from *Betjeman : Life in Pictures*,
compiled by Bevis Hillier, courtesy of John Murray

 INDEX OF LENDERS

CLARK, David
Condé Nast, New York
ESTERMAN, Leslie
Fox Talbot Museum, The National Trust
HILL, Derek
Imperial War Museum
Metropolitan Opera, New York
National Portrait Gallery, London
Michael Parkin Fine Art Ltd.

PEPPER, Terence
Salisbury and South Wiltshire Museum
Sotheby's, London
VICKERS, Hugo
WALTER, Paul

Barbican Art Gallery also wishes to thank
all those who have lent works to the exhibition
but prefer to remain anonymous

GENERAL INDEX

Page references in *italic* type refer to illustrations